ASHES AND MIRACLES

A Polish Journey

IRENA F. KARAFILLY

MALCOLM LESTER BOOKS

Canadian Cataloguing in Publication Data

Karafilly, Irena Friedman
   Ashes and miracles: a Polish journey

ISBN 1-894121-04-X

1. Karafilly, Irena Friedman. 2. Poland — Description and travel. I. Title.

DK4452.K37A3 1998   943.805 C98-931763-3

An excerpt from "Waiting for the Barbarians" by Constantine Cavafis in *Modern Greek Poetry*, edited by Kimon Friar, is reprinted by permission of the publisher, P. Efstathiadis Group S.A.

Cover: Tania Craan
Typesetting: Jack Steiner Graphic Design

Malcolm Lester Books
25 Isabella Street
Toronto, Ontario M4Y 1M7

Printed and bound in Canada
98 99 00 5 4 3 2 1

For Ranya, my daughter—for help all the way

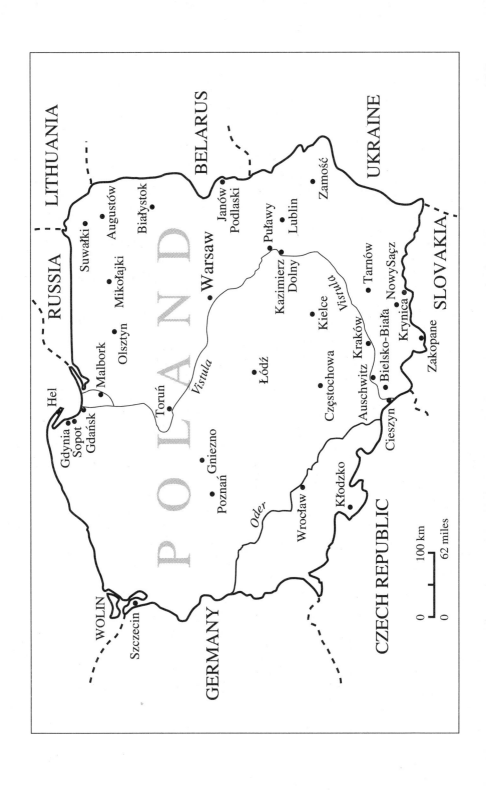

Prologue

"All journeys have secret destinations of which the traveler is unaware." Martin Buber's all-but-forgotten statement came back to me unexpectedly on a hot summer afternoon in Poland as, tired and discouraged, I found myself walking up and down a long, vaguely familiar street in Łódź, searching for my childhood home. I say *found myself* because my decision to revisit Poland after some four decades had not been in the least inspired by nostalgia, or any particular curiosity about the country of my childhood. I was so emphatically not *à la recherche du temps perdu* that Łódź—a city where I spent almost five formative years—had not even been on my itinerary when I arrived in Warsaw.

It was July 1996, and I had come to Poland with the modest plan of researching a novel with a Polish protagonist, only to find myself utterly intrigued by Poles and their turbulent thousand-year history. I knew very little about this history, but it did not take me long to realize that, with minimal planning and a good deal of luck, I had come back to Poland in what may well be one of the most exciting decades of its first millennium. Seven years after the fall of Communism, Poland appeared to me a society in flux, its new market economy beginning to flourish, its drab cities being transfigured, its citizens still reeling from the force of the decade's dramatic changes. They seemed in turn euphoric, confused, optimistic, anxious—in short, trying to adjust.

"I can't figure out what it is Poles want these days," an ex-Krakovian living in London had told me on the way to Warsaw. "I used to think I knew, but I'm not at all sure any more." He was not, he said, even prepared to state whether the majority of Poles were happier now than they had been under the Communists. Surely he was not serious?

"I am," he insisted. "I honestly don't know."

On the way *to* Poland, all this had seemed highly perplexing, not to say perverse. Could anyone possibly be wishing for the days of Soviet domination; for censorship, secret police arrests, perennial food shortages? Put like that, the answer might be a resounding no, but there are, I would soon find out, many ways of putting the question, and a surprising number of seemingly contradictory answers.

I got hooked on trying to make sense of Poles' answers; on trying to understand the country that Aristide Briand, a post-World War I French premier, called "Europe's rheumatism" and F. D. Roosevelt "the world's headache." Traveling alone by train, I visited illustrious towns and historic sites, farms, resorts, remote border hamlets. I went out of my way to meet Poles from various ethnic groups and social backgrounds—anyone who would talk, from priest to prostitute. And yet, the more Poles I talked to, the more inclined I felt to share historian Norman Davies' view of Poland as "an immensely complex phenomenon. . .a puzzle with no clear solution."

The puzzle, moreover, turned out to include a small and all but overlooked piece: my personal connection to Poland. Having left the country at age six and a half, I was embarrassingly unaware of its vast cultural riches and, even more surprising, of its imprint on my own psyche. I was born in Russia and lived in Łódź for about 10 percent of my life, yet Poland—its air and forests and architecture; its humor, obsessions, hospitality—seemed, to my endless astonishment, as familiar as home.

Some of it had to do with language. Polish is not my mother tongue, yet it often *feels* like one. Though rusty on my arrival in Poland, it is a language I speak spontaneously but imperfectly, and with a sadly meager vocabulary. Having started first grade in Israel, I learned to read in Hebrew, but English is the language of my higher education. I have lived in Canada most of my life, and yet, though English is the language I now think and write in, it does not feel like a mother tongue. I have picked up other languages along the way, but the combination of ease and familiarity and command implicit in the term *mother tongue* does not quite apply to any of them, least of all to Russian, my putative mother tongue and the only language I no longer speak.

"So what is a mother tongue?" I asked one of my childhood friends, an obstetrician with a background as complicated as my own.

"A mother tongue is the language you swear in when you're maddest!" she stated with conviction.

But I was not convinced. Given this definition, Polish is not only my mother tongue but also that of my Russian mother, and she started learning it only after her marriage to a Polish Jew. Having come to Łódź at age twenty-five, my mother mastered Polish with remarkable ease and, for mysterious reasons, has clung to its scabrous vocabulary well into her seventies, never once deigning to enrich it with equally picturesque Hebrew or English options.

I have allowed myself this small digression because it seems to me emblematic of my, and my family's, unconscious internalization of Polish culture. Paradoxically, in my mother's case, the process took place despite the fact that she never liked her husband's homeland. A Russian forced to live in Soviet-occupied Poland, she felt decidedly unwelcome in postwar Łódź, all the more as she happened to be married to a Jew. A more fervent anti-antisemite than my father, she was fond of drawing high-minded comparisons between Russians' supposed ethnic tolerance and Poles' alleged antipathy toward her husband's people.

In retrospect, it occurs to me that all this must have had more than a little to do with my odd lack of interest in the country of my childhood. Traveling through Poland, however, I found myself for the first time examining not only my own attitudes but those of contemporary Poland. Indeed, it seemed impossible not to do so, since the controversial issue of Polish-Jewish relations has, in recent years, come to occupy a prominent spot in Poland's national debate.

This, and many such issues, began to seem more interesting, more pressing, than the novel that had brought me to Poland, all the more so as my jogged memory began to yield a surprising number of dormant childhood impressions. Being half Jewish, and having been raised mostly in the West, I told myself I possessed a unique perspective, and it was not long before I decided to put my original work aside in favor of a new, altogether unpremeditated project. For better or for worse, its scope seemed to grow with every mile traveled, every new encounter. I was not merely going to write an enriched travel book, I was going to try to capture Poland in all its elusive complexity! If this was a *folie des grandeurs,* it was an oddly Polish one, born mostly of excess optimism and enthusiasm. Back in Canada, still working on the first draft, I found myself remembering François Truffaut who, in his autobiographical film *Day for Night* stated: "I always start out intending to make a great film, but end up feeling grateful if I've managed to make *a* film."

And so I too must content myself with having written what I now think of as a modest introduction to a fascinating and, as it seems to me, vastly undersold country. Since returning from Poland, I have shown photographs of the Tatras to several Canadians, all of whom mistook them for the Alps or Rockies; I showed pictures of white beaches and they said, Greece or Italy or the French Riviera. True, much of Poland is flat and geographically unmemorable, but it is a country of 120,734 square miles—quite large by European standards—-and, sadly, few travelers seem to know it has majestic mountains, pellucid lakes, and some of the finest beaches to be found in Europe.

The problem has a good deal to do with limited promotional efforts and a persistent image problem: Poland is not a glamorous destination. Not only is it scandalously polluted, but almost everything that makes it interesting is inevitably associated with suffering and deprivation, not least that connected with the recent Communist era.

All these discoveries, and such understanding as I now have of Poland, accrued over three months of intensive travel and interviews, supplemented by many hours at McGill University's Polish Library. Though my efforts suffered from obvious time constraints, I had the advantage of being able to communicate with the natives, albeit in decidedly flawed Polish. Whenever possible, the dialogues took place in English or in French, but many were conducted in Polish and are of necessity offered here in translation, the lucky reader thus being spared my own malapropisms. Some of my conversations were recorded, others reconstructed with the help of a journal, each encounter providing a new piece in the Polish puzzle. Holding the pieces together is the potent glue of Polish history, the inevitable gaps being filled with personal concerns, experiences, and curiosities about a host of related subjects. Though I have changed most of the names in the book, and many identifying details, I have tried to present a fair-minded and truthful portrait of Poland and its people.

CHAPTER 1

EVERYWHERE YOU GO in Warsaw you see the mermaid—on signs, souvenirs, trolleys—and sooner or later you hear the legend of Wars and Sawa, the industrious fisherman and his wife who are said to have lived in these parts, on the bank of the Vistula. One day, so the legend goes, a mermaid sent their way a stranger lost in the wilderness; a disguised prince who, in gratitude for their warm hospitality, bestowed on the couple a gift of land on the scenic riverbank. This was the beginning of the city called Warszawa.

Today, the Vistula runs through Warsaw, and, overlooking it from the picturesque left bank is a bronze monument to the legendary mermaid—an unusually arresting one. Unlike Hans Christian Andersen's graceful siren, or the Russian Rusalka combing her long tresses, the Vistula mermaid strikes a bold and defiant pose, brandishing sword and shield, eyes alert on the distance. She is, my guide tells me, on Warsaw's coat of arms; a timeless symbol of his beleaguered city: romantic, proud, alluring, but ever ready to defend itself.

"All you need to do is read a few chapters of our history and you see at once how appropriate it is."

My guide is Stefan Kryński, a Montreal neighbor's nephew, who has kindly offered to show me Warsaw's Old Town while his wife and young son attend some church function. He is a suave, forthright man in his late thirties; a Warsaw-born engineer who spent several years working in Libya before settling down. His features remind me of Freud's, though Stefan's eyes are vividly blue and expressive, leaping from grave reflection to abrupt merriment. Like most Poles, Stefan is enamored of irony; he is full of quaint bits of knowledge, of sardonic

1

musings. He speaks excellent English and, when I express dismay at my rusty Polish, is happy for the opportunity to practice a language he claims to love. It is a bright Sunday morning and, Stefan wryly confesses as we arrive at the renowned Castle Square, he would much rather be paying homage to historic monuments than sit cooped up in church. He seems amused by the fact that he, an atheist, should find himself married to a devout Catholic who, in turn, works as a researcher at the Jewish Historical Institute. But then Stefan seems amused by almost everything, including the famous seventeenth-century statue of King Zygmunt III, which Peter the Great reportedly coveted but could find no way to transport to St. Petersburg.

"To tell the truth, he was not one of our best kings, this Zygmunt III." Stefan throws back his head to take in the bronze statue on its seventy-two-foot-high pedestal. "But we honor him anyway because it was he who moved the capital to Warsaw." It has been the capital for only four hundred years, preceded by Kraków and, earlier still, Gniezno. Warsaw is a relatively young city, founded only in the early fourteenth century, though historic records point to the existence of a settlement as far back as the tenth. The tenth century marked the birth of Poland, a nation with a singularly tumultuous history. "The problem with Poland," says Stefan, "is it's had too many foreign masters. It's left us in a state of perpetual disorientation." He points to the extraordinary fact that, Poland having been swallowed up by its neighbors in the late eighteenth century, a Pole wishing to visit the three historical capitals of his country before World War I would have had to cross at least two frontiers: Gniezno was cut off from Kraków by the Prussian-Austrian frontier, Kraków from Warsaw by the Austrian-Russian frontier, and Warsaw from Gniezno by the Russian-Prussian frontier. This lamentable state of affairs had begun in 1772, when Russia conspired with Prussia and Austria to rob Poland of 30 percent of its territory. A second partition in 1793 brought on a national insurrection, leading in 1795 to a final partition, through which Poland found itself wiped off the map for 123 years!*

And then World War I broke out, and Poles suddenly found themselves the subjects of three warring emperors. "Imagine," Stefan says,

---

*For more information on the Partitions, see chapter 19.

2

leading me toward Warsaw's ancient defensive walls. "Imagine this: a Pole wearing a Russian uniform having to kill other Poles wearing German or Austrian uniforms." I try to imagine it, but end up recalling Rebecca West's statement: "It is sometimes very hard to tell the difference between history and the smell of skunk." Polish history has been largely shaped by the country's unfortunate geographic position. In the heart of Europe, between two powerful neighbors, Poland has often found itself the victim of Russians' and Germans' expansionist ambitions. "The only good thing about our geographical situation is we have no earthquakes." Stefan's eyes twinkle.

I stand leaning against a newly excavated Gothic bridge, photographing the Royal Castle. The seat of Polish kings and Parliament, the seventeenth-century castle was dynamited by the Nazis, leaving virtually nothing. The Old Town's souvenir stalls all sell remarkable before-and-after postcards. They show the Royal Castle and other Warsaw landmarks in their reconstructed magnificence, side by side with black-and-white snapshots taken by Polish and Soviet soldiers arriving on the scene in January 1945. What they have captured is truly mind-boggling; it leaves me shaking my head at the thought that only fifty years ago, this splendid town was a grim landscape full of smoking rubble, its bridges destroyed, its churches and palaces burnt, its historic monuments shattered. "Can you imagine?" asks Stefan. "A city like this, with virtually nothing left standing!"

If ever there was a challenge to the imagination, this is it, for the reconstructed Old Town is as much a testament to Poles' patriotic will as to the splendors of their past. Listed by UNESCO as one of the World's Cultural Treasures, today's Old Town proudly displays its great Renaissance and Baroque facades, its sumptuous palaces, its magnificent theaters and churches. It is a lively, picturesque site, full of sidewalk cafés, trendy boutiques, bars, and tubs overflowing with flowering plants. There are tourists everywhere—many of them German —and horse-drawn carriages rolling down the cobblestone streets.

Like all Poles, Stefan is intensely proud of this monumental feat, subsidized by Polish expatriates from around the world. The achievement is all the more remarkable in light of the fact that postwar planners had nothing but old documents to go on: blueprints, photographs, paintings. Warsaw's reconstruction started even before

Poland was fully liberated, and elderly Poles still speak of the extraordinary days following the Germans' retreat, when all the roads leading to Warsaw were chaotic with tanks and soldiers, and bedraggled Varsovians on foot and on farm carts, returning to homes at best reduced to ruins. It was not long, however, before a new slogan was rousing the devastated country: The Entire Nation Is Building Its Own Capital! It was a time of exceptional solidarity and purpose, with miners from Silesia, factory workers from Łódź, and Tatra highlanders rushing to help in the postwar effort. Poles of all classes and ages worked side by side for years, living among the ruins. There was little to eat, the ruins were rat infested, the walls of former homes covered with messages scribbled by Varsovians searching for lost relatives. But the work went on, most of it completed between 1946 and 1953. "Well, you can see how sentimental we Poles are," concludes Stefan, "insisting on painstakingly duplicating the past when we might have, far more easily, constructed a brand-new city."

We have arrived at Warsaw's Old Market Square, with its narrow surrounding streets and evocative alleyways. Harking back to the seventeenth and eighteenth centuries, the former merchants' houses are clustered picturesquely around the market square. They are tall and narrow—mostly three storied—their facades multicolored pastels, their slanting roofs red tiled. There are the usual stalls selling souvenirs and books, and artists peddling their paintings. Farther out, Warsaw is a welter of high-rise developments, but here the past asserts itself over the present. There are graceful gas lanterns on the streets, and mullioned windows, and wrought-iron grillwork, all affirming the Poles' passionate attachment to their past.

But Warsaw is quickly changing; more quickly, perhaps, than other Polish cities, and in ways not everyone applauds. Though Poles have recently voted in a neo-Communist president,* the drab days of the Communist regime are over. "Just think," Stefan says, "the old Communist headquarters a stock exchange now. Who would have

---

*Since this was written, Poland has held parliamentary elections, in which a coalition of two parties linked to the anti-Communist movement defeated the neo-Communists. Eight years after the fall of Communism, Poland thus finds itself governed by two men representing opposite ends of the political spectrum: President Aleksander Kwaśniewski, a former Communist, and Prime Minister Jerzy Buzek, a former Solidarity activist.

believed it before 1989!" When I point, amused, to signs saying Hot Dogs and *Drinki*—a Polonized version of "soft drinks"—he says, "We're in love, *in love*, with everything Western, even the peep shows and sex shops." He turns to grin at me and, observing my wry expression, gives a little sigh. "I don't think a Canadian can understand this," he says, "but for many Poles, these are the ultimate symbols of freedom and democracy!"

And so what can I say? I want to express my vague unease, my dawning apprehension that the price for this newfound freedom may turn out to be much higher than Stefan imagines. Eventually, I will come to see that many Poles share this particular unease; one reason, perhaps, why the neo-Communist Kwaśniewski came to replace Lech Wałęsa as president. When I ask Stefan whom he voted for, he quotes one of the Polish opposition leaders: "The choice was between cholera and the plague," he says, sounding rather sour. "But this is Poland. Do you know any other country where a semi-illiterate electrician [Wałęsa] and a famous musician [Paderewski] could end up as presidents?" He gives me one of his ironic looks, then shrugs deprecatingly. He ended up voting for Wałęsa, he admits; what else was he to do, vote for the Communists?

This conversation takes place in the shade of a Pepsi-Cola parasol, where we have sat down to rest and enjoy excellent cappuccino. As if to vindicate his decision, Stefan reminds me that only recently the United States placed Poland on its list of the ten most promising emerging markets. "The economy is booming—booming!" he says. When I venture to point out the high rate of Polish unemployment (14.5 percent), Stefan only scoffs. "Unemployment!" he says. "Try to find a painter or charwoman," he says, "or even a baby-sitter. You won't find it easy, believe me." The truth is that Poles work under the table—some of them on the dole, many others moonlighting. "Everyone these days has a TV and fridge, but now they all want a VCR, stereo, a satellite dish. And a car, of course—a car most of all!"

Stefan himself lives in dread of losing his brand-new Toyota. There are fifty thousand cars stolen in Poland a year, with police retrieving no more than 10 percent. Still, Stefan is exceedingly grateful to be the owner of a foreign car rather than the ubiquitous Polish Fiat. He is equally grateful for his new suburban home, Warsaw's fine new shops, the well-stocked supermarkets, and who can blame him? Would I want to give up any of that?

We are now strolling through the so-called New Town (founded in the late fourteenth century), and I'm still mulling all this over when, not far from the Marie Curie Museum, we come upon a little Gypsy beggar. Gypsies are a common sight in Poland, but this one, sitting alone on the gray pavement, can't be more than about eight. Unwashed and bedraggled-looking, she holds a can and a placard with a childishly printed message: I AM VERY POOR AND HAVE NOTHING TO EAT.

"These Gypsies on the street, they're all Romanian," Stefan says as we walk away. "They're much poorer than our Polish Gypsies and. . . well, people are beginning to react against them. Even the Polish Gypsies are not happy about them."

I ask where the Polish Gypsies are, and whether they are still nomadic.

They aren't, says Stefan, but he doesn't know all that much about them. There's a museum in Tarnów if I'm interested, he says.

I am certainly interested in Gypsies, but just now even more in the Gypsy girl's sign—or at least my reaction to it. Why should these words pierce me with such acute anguish? This is certainly not the first young beggar I have ever encountered, nor the first to have stirred my pity. I have given her more than the usual coin or two, but the gesture has failed to relieve my inner chaos, a stubborn feeling normally reserved for one's private griefs. It takes a few minutes, but it gradually comes to me that the child's Polish plea—its Polishness—has catapulted me back to my own childhood, toward my much younger, more susceptible self. It is as if there were two of me: a worldly, somewhat jaded adult reading a shrewd beggar's sign, the other a tender-hearted child in a soft, warm bed, listening with tears in her eyes to a bedtime reading of *The Little Match Girl*. Translated into English, the words on the placard have no power over me; in Polish, they have the force of painful revelation. This in itself is a revelation—that the very same words can, in two languages, have an altogether different emotional weight. I am intrigued by this idea, but we have meanwhile arrived at the Warsaw Uprising Monument and my focus abruptly changes.

Warsaw is a city of monuments, but this memorial to the city's heroes is itself memorable. Standing on the spot where the Polish

Home Army launched its 1944 assault on the Nazis, the bronze sculpture depicts the insurgents emerging from manholes, ready for attack, as well as their eventual retreat into the city's sewers, striving to escape the besieged Old Town. Stefan tells me many of the insurgents ended up drowning in the sewer network, some killed by Nazi grenades, others shot as they finally surfaced in the city center. Some twenty thousand Home Army fighters died in the Uprising, with at least that many wounded.

"It's generally said that the revolt was a terrible mistake," Stefan says. "And I must agree: a whole city willfully destroyed, over 200,000 civilians dead. And yet—" A Slavic shrug accompanies a quick lift of dark eyebrows. "Most of us have been raised to feel intense admiration for the insurgents' courage."

Like many Poles, Stefan is both awed and exasperated by what he refers to as "Poles' impetuosity"—their daring and flamboyance and sheer audacity. By way of example, he points to yet another famous monument. "Here you have one of them—a typical Polish hero—eighteenth century."

Jan Kiliński, a poor tailor, was made colonel by Tadeusz Kościuszko, leader of the 1794 rebellion against Catherine the Great's Russia. The insurrection ultimately failed, but Kiliński had managed a successful assault on the czarist ambassador's residence on this very street. As for Kościuszko, I am amazed to learn that he had already distinguished himself in the American War of Independence. "Oh yes, we Poles love great causes," Stefan says, responding to my evident surprise. "They've named a bridge after Kościuszko in New York, and also some kind of mustard." He gives a small, amused chuckle. "But let me tell you something about this Kiliński statue."

The Nazis reportedly looked at this monument and decided it would be prudent to dispose of what they saw as potential incitement to revolt against foreign rule. Having dismantled the bronze figure, they threw it into the National Museum's cellar, only to find, the next day, a huge inscription painted across the entire museum facade. "Varsovians," it said, "I'm here now! Signed: Kiliński."

I laugh, hearing Stefan tell this, and he too laughs, as if hearing it for the first time. "But that wasn't all," he says, enjoying himself. "Because at the same time, another notice appeared on Copernicus' monument, saying, "As punishment for the removal of Kiliński, I'm extending the winter by two months. Signed: Copernicus." Stefan looks positively gleeful. "You have to remember," he says, "this was the winter of Stalingrad. The Germans were not amused."

I am, and am still laughing when quite suddenly I am brought up short by a street chase straight out of some TV drama—the end of the chase in fact, for within two or three minutes, the young, disheveled man in blue jeans is pounced upon by the burly pursuers, who struggle to subdue their thrashing victim. At least that's what I take him to be, watching with others from a safe distance. The young man goes on struggling and the two grow brutal. One ends up sitting on the man's legs, the other astride his back.

"Why doesn't anyone call the police?" I hear myself ask Stefan. I am almost as appalled by the passive, curious crowd as by the brutality. I look up and down the sloping, residential street, tasting my own impotence. "Isn't there a public phone anywhere?" I ask. All I can see are parked cars up and down the street, publicity pillars, an old man walking a dog as if nothing untoward were happening down the street.

"A public phone!" Stefan gives a small, ambiguous sound. He seems about to add something when we hear a siren wailing behind us and turn to see a police van making the sharp corner, screeching to a halt a few feet away. At once, two uniformed policemen jump out and handcuff the apparent offender, shoving him roughly toward the blue van marked, unmistakably, POLICJA.

"So they were the good guys, those two?" I say, still a little shaky. "Did you know that?" I ask Stefan, feeling vaguely foolish.

"No," he says, "How could I? They were wearing civvies." He runs a nervous hand through his hair. "One thing I can tell you: we have a mafia here—one of the disagreeable facts about the new Poland," he admits, as we make our way toward his car. He seems somewhat subdued but all the same tells me how, soon after the fall of Communism, the Old Town's restaurant and café owners demanded police action against criminal gangs extorting protection money. It brought the problem to public attention and forced the police to take tougher measures. "These days—" Stefan flashes me a sudden grin "—our Minister of Security says we don't have a mafia in Poland any more—only organized crime, that's all."

It is by now midafternoon, and Stefan tries to persuade me to have dinner with his family. His in-laws are coming over, he says, and he thinks I'll find them interesting. Also, his wife always makes some new foreign dish on Sunday. I am sorely tempted, but, though I'd stopped in London on my way to Warsaw, I am still jet-lagged. And so Stefan drives me toward the Hotel Maria, a small, privately owned hotel on a street named after Pope John Paul II. It is a long street running through what used to be Warsaw's Jewish quarter. I did not know this when I checked into the Maria, and the information leaves me oddly moved. My father was sixteen when he arrived in the capital from his *shtetl*, and only nineteen when he escaped to Russia—nineteen! I never realized how young he was in 1939, and though many of the old streets were subsequently destroyed in the 1943 Warsaw Ghetto Uprising, the thought of his youthful presence in this area opens wider the door that the Gypsy girl's placard has recently unlocked. I had felt little connection with Poland until that moment, but by now am beginning to suspect the existence of a wide network of memory and sentiment lurking beyond that creaking door. When I tell Stefan that my father must have once lived here, he immediately suggests a very small detour.

"Just one more monument," he solemnly promises, and brings me to the bleak Ghetto Heroes' Monument. We get out of the car and walk up toward a green square surrounded by nondescript apartment blocks. The monument is made of dark granite brought to Warsaw by the Nazis for a proposed monument to Hitler. At about the same time, a Jewish historian named Emmanuel Ringelblum was living in the local ghetto, where he kept a meticulous record of what was going on. Much of our knowledge of ghetto life comes from these documents, which Ringelblum hid in milk cans and buried as the ghetto was being razed.

The conflagration took place following the Ghetto Uprising, a battle that Ringelblum described as "a contest between a fly and an elephant." Incredibly, it lasted nearly a month, despite the debilitated state of the outnumbered ghetto fighters, and their limited firepower. The ghetto by then held some fifty-six thousand Jews, though in 1941 there had been about 400,000 of them, dying of disease or hunger. After the Uprising, which ended in the suicide of most of its leaders, the surviving population was promptly shot or shipped off to the death camps.

And now, Stefan tells me, there are new louts scribbling *Judenfrei* on such monuments. "Our own homegrown skinheads. They vandalize historical landmarks, they assault gays. There's a new gay disco in Warsaw. They wait outside and. . .well, you see how it is, there's always an element that's got to have someone to bash in. Always."

I think about all this as we get back into Stefan's car, reminded that my father's entire family perished somewhere in this country; that had it not been for the Nazis, my father would never have married a Russian; that, quite simply and irrefutably, I wouldn't be here at all today, driving down this unknown Polish boulevard. Stefan tells me that after dark, Warsaw streets are mostly deserted, but at this early hour, there are many families about, walking with kids or dogs. Dogs in Poland are muzzled by law, but apart from that, this could be a street anywhere in the West. There are kids in shorts and Lion King shirts and wild-haired teens in Adidas shoes on skateboards or Rollerblades; a young couple on a street corner locked in a passionate embrace. All this, I know, my father would find hard to imagine, as he surely would the Orientals I see waiting for the streetcar. They are either Koreans brought in to work in electronics, Stefan says, or foreign students at Warsaw University. As we pull into the hotel's driveway, he comes around to open my door and invites me to stay with his family on my way back. "It's a big house, and my wife will be pleased to practice her French a little. Also," he adds, "my mother-in-law was a history teacher. She'll tell you interesting stories."

"Well, maybe," I say. "I—"

"No," he insists. "You must. You know what the Poles say: A guest in the home is God in the home, right?"

I laugh at that. "But you don't believe in God!"

"True," he says, "but I do in Polish hospitality." He gives one of his most disarming smiles, so I find myself promising to stay with them in Piastów. I also find my hand being kissed in farewell—one of the Polish gallantries that have somehow survived all the recent changes.

"By the way," he says, "you'll get better service if you speak English at the hotel." This is something I have heard before and indeed have acted on, though mostly because I am still self-conscious about my Polish. I thank Stefan for the tip, and for the lovely tour, and stand watching him vanish in his very shiny, very red Toyota.

❁

There is a postwar photograph of me and my parents, taken in Łódź in 1947. It is, it seems, our first Polish photograph. We had just moved from some temporary quarters to a new flat in the center of town, and judging by my mother's face, she knew herself to be exceptionally lucky. Dressed in a tweed skirt and angora sweater, she leans against a shiny black piano, smiling radiantly, a crystal vase of roses visible in the background. She did not yet know that the vase, the piano, the crystal chandelier—every piece of furniture in the elegant flat—had once belonged to a Jewish family shipped to Treblinka. She believed everything had been bought by the Germans who lived in the flat during the war and whose possessions she was delighted to have inherited. The photograph was taken some months after our arrival from the U.S.S.R., when a new child—my mother was two months pregnant with my brother—and a beautiful new flat were still enough to make my mother glow.

But my father must have known. It may even account in part for the expression on his face. Standing on the other side of the piano, he wears a gray suit and tie, staring into the camera with dark, deeply set eyes. There is something both mournful and beautiful about these eyes; something at once brilliantly evident and inexplicably opaque. Where is the pain, one feels compelled to ask—the dark pupils, the heavy eyelids—where? Impossible to say, but the facts say it all. This is a twenty-seven-year-old man who has spent some of his best years in a Soviet labor camp; who has no one left in the world except for this fair-haired young woman and the two-year-old toddler seated with her legs stretched out on a piano stool, where just a few years ago an older Jewish child probably sat playing.

Though I was much too young to know any of this, my own features are eloquent with some vague apprehension. I have no conscious recollection of the long journey from Orenburg but have been told that it left me rather traumatized, subject to frequent nightmares. The journey took two weeks, the ancient train crawling all the way from the Urals through a war-ravaged landscape—scarred towns and torched forests, and Ukrainian villages often reduced to rubble. The passengers were mostly Poles and Polish Jews returning home, uncertain of what awaited them. Some of them wept through much of the journey.

I dream of this journey on my second night in Warsaw and wake up inwardly shaken, aware of an odd, progressively louder rumble, and a clanking sound I eventually identify as an approaching trolley. My watch has stopped, but it is daylight outside, and going to the window, I see Varsovians standing on street corners, waiting for buses, trolleys. Having eaten only a sandwich before turning in, I am ravenous. I shower quickly, dress, and go down in search of a good Polish breakfast.

What I find is the night clerk wrapped up in a brown blanket, asleep on the vinyl sofa before the reception desk. The lobby is dark and deserted and, having heard my footsteps, the clerk stirs, rubs her eyes, and sits up, blinking at me. She looks at her watch; she frowns.

"Good morning." I speak English, hoping I might be more readily forgiven this rude awakening.

"Good morning," she says; then, getting up and folding the old blanket, "Can I help you with anything?"

"Well. . .I was just hoping to get some breakfast. I suppose I'm too early?"

The clerk looks at her watch again. "*Madame*," she says, giving it a French emphasis. "It's not even five a.m."

"Five a.m.?" I echo.

"Four fifty-five." She gives a rueful smile.

Oh God. I stammer out my apologies and urge her to go back to sleep. Four fifty-five! Do people in Montreal go to work at such an ungodly hour, in such numbers? I wonder, eating some crackers by the open window. I have about two hours to wait for breakfast and spend them packing and looking through my mother's Polish photographs. Taking the small album was a last-minute impulse, inspired by the purchase of gifts for a couple of childhood playmates. The two sisters are both in the album, as are others connected with our shared past. Most of the photographs, however, are of my own family, and, forgotten for at least two decades, they leave me feeling much like Poland will: it is all so familiar; it is all so strange.

When the fragrance of freshly brewed coffee finally reaches me, I hasten downstairs and across the hotel lobby, toward the plant-filled dining room with its long wall of sunny French windows. The porter wishes me good morning in Polish and I answer in English, beginning to feel the strain of my charade. Fortunately, the waiter addresses me in

English, offering sausages, which turn out to be wieners, eggs, black currant juice, coffee. Poles like to eat a substantial breakfast and then to snack on various sorts of buns as the day wears on. Some may have a sandwich around noon; most wait until the main meal, which is eaten anywhere between three and six o'clock.

I am halfway through my breakfast when other guests arrive. There is a Japanese man with a blond woman, speaking German, a group of American academics on my left, and on my right a bespectacled Pole who is soon joined by another, white-haired Pole, both here to attend some sort of national convention. Warsaw is a popular convention center and, I gather, the two have not seen each for some time. Asked how things are in Gdańsk, the bespectacled Pole gives a typically Polish answer.

"It's not so bad that it can't be worse."

In fact, for many in Gdańsk, things are grim indeed. The famous shipyard has recently gone bankrupt, with two thousand workers finding themselves without jobs. Inevitably, the conversation turns to Wałęsa who, after losing the 1995 elections, declared his intention to once more earn his living as an electrician, in ostentatious contrast to the lavish lifestyle of other ex-presidents. What the two men can't quite decide is, was Wałęsa being hypocritical; or is it simply that he had forgotten what the life of a blue-collar worker was like? People do forget, they eventually conclude; how else is one to understand so many Poles wanting the Communists back?

As for Wałęsa, he reportedly arrived at the shipyard in a limousine, worked for a day, then went to visit the United States. When he came back, it was to express his sudden reluctance to deprive some desperate worker of a much-needed job. Then the shipyard closed and there was no more talk of Wałęsa leading a simple life. The two diners chuckle over this, then go on to discuss industrial conditions, pollution, national politics. Eating ham and eggs, they argue a few points, but strongly agree on one thing: it was a grave error not to purge the system of former Communists, as the Czechs have done. The issue of "decommunization" is a highly charged one in Polish politics, with much of the debate focusing on the views promulgated by Poland's best-selling daily, the *Gazeta Wyborcza*. Adam Michnik, its controversial editor, is a former Solidarity theoretician and political dissident.

Frequently jailed under the Communist regime, he is now accused by the extreme right of being a Communist collaborator. This is partly due to his apparent friendship with both President Kwaśniewski and General Jaruzelski, the man responsible for declaring martial law back in 1981. Though Michnik was one of Jaruzelski's most publicized targets, and despite the fact that he has in recent years fallen out with Wałęsa, Michnik is passionately committed to resolving the pernicious conflicts dividing Polish society; to bridging the gap between the post-Communist and post-Solidarity camps.

This "let bygones be bygones" attitude is, however, plainly not shared by my two breakfasting neighbors. The one from Gdańsk dismisses the *Gazeta Wyborcza* as a cheap tabloid; the Krakovian calls Michnik an irresponsible egotist. And then, breaking a bread roll, he nonchalantly asks, "Did you know that he is a Jew?"

"Well," says his bespectacled companion, "I've heard it said, but—"

"No, no," interjects the first. "He really is. I saw him on television at Stryjkowski's funeral and he was wearing a Jewish skullcap."

"Stryjkowski was a Jew?" the one from Gdańsk asks over his cup of coffee.

"He was." This is said in an utterly neutral tone.

The bespectacled guest states that he never suspected Stryjkowski the writer could be a Jew; for that matter, he never believed it about Michnik either.

"It just goes to show you," says the white-haired Krakovian. "For all we know, Kwaśniewski too is a Jew, just like Wałęsa said."

"No, no." The younger man wipes his mouth. "He had three priests at his mother's funeral—three!—and—"

"Well, the thing is, you never know," states the other. He goes on to talk about Kwaśniewski's various promises, but I have finished my breakfast and leave them in midconversation. Though there was no rancor in the two men's tone, I can't help musing on the Poles' famous obsession with the Jews. There are, it is said, no more than five thousand Jews left in Poland, but the word *Jew* has gradually come to mean different things to different people. To some, it's quite simply synonymous with liberal; to others a person of power and influence; for many it's just a pejorative applicable to absolutely anyone.

These are the things I reflect on as the porter, who doubles as occasional chauffeur, drives me to the train station. He keeps speaking to me in broken German, and I find myself tempted to help him out by confessing to my knowledge of Polish. I feel surprisingly uncomfortable with this small deception, but then it occurs to me that had they not heard me speak English to the waiter, the two Poles in the dining room might not have conversed quite so openly. Speaking as I do several languages, I have sometimes found myself in the position of the proverbial fly on the wall. On at least one occasion—on a remote Greek island— the experience led to a story I could not otherwise have written. And so, by the time we reach the train station, I find myself wondering whether I would not in fact learn more about Poland if, at least some of the time, I played the aural equivalent of "Candid Camera." I decide that I probably would, but remain ambivalent. It feels immoral somehow, like spying on someone through a window, or reading a person's mail. I remind myself that art transcends moral considerations. Or so they say. Personally, though I've decided to give it a try, I still have my doubts as I enter Warsaw's train station. I have a ticket and forty minutes to wait, and so walk about, finding myself in a waiting room occupied by local vagrants. There are about 300,000 homeless people in Poland, fifteen or so of whom have taken shelter here at the Central. Half of them are asleep, the others chatting or staring vacantly. One barefoot woman in a faded red polka-dot dress is feverishly tidying up clothes, paper cups, newspapers. She is muttering to herself as she bends and stretches, seemingly determined to triumph over the pervasive chaos. It is an oddly domestic sort of chaos, with undershirts and socks hanging over the windows, and a beer bottle with several daisies standing on an overturned crate. Much later, I will meet a sociologist who will tell me that the number of homeless people has been steadily rising since Communism's collapse, one of the more worrisome facts of life in the new Poland.

I sit down to wait in the main lobby, watching the long queues in front of the ticket counter. A few feet away, a curly-haired boy of three or four is playing with a black rubber spider that jumps at the end of a rubber tube. Every now and then, the boy calls out in Polish, "Look, Papa, look at how it jumps!"

I turn to look at the father, amazed to see a dark, mustachioed man speaking Arabic to a Muslim woman wearing a long, shapeless dress and a white hijab. I speculate that the Arab is a graduate student at Warsaw University; that the child attends a Polish nursery. But then a Polish woman in a sleeveless T-shirt and jeans appears from the direction of the wickets and the child calls out, "Mama, Mama, look at my spider!" The woman smiles, comments on the toy, then joins the Arab couple, speaking in Polish to her husband, in English to the woman whom I now guess to be her sister-in-law. I watch this unlikely tableau with much interest, for despite the difference in their dress and style, the two women seem perfectly amicable. They laugh, sharing an anecdote about the ticket clerk; they touch each other fondly. And then the man glances at his watch and calls the child over, and the four of them start heading for the stairs. It is only when the Muslim woman turns that I see the large white bag that she is carrying. It is a plastic bag—perhaps a newspaper publicity bag?—and on it, in black English letters, appears the following, indisputable statement: TIMES ARE CHANGING.

CHAPTER 2

TIMES ARE CHANGING in Kraków too, but one of the first things to strike me on arrival in the Old Town is the great number of nuns on the crowded streets. I run into a cluster of them just outside McDonald's, blithely making their way among the milling tourists. Having spent much of my life in Montreal, I am not unaccustomed to seeing nuns in public places, but not such jolly, attractive ones, laughing together as they cross the street, looking flushed and wholesome and a little improbable—like actresses who have just stepped off a Hollywood movie set.

The observation amuses Olga Podlaski, a native Krakovian who spent two years in Canada, studying and working as an au pair. When I remark that there seems to be a church on just about every corner, Olga laughs and says, "In Canada, you have a bank on every corner; in Kraków, we have a church. What else would you expect from a city that gave the world its first Polish Pope?"

Indeed. Unlike Warsaw, where the tallest buildings are steel-and-glass skyscrapers, Kraków boasts gleaming church spires. Its history goes back to A.D. 965 when Mieszko I, and with him all of Poland, embraced Christianity. Though devastated by several invaders, Kraków was rebuilt each time to greater splendor, to be known eventually as the City of Kings and, after the founding in 1364 of its university, as a center of high culture and learning.

Today, Olga Podlaski is an English lecturer at this venerable institution. She is an energetic, dark-haired woman with Slavic cheekbones and slanted eyes; a descendant, she feels sure, of some marauding Tatar. She is impressively pregnant. Olga has a two-year-old daughter and is married to a pediatric psychologist whom we are to meet for dinner. Meanwhile, we stroll through the university's oldest surviving building—a fifteenth-century Gothic edifice with a splendid arcaded courtyard. Though we pass a new shop selling the usual university memorabilia, the hushed interiors have a cloistered medieval atmosphere. Olga names a few illustrious students—Nikolaus Copernicus, the astronomer; Jan Matejko, Poland's most famous painter—then takes me to the Alchemy Room where Dr. Faustus, the fabled scientist, reputedly performed his magical feats. The past lives on in every room we visit: from the Treasury, with its 1510 Jagiellonian globe (the first globe to show the existence of the American continent), to the portrait-packed Assembly Hall with the Latin inscription over its Renaissance portal: "Wisdom Rather Than Strength." This was the room where Czesław Miłosz and Pope John Paul II received their honorary doctorates. Olga surprises me with the further information that Karol Wojtyła, the man who would be Pope, was, during the Occupation, an actor in the underground theater, as well as a poet and playwright.

It is fitting that Kraków be the former home of the Polish Pope, for until World War II, the city was widely known as the stronghold of Poland's Catholic, conservative intelligentsia. Even today, its students are said to be more conservative than those in the capital. When the abortion bill was before Parliament in 1992, Olga was amazed to discover that the majority of her own students were anti-abortion, and some against contraception too. She herself is against what she sees as Poles' "rampant hypocrisy" on this subject. She tells me about the large numbers of Polish women traveling east for a cheap abortion, or, those who can afford it, west to Berlin. Some of these women suffer from complications and end up in hospital; in villages, there are those who practice infanticide. All this is common knowledge, but the government, under intense pressure from the Catholic Church, ended up passing the most restrictive anti-abortion law in Europe. This law, however, has many vociferous opponents, among them Jerzy Urban, publisher of the notoriously satirical periodical *Nie*. Back in 1992, when the abortion bill seemed imminent, Urban offered 50 million złoty (at the time, about U.S. $4,000) to any woman prepared to go public about an affair with a member of Parliament that had resulted in an abortion, preferably paid for by him. The next morning, there were many panic-stricken faces in Parliament, but the anti-abortion bill was passed all the same.* Olga quotes Zygmunt August, a sixteenth-century Polish king who stated, "I'm not the king of your consciences." He was, she hastens to point out, speaking about religious freedom, but his pro-choice stand is highly relevant in today's abortion debate. Poland, alas, no longer has leaders of that caliber; no one who could possibly qualify as either wise or strong.

This is a sentiment one often hears expressed by Poles, who seem to live perpetually in the long shadow cast by their kings and heroes. One of the most revered in the royal pantheon is King Władysław Jagiełło, after whom Kraków's university is named. Interestingly, Jagiełło was originally a heathen Lithuanian and one whom the fourteenth-century princess Jadwiga was most loath to wed. Set on marrying Wilhelm of Hapsburg, to whom she had been betrothed at the age of ten, Jadwiga was whisked away and locked up in Wawel Castle, the hilltop royal residence. Though the door to her chamber still bears the markings of the ax Jadwiga wielded in her attempts at improbable escape, the eventual union with the converted Grand Duke of Lithuania vastly expanded Poland's territory, placing it among the Great Powers of Europe, a status it was to enjoy for three hundred years. Though Jadwiga herself died young, her marriage marked the beginning of what was to become known as Poland's Golden Age. She died childless, but it was the Jagiellonian Dynasty that established Poland's fame as a center of learning and religious tolerance, attracting scholars from all over Europe, in many parts of which religious wars were still being waged.

In royal circles, however, the Jagiellonians were above all renowned for the magnificence of their Kraków court, which reputedly dazzled foreign visitors. It still dazzles today, attracting local and foreign tourists with its vast store of art treasures, tapestries, and historical relics. Legend has it that the original castle was built by a prince named Krak who succeeded in vanquishing a voracious dragon living beneath the castle. He gave the city its name and also a daughter whose own name was to become emblematic of Polish patriotism: Wanda drowned herself rather than marry a German prince. Her story became an enduring

---

*Poland's abortion law has recently been amended, allowing women to undergo abortion for financial or social reasons.

folk song, so popular in its day that even Napoleon learned it by heart from his Polish soldiers.

"Of course you realize that if she lived today, Wanda would probably take the first flight west to marry her German prince."

Olga's cynicism is due, at least in part, to her acknowledged dismay that Poland should, after centuries of victimization, consider Germany her best Western ally. One of Olga's uncles ended up at Auschwitz in 1939, after the Nazis closed down the Jagiellonian University. They were, in those early days, as eager to wipe out Poland's intellectual and spiritual leadership as they were to eliminate the Jews. Their plans foiled, the Germans tried to blow up Kraków, but the city was miraculously saved by the arrival of the Soviet Army. It was too late for Olga's philosopher uncle. He had perished along with 50 percent of Poland's academics.

We have arrived at Floriańska Gate—part of the city's original defensive walls—when Olga asks whether I intend to visit nearby Auschwitz. I do, though I am frankly not without inner doubts. I am reluctant to go but feel I must; feel guilty at my own ambivalence, as if I were simply shirking an unpleasant responsibility. Olga says that people who had never thought of visiting Auschwitz started to do so after seeing *Schindler's List*. The film caused a stir in Poland, particularly among the young, who had known very little about the Jews. Now, there are popular Schindler's List Tours, guiding people through the Kazimierz district, where some of Spielberg's filming had taken place. The formerly Jewish district had stood dilapidated, but now they have a new action plan to save it. "There you have it," says Olga. "The power of art!"

I have been to Kraków once before, several decades ago. I was five years old, and if I remember it at all, it is partly because there is a photograph of my brother and me outside Wawel Castle, but also because, throughout my childhood, the visit to Kraków was the subject of occasional amused reminiscence. For years, my parents would chuckle over my childish mulishness in refusing to eat at a restaurant—any restaurant—while visiting Kraków. I may have been mulish, but I was also proud and would not divulge the reason for my reluctance. I was afraid to enter a restaurant because in those days all Polish waiters wore white jackets similar to those worn by doctors. Only a few months earlier, I had been taken to a Łódź surgery where a beguiling dentist persuaded me to open my mouth, assuring me that all he wanted was to have a look. I believed him, utterly unprepared for the flash of sharp pain as all at once the soft, friendly fingers hardened, pulling out a stubborn milk tooth. There was the alien taste of blood in my mouth, and of rising, murderous rage. The dentist was pressing a cotton ball to my bleeding gum when I bit his thumb—not so much for hurting me as for betraying my trust.

I tell Olga this story as we sit drinking Sprites at a sidewalk café where the waiters are all clad in white. Both of us would have preferred juice, but only the Cokes and Sprites and Fantas are available cold. This is a common problem in Poland, where the new craze for American drinks means the shunned local juices get left out of small coolers. When Olga asks how my parents dealt with the restaurant problem, I confess I eventually allowed myself to be bribed with a somewhat unusual doll. The Wawel photograph shows me cuddling this new possession—a cloth doll dressed in a dashing sailor outfit. Evidently, my longing for the doll was stronger than my fear, but for a long time, I would deeply mistrust all dentists and doctors. Ironically, I eventually married a dentist, though this may have had something to do with the spell cast by a prolonged stay on a Greek island. Still, I trusted him despite his priestly white jacket—and still do, for that matter, divorce notwithstanding.

"So—" Olga laughs at my story "—at least you got over your phobia," she says.

"I did. It helped that he looked like Omar Sharif and wrote poetry. . . and took me for long walks on the moonlit beach."

"Ah yes." Olga sighs softly. Two years ago, she and Marek visited Greece and came back fervent Hellenophiles. This is how we end up changing that day's dinner plan from Polish fare to Greek. Olga calls her husband, and we arrange to meet him and his sister, Danuta, with whom I am to stay. Olga and Marek live in a two-bedroom apartment, but Olga's elderly mother lives with them and their daughter, so the choice was between a living-room sofa and a guest room at Danuta's. It is not really a guest room. Danuta, who is single and recently lost her job, has a lodger who is away on vacation. The room is empty and, it was made clear, I would be most welcome. Though Poland no longer suffers from the cultural isolation of Communist days, Poles remain eager for contact with the outside world and grateful for opportunities to practice their language skills.

Danuta and Marek are already on the terrace when we arrive, drinking retsina and watching the pedestrian traffic along the Floriańska mall. The restaurant may offer Greek meals, but it is owned by Palestinians, as I eventually discover when I try to engage them in Greek conversation. When Olga and I arrive at the terrace, Marek stands up and I stop in utter amazement: the man holding out his hand is a dead ringer for Anthony Hopkins; younger—Marek is only in his thirties—but startling in his resemblance to the British actor. When I ask whether he has been told this before, Marek admits that he has. Some of the adolescents he sees at the clinic began to call him Hannibal after *Silence of the Lambs* came out.

We talk for a while about Marek's work at a pediatric hospital, where there has been a steady increase in the number of troubled children and adolescents. The outpatient clinic where he works gets seven hundred new referrals a year. Marek attributes this in part to parental neglect. There are those who work very hard these days because their business is flourishing, and those who do just to make ends meet. The upshot is that both poor and affluent kids see little of their parents.

But there is more to it, Marek explains. The rapid changes in Poland have brought about a new crisis of values. The old days of social conformity may be gone, but so are the old certitudes. Parents as well as children find themselves floundering in the face of growing Western influence. When I ask about drugs—an issue that concerns me personally now that my own daughter is a teenager—Marek says that drug abuse is certainly on the rise, a problem for which Polish professionals lack both training and experience. Otherwise, they have a good success rate with their young patients.

Throughout all this, Danuta and Olga have been quietly listening and eating their moussaka, glancing from time to time at the passersby. There is a steady flow of tourists and shoppers, though it's difficult to see how Poles can afford to shop on upscale Floriańska. My hosts assure me, however, that there are many *biznesmeni* who have grown quite rich, not to mention the local mafia. A few minutes later, Marek draws my attention to two passing couples, whispering "Mafia." The men have slicked-back hair and wear impeccably cut suits with rather flashy ties; the women, who look like sisters, are both statuesque and deeply tanned, with bleached hair and a great deal of gold jewelry and makeup. One of the men is talking into a cell phone, frowning with the effort of shutting out the sound of Peruvian pan flutes. There are many teenagers on the street, wearing jeans and nose rings, but just as many Gypsy beggars, and peasants selling smoked cheese, and Belarussians peddling watches and Chinese kitsch. Since the opening of the borders, Belarussians have been coming to Poland in droves, and watching one of them accost tourists, Danuta turns to me with a frown. There are teenage hooligans in Poland for sure, she tells me, but the real problem is the rise in serious crime. Just last week, someone broke into the cellar in her own building and tried to steal a bike. Fortunately, he got caught. "And sure enough it was one of them—another one from across the border."

And so I am reintroduced to one of Poland's greatest preoccupations: the steadily rising crime rate, and the prevailing belief that most of the perpetrators are itinerant Belarussians and Ukrainians, and of course Gypsies. They come to Poland, Danuta says, and sleep on park benches and help themselves to anything they can get. In some places, boys as young as six can be seen lurking on crowded streets, cigarettes dangling out of their mouths, watching for pickpocketing opportunities.

Olga agrees crime has become a problem. Her elderly mother is afraid to visit her father's grave in broad daylight. Women are often mugged in cemeteries; even flowers are stolen from the graves. "But," she says, "I don't think we should blame it all on outsiders. There are many poor Poles who have turned to crime. We have to recognize this."

Marek agrees. The new political realities have yet to improve everybody's living standards, but they have dazzled Poles with glimpses of Western consumer goods, tempting some of them into petty crime. Danuta shrugs and asks how things are in Montreal these days, and I have to admit that though the incidence of crime is low by American standards, we have our share of holdups and muggings and frequent burglaries. I tell them about the automatic lights I bought before leaving home, and that I tried to find an inflatable, lifesize doll to seat in front of the window. Somewhere I had heard about them, I say, but didn't know where to find one.

"Oh." Danuta looks up from her baklava. "They sell them in sex shops in Kraków."

"Sex shops!" I echo, amazed.

"Yes," says Danuta. "You can buy one and take it home."

I say that they probably sell them in Montreal sex shops too; I hadn't thought to look. But I have trouble imagining Danuta inside one of them. She is a plump, graying woman in her midforties—distinctly maternal-looking, though she is childless and has never married.

As for the Sex Business, it is apparently flourishing all over Poland. Prostitution is illegal, but the trade is said to be alive and well, though there are frequent complaints of Bulgarian and Ukrainian prostitutes undercutting local women. I can't help reflecting that this echoes the old resentments against Jewish merchants who allegedly cut prices. We have meanwhile finished our Greek dinner and decide to satisfy Olga's craving for ice cream. I am about, they tell me, to taste the best ice cream in Kraków.

And so we walk toward the ice-cream parlor, taking the King's Way—the route used by the royal entourage on its way to and from Wawel. There are many historic buildings here, among them the oldest hotel in Kraków. I am told that Liszt and Balzac and the occasional czar have stayed at the Pod Różą, but the hotel looks surprisingly modest. These days, it is known for its new casino, Marek says; no one pays attention to its lovely Renaissance portal or the Latin inscription that says: "May this house stand until an ant has drunk the oceans and a tortoise has circled the world." My hosts insist on showing me Kraków's McDonald's—a truly original branch whose lower level has been built into a medieval cellar. This is Kraków, they say; where else would you get an American Big Mac in a six-hundred-year-old brick vault?

Renovated cellars are all the rage in Kraków, and we soon visit another one, the famous Jama Michalika, a cavernous café with marble-topped tables and walls lined with caricatures and paintings. In Communist days, the Jama had a cabaret famous for its satirical shows, but it has been a favorite bohemian haunt since the turn of the century. A dimly lit, oddly cozy place, it has managed to retain its fin de siècle café atmosphere, though—Poland having passed a recent law banning public smoking—it is far less crowded than it used to be.

As we move on, Olga expresses disappointment at the shortness of my intended stay. Four days are hardly enough, she says, given the city's treasures. Just walking through Old Kraków, however, is a true visual treat, for this city, with its ramparts and towers and dungeons and churches, offers seven centuries of Polish architecture, an overwhelming statement of its layered history.

The ice cream, alas, is a disappointment, though this perhaps has something to do with aroused expectations. One of my most vivid childhood memories is of a Łódź café where now and then I would stop with my mother for an ice-cream treat. It was rich and creamy and served between two homemade wafers whose fragrance greeted us long before we reached the café entrance. There have been a few occasions—in Paris once, and in Montreal—when the fragrance of coffee and fresh waffles excited my dormant senses, but there was no ice cream to be had—only the tantalizing, evocative promise, never to be fulfilled.

Still eating our ice-cream cones, we make our way toward Kraków's Market Square, the largest medieval square in Europe, surrounded now by lively cafés and international restaurants, banks and Italianate courtyards. Designed in 1257, this square was for centuries the center of social, commercial, and religious life, as well as a place of public executions. It was here that the Teutonic Knights made their 1525 vow of allegiance to Poland, and two centuries later that the heroic Kościuszko issued his rallying cry against czarist Russia.

As we cross the street toward the square, a horse-drawn carriage comes rolling down the street, in its wake a Krakovian in traditional costume swiftly collecting the horse's droppings. Danuta tells me there was an article in the paper about this Krakovian who reportedly approached the carriage owners' association, asking for the job. He loves horses, he said, and he loves his city and likes to see it clean. And so he spends his days, this scrawny *vieillard*, jogging in his striped balloon pants and embroidered tunic, ever ready with his broom and pan, occasionally tipping his plumed hat at gaping tourists.

In the square, a crowd has gathered around a turbaned snake charmer, watching him sit cross-legged on the ancient flagstones, playing his flute, while a thin, striped snake uncoils itself slowly and begins to dance. Beyond the crowd, children chase the multitude of pigeons, and tourists stand photographing the renowned St. Mary's Church. Apart from flower sellers, the old market stalls are all gone now, but the central Sukiennice, an ancient merchants' hall, contains shops and souvenir stalls and is as crowded with shoppers as it likely was centuries ago. A long, two-story structure, it was a famous medieval trading center, rebuilt during the Renaissance and today housing a National Museum art gallery. I decide to buy a souvenir for my daughter, bemused by the thought that the spot I stand on once saw Polish knights trying on new armor.

As if this wasn't enough to fire my imagination, I suddenly hear a trumpet sound high up in one of St. Mary's towers, an oddly plaintive call commemorating a thirteenth-century Tatar invasion. The Tatars were the first foreigners to devastate Kraków, and according to legend, one of their arrows hit a sentry as he tried to sound the alarm from this very tower. And so to this day, every hour on the hour, the familiar bugle call is heard in the square, breaking off abruptly at the precise moment when the arrow allegedly pierced the trumpeter's throat. The tune has become Kraków's musical symbol, and listening to it play, people in the square stand alert and still, heads raised toward the tiny window in the 266-foot tower.

Only when it is over do we realize that Marek has disappeared, even Olga has no idea where. We turn around and scan the crowd, but he is nowhere to be seen. Olga glances at the statue of Adam Mickiewicz. This monument to Poland's greatest poet is a popular rendezvous spot, and the place where she and Marek used to meet when they began to date.

Olga tells me this, frowning a little, still scanning the immense square. And then she sees him—we all do—hastening toward us from behind one of the flower stalls, grinning with boyish satisfaction. Olga begins to smile; she shakes her head with a look of amused indulgence. Marek comes then and, with a little mock bow, presents each of us with a rose. They are exquisite yellow roses, with an intoxicating fragrance and the longest stems I have ever seen—about four feet! It occurs to me there is something to be said for Poles' gallantry, as well as their determined joie de vivre. In 1945, Allied observers reporting from Warsaw expressed astonishment at the great number of stalls selling fresh flowers. The city was in ruins, people had little to eat, but Varsovians were nonetheless buying carnations and roses. Olga says this was true all over Poland, even in times of acute food shortages.

"When you can't fill your belly," she says, "you have to think of your soul, don't you?"

❧

In Danuta's living room hangs a framed copy of a prewar oil painting. Done by one of her nephews, it shows a typically bucolic scene: a village with willows and wooden huts, two cows grazing in a green pasture, a church spire in the distance. It is titled *Mogiła*, the name of an ancient village that once stood outside Kraków, a stone's throw away from what is now Danuta's neighborhood. Today, all that remains of the village is a majestic Cistercian monastery dating back to the early thirteenth century. Surrounding it is a vast suburb of what the Poles call "anthills"—indistinguishable concrete apartment blocks, built by the Communists on the outskirts of Polish cities. Nowa Huta, where Danuta lives, was quickly constructed after the war to accommodate the thousands of blue-collar workers brought in from the countryside to work in the new Lenin steelworks.

The foundry—the largest in Europe—was built just outside Kraków in utter disregard of the exceptional fertility of local soil and the overwhelming evidence that virtually all raw materials would have to be brought in from other locations. If this was folly, it was not unpremeditated: the Communists were determined to replace Kraków's educated Catholic establishment with a new wage-earning Communist proletariat. As it turned out, Nowa Huta, with its 200,000 inhabitants, became a center of trade union agitation, a subversive force feeding the growth of the national Solidarity movement. It was by then clear, moreover, that Nova Huta, with its forest of smoking chimneys, was an environmental disaster area. Built in the early 1950s with already dated technology, the Lenin steel mill soon had an annual emission of 170 tons of lead. Kraków lies in a valley, and every winter a blanket of polluted air would envelop the city. Monuments that had survived Tatars, Swedes, and Nazis began to be eroded by noxious fumes and acid rain. To the end, however, Communists gave little thought to pollution control. Even the filters fitted on chimneys to control the escape of dust were usually turned off at night to save electricity.

This last bit of information comes from Danuta, who worked at the foundry for some twenty years. Krakovians, she tells me, had four times as many colds as other Poles and three times as much asthma. "Many—many—people suffered from lung cancer and bone disease."

If Danuta uses the past tense, it is because, in recent years, a new industrial management has been taking measures to modernize the steelworks. With Soviet subsidies and its market gone, Nowa Huta's foundry—like much of Poland's industry—had become unprofitable, too antiquated to compete in the free market. *Restructuring* has become the new buzzword in Poland and, while it has arrested the swift decline of the steel industry, it has also brought about massive unemployment. Some fifty thousand employees have been let go in the steel industry, eighteen thousand of them in Nowa Huta. Danuta, a metallurgist, is one of them, but surprisingly, she acknowledges the inevitability of the recent changes.

"People like my father," she says, "would tell you it's better to have pollution and jobs than clean air and thousands of unemployed, but . . .well, that's another generation." She shrugs, smiling bravely.

Danuta and Marek's parents are now back in the village of their birth. Their father, who had a grade-school education, was among the thousands recruited in the 1950s. He was, and remains, a Communist supporter, though, like many such Poles, he participated for years in the American visa lottery. Danuta's parents are now too old to contemplate emigration, but every year thousands of Poles win an entrée to the U.S. this way. The Communist supporters among them see no contradiction between their political stance and private aspirations. What fuels her father's fervor, Danuta tells me, is above all his children's elevated status. Danuta may be unemployed, but all three of his children—there is an architect brother in Nowy Sącz—are educated professionals, with diplomas from the Jagiellonian University.

"This would not have been possible before the war," Danuta points out. "Not for working-class people, and certainly not for women. There were many good things about Communism. It's not as black and white as some people like to think."

Danuta is one of those Poles who favor "the third way"—a system that would combine socialist advantages with the benefits of the free market. Certainly, the bold economic reforms are finally bearing visible fruit. Since 1992, the Gross Domestic Product has been steadily growing. People have possessions they used to see only in the movies.

If Danuta is not as bitter as she might be, it is perhaps because she is one of the "unemployed" workers Stefan Kryński alluded to in Warsaw. She works several hours a day as a consultant, has taken a lodger in—she manages, she says, but concedes it would be more difficult if she had children and was the main breadwinner; if her parents were unable to send occasional provisions from the country.

Having spent the afternoon in Danuta's company, I have heard a good deal about her family. Also, about her fiancé who, over two decades ago, was hospitalized with appendicitis and died soon after, having contracted jaundice from an infected needle.

"That's one thing I *am* bitter about," Danuta has confessed, though she seems more resigned than bitter. There is about many Poles an air of quiet dignity and remarkable forbearance. Though the long lines for food have gone with the Communists, there are still lengthy waits in banks, railway stations, post offices. I accompanied Danuta on some of her daily errands and, contrary to stereotype, saw nothing but civility, solicitude, patience. Though the small supermarket in Danuta's neighborhood was fairly well stocked, most people in this part of town apparently subsist on eggs, vegetables, and pierogi, with meat and fish served only on weekends or holidays. Still, Danuta hastened to add, it is good to go to the shops and not to have to look at empty grocery shelves. When I asked Danuta what was the first new item she remembers finding in the shops after the fall of Communism, she paused for the briefest moment.

"Toilet paper!" she laughed. "And then good shampoo."

Most Poles may not yet be in a position to buy new furniture or appliances, but they are enamored of the color and variety of domestic products. Danuta's bathroom is full of jars and bottles—several kinds of shampoo and hair-care products, cosmetics, cleaning agents. The small bathroom overflows with these, perhaps because there is so little storage space. Like all such apartments, Danuta's was constructed with little regard to aesthetics or even efficiency. There are no bathroom cupboards and only a small bedroom closet. After all, says Danuta, they were not expected to have anything, were they? She is quick to point out, however, that her own parents had to use an outhouse before the war; there was no running water in their wooden hut. "My life has been much easier than my mother's, believe me," she says.

Danuta has cold and hot water, the latter available through a gas-fueled tank suspended beside the bathtub. To save energy, Danuta turns it on only when she is about to take a bath or do a white wash. Space being at a premium in this part of the world, Poles have had to become remarkably ingenious at maximizing their resources. Danuta has a collapsible clothes rack attached to her bathroom ceiling. A tug on a cord opens it up, allowing clothes to drip into the tub below. There is a semi-automatic washing machine in the tiny bathroom, but the water tank is old and a smell of gas lingers in the apartment. Danuta has called several times for a repairman but is still waiting.

"One thing Communism taught us is patience," Danuta says with a smile.

She smiles too when I tell her I have never had the patience to make pierogi, though I love to eat them. Danuta's are made with meat—I suspect for my benefit—and she has served them with sour cream and a wilted cucumber salad the Poles call *mizeria*. She also made cold sorrel soup and a honey cake. As we sit having our dessert, there is a knock on the door. A neighbor has an ailing cat and has come to ask whether by chance Danuta has any antibiotics.

"Oh," I say. "Do you have a cat?"

"No, no." She had bronchitis last winter, Danuta explains, and the neighbor thought she might have some pills left over.

We talk for a while about domestic pets—a status symbol now that pet food is available. And then we become aware of a quarrel next door. The walls in these buildings are made of plaster, and every word is perfectly audible: the man shouting abuse, the woman's shrill attempts at self-exculpation. Danuta's mouth tightens as she listens. Meeting my eyes, she sighs. "This is what happens when men lose their jobs," she says with sudden weariness. "There's nothing left but vodka."

The man continues to swear, and partly to lighten the mood, I speak of the oddity of most Polish curses. *Dog's blood* is a common one;

another, *pale cholera*. "Why *pale* cholera," I ask Danuta across the white-cloth-covered table. "Is there such a thing as dark cholera?"

"I don't know." Danuta smiles, saying most Polish curses have to do with calamity. Just then, the neighbor's booming voice spits out, "May lightning strike you!" and we burst out laughing as we collect the dinner dishes. Danuta, however, does not permit me to do more than carry my plates to the kitchen. When I approach the sink, she stops me with an impatient gesture, reminding me I am the guest.

I am perfectly familiar with this generous hospitality but can't quite bring myself to sit back and enjoy it. It has been a hot day and Danuta was up at five to go to work, cleaning the apartment before I was even up. She cleans it every day, she tells me, for despite the changes taking place at the steel mill, there is still considerable pollution, and the apartment gets very dirty. Most Poles take great pride in domesticity and Danuta is no exception. One of the worst things you can say about a Polish woman is, "she doesn't love her home."

Thin walls and gas smell notwithstanding, Danuta clearly loves hers. Her tablecloth and bedsheets are immaculately white, starched and ironed to perfection; there are doilies on every surface and cloth roses on the television set. The television stands across from the sofa bed, where Danuta—like most adults here—habitually sleeps. When I ask what she does in her free time, Danuta says she reads—English and Russian books, as well as Polish—and watches television. Sometimes she goes to see her parents in the country. I ask what she likes to watch, and she says documentaries and travel programs. If she ever has money, she would like to see the world. So far, she has been only to Hungary and Bulgaria.

"It was nice," she says, "but too much like Poland. I want to see new things. *America*," she says, and gives me a smile that says she is asking for the moon and knows it, but there is no harm in dreaming, is there?

The way Danuta smiles, and arranges her aluminum pots on the floor, and calls out the window to some neighborhood child to come up for cake, gives me a feeling I will experience many times in Poland; a longing to give these people whatever it is they so quietly, so modestly, dream of. There is something about Poland that I find oddly moving; perhaps it reminds me of my own mother's struggles after we left for Israel—the meals cooked on Primus burners, the laundry done in the bathtub. But there is also something about Poland that appeals to my dormant European self. Despite all the changes, this is still a country where adolescents give up their bus seats for their elders, and mothers leave baby carriages outside busy shops. It all seems so rare and precious, like all things on the verge of extinction.

The child who has been skipping rope outside Danuta's entrance is the daughter of a neighbor Danuta has barely met. He works long hours and the girl is left to fend for herself in the summer, her mother having died of cancer last year. She has an aunt in Silesia and an uncle in Chicago. Her father hopes to move there someday. All this Danuta has learned from Ela herself, who followed her up one day, asking for a story. Ela, who is eight, keeps staring at me as she eats her cake but doesn't speak until she has finished, when she asks permission to watch television.

And so Danuta turns the TV on and we sit, all three, on the red-plush sofa bed to watch a televised concert. In recent years, Polish folk music has become increasingly popular, but on this occasion the costumed folk band has teamed up with the reggae musician Norman "Twinkle" Grant to produce music that is as improbable as any of this decade's changes.

And then the telephone rings and Danuta answers, covering the mouthpiece to tell me it's her brother calling from Nowy Sącz. They speak for a few minutes, during which Danuta learns that her nephew—an economics student in Warsaw—has come home for a holiday and is planning a short trip to Kraków. Danuta in turn tells him about her Canadian guest, and they talk a little longer. When she hangs up, she announces that I have been invited to stay in Nowy Sącz.

I thank her and say that I wasn't planning to go to Nowy Sącz, but she says it's near Tarnów, where I have told her I hoped to go, and has an excellent ethnographic park. "Anyway," she says, "he said to be sure to tell you you'll be very welcome."

Homer called it "divine" and Plato declared it "a substance dear to the Gods." It was certainly dear to man, I gather from the guide to the Wieliczka salt mine; there were times when salt was considered more precious than gold. Some of the world's oldest trade routes were created for traffic in salt, and in many parts of the world, cakes of salt have been used as money. All this is new to me. I have never given salt much thought and am here, at this ancient salt mine, on Olga Podlaski's recommendation.

Wieliczka is 9 miles out of Kraków, a small village with a salt industry that has flourished for at least seven hundred years; some say since A.D. 800. According to legend, Queen Kinga dropped a precious ring down from her window and demanded to have it retrieved. This was how the salt deposits are said to have been discovered.

The guide tells us the legend as we stand in a long queue, waiting to be admitted. The mine admits only official groups, so I have joined an Orbis tour guided by a squat, peremptory woman who speaks barely intelligible English. The Danes and Brazilians and Italians don't under-stand her at all, but people are soon referring to her as the General. The mine is overrun with tourists from all over the world, and as we are finally ushered in, I hear an American talk about an Italian girl who reportedly got lost here the other day.

"What happened—did someone find her?" his companion asks.

"I don't know," the young man answers. He has barely spoken when another, older, American voice is heard. "She didn't turn into a pillar of salt, did she?"

Everyone laughs, but the guide is fiercely, stubbornly, humorless. She pauses abruptly and wheels about, her eyes flashing. "She wasn't lost," she says, "and it wasn't at Wieliczka. She went to make a phone call and couldn't get through. That's how all American propaganda starts," she adds in Polish to the accompanying miner.

A miner accompanies all such tours because, in fact, it would be all too easy to go astray in this vast, crystalline labyrinth. There are nine levels and approximately 185 miles of tunnels, stretching over an area some 6 miles wide. Only three levels are open to the public, however, leading down to a depth of 440 feet. A UNESCO World Heritage Site, the mine is a remarkable, eerie place made up of salt-rock passageways and chambers hewn between the seventeenth and nineteenth centuries. The guide leads us toward the stairs, visibly miffed to have her dis-course interrupted by a horse's neigh. Though the mine's lower sections are now mechanized, an occasional horse is still used for transport at the upper levels.

It is a spectacular, chilly descent. At first, there was nothing but relief at this unexpected refuge from the summer heat. But as we keep going down, the chambers become uncomfortably cold and our legs grow limp. Who would have thought going down could be so strenuous? Who would have believed a salt mine could be so fascinating? There are rooms full of salt sculptures, and subterranean lakes, and chapels carved out of salt. The most impressive of these is the ornate Blessed Kinga's Chapel, which stands 39 feet high and measures 177 by 55 feet. Everything inside the chapel is also carved out of salt: the altar and illuminated crystal chandeliers, the stairs and banisters. The chapel was thirty years in the making, with some twenty thousand tons of salt being dug out in the process. Its acoustics turned out to be so superb that the chapel is occasionally used as a concert and banquet hall. This, of all places, is where President Bush was once feted, in a show of gratitude for his contribution to antipollution efforts.

After an hour or so, everyone is cold and exhausted, and we are given a coffee break at a crowded snack bar. I like the look of our miner and go to sit beside him on one of the picnic benches. A tanned, lean man in blue overalls and construction hat, he sits surrounded by foreign tourists and looks pleased to find himself addressed in Polish. The mine, he tells me, still produces tons of pure salt a day but is likely to be depleted in ten to fifteen years. "It's a good thing we have a growing tourist industry." He smiles.

Surprisingly, they also have an underground sanatorium at Wieliczka, specializing in respiratory illnesses: saline air is especially beneficial for asthma and allergies. More astonishing still, there is a huge chamber here, used by the Germans to manufacture spare aircraft parts during World War II. "In a salt mine!" I exclaim on hearing this from the miner.

"Leave it to the Germans," he says with an eloquent gesture.

And then the guide's voice booms over the chatting tour groups, calling out our number, and we all shuffle to join her, like recalcitrant children on a school excursion. The group's American wit is right behind me as we take the stairs. "Back to the salt mines," he says and I laugh, telling him I have recently learned the Polish equivalent of this expression, which is "Back to the prose of life." This delights him; he used to speak Polish but has forgotten most of it. "That's the problem with the General," he then says. "There's no poetry left in her."

His name is Abe Klein and he is from New Jersey, he tells me as we go down the narrow, winding stairwell. He is one of those elderly, chatty Americans one often meets on such tours; a retired high-school teacher who likes to read, cook, travel. By the time we reach the lowest level, I know he is a widower with grandchildren, that he was born in Warsaw, that he is a MENSA member.

In the museum, there are wooden treadmills on display, and wagons and mining tools that date from the thirteenth century. I am fascinated, too, by the geological exhibit, which shows salt crystals with embedded corals, fossilized dates, pine cones.

"These go back twenty million years!" The guide speaks with evident pride, but everyone is so cold by then that it is hard to match her enthusiasm. Someone asks the guide whether she believes in the ghosts that are said to lurk in old Polish mines. He is clearly baiting her, but the guide says some of the miners insist that they do exist. Occasionally, a lost miner has reported being guided by a long-bearded figure carrying a lantern.

"May I have the pleasure of guiding you out of this labyrinth?" a familiar voice says. Abe Klein is once more beside me and, true to his word, accompanies me up in the ancient elevator, back into the warm sunshine. He sits beside me on the tour bus and starts educating me. Early in the history of the Roman army, both officers and soldiers were given a regular allowance of salt. It was called, he says, a *salarium* and eventually came to be replaced with a monetary allowance toward the purchase of salt. "That's where the word *salary* comes from," he informs me. "You didn't know that, did you?"

Before I can answer, the guide informs us that we are about to pass the former Płaszów concentration camp. Built on the site of two Jewish cemeteries, Płaszów was ruled by Amnon Goeth, the sadistic Nazi featured in *Schindler's List*. Toward the end of the war, it held twenty-four thousand prisoners, both Jews and Poles, many of whom were eventually killed at Auschwitz. The camp having been leveled after the war, all we can see from the road below is a large memorial to the camp's victims. It is enough, however, to cast my ebullient companion into abrupt melancholy.

"My grandparents both died in the war," he says with a sigh. "I wish I knew where, at least."

"Yes," I say vaguely. "I know what you mean."

We sit staring out the window.

CHAPTER 3

THE SKY is the first of many surprises: cloudless and blue as a peacock's neck when my inner script apparently called for the leaden sky of wartime photographs: I am on my way to Auschwitz. Having decided against an organized bus tour, I head toward Kraków's old railway station, unreasonably jolted to find my destination—a name haunting millions—printed above a Polish ticket counter.

Today's Auschwitz—Oświęcim in Polish—is a small industrial town serviced by a commuter train full of Poles bearing magazines, flowers. Wearing sandals and dark dress, I stand in a long queue; then, speaking Polish, say the improbable words, "One-way to Auschwitz, please." I say *one-way* because the schedule makes a return by bus more convenient. *Auschwitz*, I say, and no one blinks or winces. Just another name on an ever-changing map.

I get on the train, sitting across from a red-haired woman frowning over a crossword puzzle. She glances up from her magazine, taking in my English paperback, my well-cut dress. I am clearly a foreigner and she smiles brightly, soon offering me a home-baked cookie.

Her name is Zofia Russak and she is a schoolteacher in Auschwitz. Her father having been a railroad man, the family was allowed to stay on in Auschwitz during the war, after most Poles had been relocated. Russak is too young to remember the war, but her parents often speak of it, she tells me. Her sons, on the other hand, are tired of the subject. "You can teach kids their ABCs," she says, "but not the lesson of history."

"What *is* the lesson, exactly?" I ask.

"Doubt yourself." Russak brushes cookie crumbs off her skirt.

"Doubt yourself?"

"Your cause, anyway," says Russak, reminding me of Bertrand Russell who, on being asked whether he would die for his beliefs, exclaimed: "Good God, no! I might be wrong after all!"

"So you think Hitler—"

"Not only Hitler," she interjects with a didactic shake of her head. "The worst slaughters of history were committed in the name of some worthy cause, no?" She gives me a grave, penetrating look.

"Yes," I say; then, "my father's family perished in the war."

"Ah—" sighs Russak, the conductor's arrival forestalling further comment. The train clanks, whistles, chugging along past haystacks and grazing cows and long-skirted peasants gripping black pitchforks. Having only yesterday walked through Kraków's old Jewish district, I find it unnerving to ride, a book in my lap, the very railroad Americans had declined to bomb, unable to believe the reports from Europe. But a trip to Auschwitz is a pilgrimage to the realm of the unbelievable, a mental surrender which perhaps explains the almost-hallucinatory moment I experience on getting off at the Auschwitz station.

I have come up to the second floor for directions, to a vast area with wickets and tropical plants. Though I am well acquainted with these plants—palms, philodendrons, dieffenbachias—the sight of them stops me dead in my tracks. Never, except perhaps in some botanical garden, have I seen indoor plants grown to such monstrous proportions—all the way up to the cathedral ceilings, aggressively spreading left and right. True, the light is excellent, the pots enormous, but is that enough? It probably is, but standing here, on the edge of Auschwitz, these prodigious plants seem oddly macabre; a row of robust but portentous sentries on the threshold to a nightmare.

I have no relatives on my father's side—no grandparents or aunts or uncles, no cousins—not even their photographs. Though I do not know where any of them died, I soon find myself at Auschwitz-I, doggedly looking for them among the countless snapshots. There are long corridors in the brick barracks, closely lined with the inmates' faces. I pause before each photograph and scan the features, names. There are dark and pale faces, plump and gaunt; humble and grim and defiant faces.

"As you can see," says an elderly woman to her younger companion, "a lot of them were Polish." And she is right, though the vast majority of victims in the Auschwitz complex were certainly Jewish. According to recent studies, a million and a half prisoners are said to have died at Auschwitz,* 10 percent of them Soviet prisoners of war, Polish political prisoners, Gypsies. I am briefly astonished to find that the camera has caught some of the inmates smiling. But then it comes to me: the snapshots were taken on arrival, with many of the prisoners still crediting the Nazis' relocation myth. There is, in one of the barracks, an enormous room full of chipped cookware, another with a mountain of old suitcases, the owner's name and address inscribed in white. The prisoners' possessions, confiscated on arrival, were sorted out in an area known as Canada—symbol of abundance in Poland. They are empty now, these old suitcases, but the handwriting on them is brutally evocative, its individuality so eloquent that it instantly calls up a vision of men and women in chaotic rooms, feverishly packing up for an uncertain journey. But this is a post-*Schindler's List* visit. It is difficult to be sure what the imagination would yield without Spielberg's memorable direction.

My father grew up in a small town called Kazimierz Dolny, son of a religious scholar named Shulom and Braha, his sharp-tongued, resourceful wife. There is not much more I know about my grandparents, but I can't shake the feeling that somewhere, in one of these old barracks, I will stumble upon their faces. When I finally give up on the photographs, it is with the wry thought that had this exhibit been organized by the Germans, the photos would likely be displayed in alphabetical order. Nor am I alone in my adherence to stereotype. Just yesterday, a taxi driver told me, "Poland would be in fine shape today if only it had managed to keep Poles for labor, Germans for administration, and Jews for commerce."

The Jews are almost all gone now, but their surviving possessions suddenly threaten my stubborn composure. What finally does me in is the display of children's clothes: tiny, doll-size vests and dresses, much like those once worn by my infant daughter. And then the mountains

---

*The previous, commonly cited, figure of four million was officially revised after the fall of Communism. See Franciszek, Piper, "Estimating the Number of Deportees to and Victims of the Auschwitz-Birkenau Camp," *Yad Vashem Studies* 21 (1991): 49-103.

of shoes, artificial limbs, wire-rimmed eyeglasses, hair. There is a sample of cloth woven from inmates' hair, and examining it, I feel an inner compulsion to seize some Holocaust denier; drag him up to the glass enclosures, the fading, spurned evidence. Would he, I wonder, deny the denials?

"That's really sick," says a tall American girl in white stretch pants. "Imagine using cloth made of my hair!"

The girl's hair is long and dark, glossy as a chestnut. It would have been handled by one of the so-called crematorium ravens, the Jewish squads forced to work on corpses, cutting long hair, pulling out gold teeth, artificial limbs. In time, these *Sonderkommandos* too would be gassed, but meanwhile, their teams played soccer against SS teams!

I go out and take a deep breath at this point, looking out at the clear sky, the bleak grounds full of milling tourists. There are elderly couples with halting steps, students in jeans, many Germans and Japanese with video cameras. They walk from one barrack to another, pausing to consult their guidebooks, pose for photographs. I sit on the stone steps, watching all this, surprised to see families with children, some young enough to be clutching teddy bears. Having occasionally been accused of being an overprotective mother, I now ask myself, How old *should* our children be before we acquaint them with life's ultimate horrors? When my own daughter was small, I could not even bring myself to tell her that an animal had been slaughtered so she could enjoy her favorite lamb chops. It seemed such a shameful secret, the suffering inflicted on helpless animals.

I ponder this as I go to use the public washroom, taken aback by the cooking aromas wafting from the kitchen. Yes, there is a cafeteria at Auschwitz, crowded at this hour with noisy diners. Though I too am hungry, the sight of the heedless lunch crowd fills me with aversion. I feel I will be unable to eat for hours, days, possibly not until I get back home! And then—perhaps because of my recent musings—I recall my first trip to Greece, where I saw lambs grazing beside their mothers, then butcher shops with lamb carcasses hanging on hooks, attracting summer flies. It was not, in subsequent days, as easy to shut out the brutal facts as it had been while shopping at Canadian supermarkets, but did I—I who had felt shaken by the sight of dripping lambs' blood—quit eating meat? I didn't. When all is said and done, it is not all that difficult to shut out the knowledge of others' pain; to silence, when it suits us, even an exigent conscience.

The grim relevance of all this pounces on me as I make my way back toward the Auschwitz barracks. What troubles me above all is the bald fact that any issue is open to rationalization, the insidious process through which we reach moral compromise, often abetted by society. And yet we ask—how can we not ask, visiting Auschwitz—how intellectual giants like Heidegger fell in with the Nazis; how thousands of ordinary, decent people could go about their everyday lives seemingly unperturbed by others' agony. The answer, as Sir Isaiah Berlin suggested, is not to be found in the common depiction of the Nazis as mad, pathological cases, but rather in the diabolically successful brainwashing of a normal populace persuaded that Jews were a subhuman species inimical to their own survival.

Certainly, any reader of Nazi diaries is bound to be struck by the pervasive sense of moral rectitude. Engaged in mass shootings and gassings, most Nazis apparently perceived themselves as positively heroic. They carried out what they saw as loathsome but essential tasks, cultivating a self-image invulnerable to the most gruesome contradictions. "It is not the German way to apply Bolshevik methods during the necessary extermination of the worst enemy of our people," states a military court verdict against a notoriously sadistic German officer.

It is this warped vision—the human capacity for self-deception—that makes me recall Zofia Russak as I go on to visit Auschwitz's Surgical Department. It was in this building, a putative infirmary, that the infamous Dr. Mengele carried out his experiments on human prisoners, whistling operatic tunes. The place quickly became known as the crematorium's waiting room, Josef Mengele as the Angel of Death. The dashing doctor, however, steadfastly saw himself as a dedicated scientist engaged in valuable medical experiments. *Doubt yourself.*

As I leave the infirmary, my thoughts turn to the medical research institute where I once worked as a young student. Though I was often unnerved by the condition of postoperative dogs, I did not question the scientists' moral right to conduct the experiments. I feel I must question it now, even as I wonder: Were my own daughter desperately ill, were it possible to save her through the sacrifice of some animal, would I not jump at the opportunity?

These are the questions that plague me as I pause before the Black Wall, where prisoners—mostly Poles, many of them Resistance fighters—were executed, crying out, "Long live freedom!" Today, tourists stand photographing the lit candles and wilting bouquets, the high windows boarded up to block prisoners' view of the courtyard. My own camera, full of images of monuments and cathedrals, is back in Kraków. I have brought a notebook but rejected the thought of taking photographs. Why should note-taking seem a more respectful way of recording impressions than photography?

As I mull this over, two young Englishmen and a girl arrive and start snapping pictures. Standing before the wall, one of them slaps his hand against his chest and falls sideways, an imaginary victim of the firing squad. The girl laughs, then turns and asks would I take a picture of all three of them.

"Sorry," I say and hasten away, shaken, stopping only when I arrive at the old camp gate with its famous sign, ARBEIT MACHT FREI—work brings freedom. Here too the photographers are at work, posing, gesturing, laughing. It is clear that to the young, World War II is ancient history. They are as morbidly curious, as unmoved, as schoolchildren in the Tower of London.

"Oh look, look—what's that?!" a young woman's voice cries out suddenly. She stands shielding her eyes from the sun, pointing toward one of the watchtowers. Despite the sun and the summer sky, the towers look as sinister as they do in war films. It is impossible to look up and not experience fleeting surprise at not seeing a truculent face, a pointed shotgun. But what I actually see is a bird nest—a large, round straw nest in which two storks are plainly visible.

"Listen to those tourists," a Polish woman says to her husband. "They've probably never seen a stork before."

"Probably," says the husband. He sighs. "We won't be seeing them much longer either if they don't do something about the pollution."

I run into the same couple at Auschwitz-II, known as Birkenau. They are standing in front of the main guardhouse, a forbidding, familiar structure known as the Gate of Death. It was here that new prisoners were made to disembark, after days of travel in cattle cars, to face the selection committee that would decide their fate; here that families found themselves irrevocably separated.

"Left, you died; right, you became a slave," says the bespectacled Pole. He speaks knowledgeably about the camp, telling his wife a fact new to me: some of the Jews actually had to pay for the ticket that would bring them here! I have hung about, eavesdropping on their conversation, aware of a growing reluctance to go through the gate. Birkenau by all accounts was the ultimate hellhole, the most horrific part of the Auschwitz complex, with four steadily smoking crematoria.

"In comparison with Birkenau, Auschwitz-I was a resort," a passing tour guide says, eliciting rueful chuckles. When one of the tourists asks where the Carmelite convent stood, the guide points vaguely over his own shoulder. He is not, his gesture makes clear, about to plunge into this particular controversy, not with Elie Wiesel's speech still echoing all over Poland.

The Nobel Peace laureate, in Poland for the fiftieth anniversary of the 1946 Kielce pogrom, has stirred up an old hornet's nest with his demand that all Auschwitz crosses— "an insult to Jews"—be removed from the former death camp. The Poles, having reluctantly moved the nuns (but not the twenty-three-foot crucifix standing on the site), as well as halted plans for a nearby shopping complex, have been in an uproar over Wiesel's latest demand; a little cowed by the notoriety dredged up at Kielce but equally resentful of Wiesel's opportunistic timing. The ensuing controversy has raised few moderate voices, surprising among them that of Marek Edelman, a commander in the Warsaw Ghetto Uprising. "Poles, too, died in Auschwitz and it's understandable that they should want to have their monuments too," he stated. "Remarks like those made by Wiesel incite people to xenophobia, nationalistic feelings, and religious fanaticism." Edelman shied away from using the more charged *antisemitism*, but sentiments have been running high. On the train from Warsaw, I overheard a heated discussion between two couples, fetching up the war and much else besides.

"What does he mean 'an insult' anyway?" one of the men argued. "Why should a cross be an insult but not their star—are their dead more important than our dead; is their suffering greater than ours?"

"That's how it is," his wife stated. "Don't get so worked up about it," she pleaded. "It's not worth risking a heart attack, is it?"

I have followed the tour group into Birkenau, a shockingly vast area bisected by a railroad track and enclosed by a barbed-wire fence, towers. The ruined camp grounds are punctuated by the remnants of burnt or demolished barracks, of which only sixty-seven have survived intact. There were once three hundred of them, made of brick or timber, standing in long grim rows in an open, 430-acre field. Originally used as stables designed to shelter fifty-two horses each, the barracks came to house hundreds of inmates, sleeping on straw in three-tier bunks, subsisting on turnip soup and bread. A Toronto friend has a snapshot sent by a surviving uncle. It shows several live skeletons reclining on the pine planks, valiantly raising their heads to look into the eye of their liberators' camera. "Don't ask what I had to do to survive," said the accompanying letter. What I do ask, imagining the striped figures scurrying in the mud, the crematoria smoke, the heaps of dead bodies, is the obvious question, How could anyone who did survive go on to lead what we think of as "a normal life"?

"You can't imagine the daily degradation," an Auschwitz survivor told me years ago. "The fights over the slop bucket, a scrap of dry bread from the garbage dump." Mrs. S. survived because, after weeks spent digging trenches, she was transferred to work in the camp's kitchen. She would never stop dreaming, however, of whips and gongs and whistles; the endless dread of finding herself among those selected for the gas chambers. "It was hell on earth—you really *can't* imagine," she said yet again.

And perhaps she was right just then. With the benefit of countless books and documentaries, however, I find myself imagining it all too vividly now. I also find myself somewhat disconcerted that it should be so easy, though I am for the moment prevented from exploring all the reasons for my vague discomfort.

What distracts me is the voice of an elderly woman who stands with her back to one of the ruined crematoria, pointing to what used to be the Birkenau women's camp. It was their barracks' proximity to the chambers of death, she says, that made it doubly difficult for the women to hold on to their sanity. Some of them just couldn't take it and tried to escape, or else threw themselves against the electrified barbed wire. The elderly survivor tells all this to an English teenager—perhaps her granddaughter?—to whose arm she clings and clings. One day, she says, one of her own friends made a dash for the barbed wire, only to be pounced on by the SS guards' vicious dogs.

The woman begins to weep, and I turn away, swept by a sudden, peculiar sense of shame. I may be a Holocaust survivor's daughter, but I have come here with a notebook in my bag, a fountain pen full of ink. I have come to pay homage, I thought, but all at once feel like a trespasser, one groping to make sense of my own chaotic feelings.

Overcome by the need to be alone, I walk away briskly, eventually coming to a small pond where ashes from two of the crematoria were routinely dumped. But here, too, tourists come and go, among them an adolescent boy with. . .*a Walkman*? Yes. He pauses with his parents and looks down at the gray water, then strolls away, his fair head bobbing rhythmically. This is one of the most unnerving things I see at Auschwitz, and it reminds me of the Nazis' own passion for music: the waltzes and tangos that greeted new arrivals at the Gate of Death, the concerts that gifted inmates routinely put on for their jailers' pleasure. In her fine memoir, *Playing for Time*, Fania Fénelon, a French singer, recalls her experiences as a member of Birkenau's women's orchestra. It was headed by Alma Rosé, Gustav Mahler's niece, who had been unexpectedly arrested on a musical tour in Holland. When the distinguished musician died at Birkenau, her corpse was ceremoniously laid out and blanketed with flowers; a great profusion of white lilies ordered by the grieving SS. The uniformed officers all came to pay their respects, filing past with bowed heads, many of them in tears.

It is the thought of this scene, its power to shock, that eventually leads me to an inner articulation of what has been bothering me. Simply and brutally put, it is the awareness that Auschwitz, a fifty-year-old metaphor, has gradually become a grim cliché. This may seem an offensive observation to some, and an obvious one to others; to me, it is underscored, and made intolerable, by the presence of flesh-and-blood survivors in this haunted landscape. And there is something else, equally disconcerting: one cannot write about the horrors of Auschwitz any more. One can only write about the difficulty of trying.

It is late afternoon when I retrace my steps, leaving Birkenau. Slowly, I make my way back toward town, eventually arriving at the apple orchard blocking all view of Auschwitz-I. In the dappled shade, birds sing and doves call and the apple trees spread their fruit-laden branches over the fence. I think of Yevtushenko reading his poem, "Stolen Apples," his face aglow, recalling the incomparable taste of forbidden fruit. Impulsively, I reach out and pluck my own red apple; then stop, look at it and, once more filled with repugnance, throw it over the fence.

Only then do I see the child watching me from the house across. I look at the houses—the flower boxes, the billowing curtains—and find myself thinking of Zofia Russak's family, sitting down to a Sunday meal, with the smell of roasting flesh carried in by the summer breeze. I imagine them awakened in the night by trains, watching through drawn curtains the unfolding of others' nightmare. I see them shuffling back to warm beds, eventually learning to sleep through it all.

I imagine all this, and an old Holocaust poem echoes in my head, vying with theologian Michael Wyschorgrod's words: "It is forbidden to make art out of the Holocaust because art takes the sting out of suffering."

To be sure, but is there any virtue in perpetuating suffering? Haven't people often turned to art precisely in order to make the unbearable less so?

This is the last question I ask myself as I board the bus, looking out the window at this place called Auschwitz. It is a disconcertingly ordinary town, on whose streets children ride bikes, dogs bark at cars, and women pause to chat under shop awnings. The bus stops, an elderly man gets on, and a soldier jumps up, offering his seat. Beside him sits a flushed woman, steadily wiping perspiration from the face of her Down syndrome daughter. Just over half a century ago, girls such as this were among the first to be herded into the gas chambers. But half a century is a very long time, and this is the sort of summer day on which the Romantics couldn't resist putting pen to paper. Across from me, on the bus, the Down's girl hums to herself. People smile kindly. Outside, in front of a cornfield, an arrowed sign says: TO THE MUSEUM.

CHAPTER 4

ONE JEWISH GIRL who would have likely ended up at Auschwitz was saved in the city of Nowy Sącz by a Polish watchmaker. Like other ancient Polish towns, Nowy Sącz has a central marketplace with a town hall, a massive neo-Gothic structure with a tall tower where the young girl sat hidden for two unimaginable years. She was, I am told, hidden in the cupola, above the erratic clock that required regular adjustment. Or so the watchmaker claimed, using this pretext to make frequent trips up the clock tower to feed the girl.

Janusz Krenz, Danuta and Marek's brother, remembers the story on learning that my own father started out as a watchmaker in Poland. The hidden girl survived the war and went on to live in Israel. "She still comes to Nowy Sącz to visit," says Janusz, "but to this day can't bear to be anywhere near a ticking clock."

I like the story and I like Janusz, and am glad I let Danuta talk me into stopping in Nowy Sącz. Janusz and I speak French, which he learned while working in Algeria. He settled in Nowy Sącz because there was a construction boom in those days, and because his wife's family had lived here for generations before being deported to Wrocław. It was all part of a 1947 Communist campaign aimed against the Ukrainian Resistance Army. The Bieszczady and Beskid Niski regions had sizable Ukrainian communities in those days, allegedly collaborating with the rebels under the slogan Neither Hitler Nor Stalin! The infamous Operation Vistula succeeded in destroying the rebels' base, but in doing so victimized two subethnic groups living in southeast Poland. The Boyks and the Lemks—of whom Janusz's wife is one—found themselves deported along with thousands of local Ukrainians, either east to the Soviet Union or west to the recently liberated German territories.

Both Lemks and Boyks are descendants of nomadic shepherds who settled in Poland in the thirteenth to fifteenth centuries. Unlike the majority of Poles, who are Roman Catholic, they are either Russian Orthodox or Eastern Catholics belonging to the Uniate Church. The Uniates—including Greek, Armenian, Syrian and Coptic Catholics—uphold the supremacy and infallibility of the Pope but have their own liturgy, religious rites, and customs: *their* priests are allowed to marry.

I learn all this while Janusz takes me around his adopted town. Capital of the Beskid and Sądecki region, Nowy Sącz was founded in 1292 on the Dunajec River. A pleasant provincial town, it has several sites of touristic interest, notable among them the local *skansen*—a vast open-air museum of a type seen all over Poland. Nowy Sącz's is an impressive one, its recreated villages representing the region's diverse ethnic cultures. As in all *skansens*, the interiors have been faithfully furnished and decorated, offering insight not only into rural architecture but also the lifestyle of various social classes. We see everything from a farm laborer's thatched cottage to a seventeenth-century manor house transported to the park with its original interior and wall paintings intact. Eventually, we arrive at two Gypsy huts, set some distance away from the simulated village as they would be in fact. Transferred from their original mountain site, the two sheds are but a small part of a Gypsy hamlet-in-progress.

"The Carpathian Gypsies are the poorest in Poland," Janusz tells me as we study one makeshift dwelling. Coated with clay and white-washed, the room we stand in has wrapping paper nailed to the ceiling, and walls decorated with postcards and newspaper clippings. There is a primitive cooking stove and minimal furniture: an iron bed with a straw mattress and blankets, a hand-hewn shelf, a bench. When he learns that I am planning to see the Gypsy exhibit in Tarnów, Janusz excuses himself to make a phone call and comes back to tell me he has invited an ethnographer friend for tea.

"He's bound to know more about them than I do," he explains with utter simplicity.

I have come to Poland with only five contacts but am beginning to see that these five are very likely to be compounded, given the exceptional kindness and hospitality of people along the way. In contrast with the frequently grudging attitude of people in the service industry, Poles in private life often go out of their way to be helpful. Even perfect strangers on the train to Kraków urged me to visit them in Olsztyn so they could show me the Mazurian lakes. In Nowy Sącz, Polish hospitality reaches unexpected heights.

We had agreed that I would call and let the Krenzes know the precise time of my arrival, but—and this would prove to be a frequent problem with Polish phones—I couldn't get through to them. I arrived in Nowy Sącz in the evening, during a cold, rainy spell, and stood searching for their bell in the fading light. The Krenzes live in an outwardly dreary "anthill" with a typically rundown exterior: the floor and stairs bare concrete, the small entrance dark and ill ventilated.

The Krenz bell was out of order, but someone let me in. As I made my way up to the fourth floor, the timed light went off, forcing me to climb the remaining stairs in the musty dark. When I finally stepped into the Krenz home, I felt the way a weary desert wanderer must feel, arriving at an oasis.

I was greeted by a slight, fair-haired woman of great charm and warmth, wearing an apron and holding a soup ladle. She had been stirring a pot of jam, and the entire apartment was filled with the delectable aroma of stewed apricots. The apartment seemed typically small, but exceptionally inviting, full of books in several languages, pictures, countless flourishing plants.

Anna invited me into the kitchen, telling me to call her by her first name—an unusual request, coming from a middle-aged Polish woman. Her kitchen was bright and spacious, cluttered with pots, pans, huge jars of homemade pickles, drying mountain herbs. She sat me at the kitchen table and fed me delicious cream of vegetable soup and blintzes, stirring the jam as we chatted and peeling garlic for the pickle jars.

Anna is a poet with two published books to her credit. When I asked her what name she wrote under, she hastened to assure me she was not at all well known, except perhaps in tiny literary circles. In any case, poetry—in fact all serious literature and art—is quickly becoming a luxury, she stated, appreciated by an increasingly shrinking public. In Communist days, there were of course many imposed restrictions, but artists could count both on state subsidies and a devoted readership. Now they have the freedom to write anything they want but no one to write for. "We're well fed these days but are quickly becoming redundant," Anna concluded.

This conversation (which took place about three months before Wisława Szymborska won the 1996 Nobel Prize for Literature) reminded me of a Writers' Union meeting described by Eva Hoffman in *Exit into History*, an event that took place in Warsaw right after the fall of Communism. Poignantly, Hoffman speaks of an elderly writer's dawning realization of what the free market might mean to the likes of him. Having grown accustomed to a system that paid writers, regardless of quality or popularity, on a per page basis, the dismayed writer stood up to exclaim that "under the new system, it's possible that good, serious books may make less money than mediocre or even very bad ones!"

And, of course, it has come to pass. Polish writers, like their Western counterparts, must now compete not only against the ubiquitous television but books by Krantz, Ludlum, Steel.

"At least my cakes and jam are still wildly popular," Anna joked as her husband came in from the rainy night, sniffing appreciatively around the giant pot. A tall, dark-haired man with soft features and a laid-back air, he was soon followed by his sons: twenty-two-year-old Staszek, the economics student, and twenty-year-old Paweł, a computer science student in Kraków. Though Danuta had assured me that space was not a problem, I suddenly registered that I was to occupy the only bedroom, one shared by the two boys throughout their childhood. We chatted for a while—in French with Anna and Janusz, English with their sons—and then got ready for sleep: I on one of the bunk beds, the two brothers in the living room, on a double mattress set on the floor, between their parents' sofa bed and the dining table. I was deeply moved, all the more because they contrived to be so graciously offhand as to seem not at all inconvenienced. I asked myself, Do I know anyone back home who would be willing to be put out like this for a perfect stranger? I don't. Perhaps not even for a friend.

Anna turns out to be one of the best cooks I have ever met. She has spent the morning shopping and cooking while her sons were hiking in the nearby mountains and Janusz and I drove around Nowy Sącz. When we come back for dinner, it is to be greeted by another tantalizing aroma; a familiar one that, the moment I enter, flashes me back once more to my Polish childhood: my mother in the kitchen frying wild mushrooms in butter, filling our home with an incomparable, unforgettable fragrance. I close my eyes, utterly transported, learning that Staszek and Paweł have brought the mushrooms from the mountains. I am shown one of them—a huge one, almost a foot in diameter—which, alas, is wormy; the others Anna has quickly washed and fried to accompany her schnitzel. But first there is an exquisite celery root salad and a cold cherry soup. A late-afternoon feast during which we speak mostly Polish, talking about life in Algeria, Canada, Poland; inevitably, about politics. I learn that 40 percent of Poles did not vote in the 1995 elections, Janusz being one of them. This does not prevent him from arguing with his wife and sons, each of whom holds a slightly different point of view. On one thing they all agree: Poland is changing at a dazzling speed, but people haven't yet learned their way around the new system.

Before 1989, says Janusz, Poles knew how to milk the system for all it was worth. In his field, materials were habitually stolen by construction workers, and even those put in charge. The foreman, for example, might offer his engineer and architect cognac provided by some grateful beneficiary; someone who had himself obtained free construction materials in the past. "And so it went, you see, a vicious circle." He makes a vaguely scornful gesture. When I ask how architects are faring these days, he admits it is not easy, for the usual reasons: housing subsidies have ended, and the private construction industry has not yet taken off. He seems about to elaborate when Staszek looks up at me with a popular riddle.

"Why has there been no spring this year?" he asks, smiling ironically. When I plead ignorance, he says, "Because Kwaśniewski promised us new housing by spring!"

We all laugh, but when Anna tries to defend Kwaśniewski, Staszek scoffs at her. "Don't listen to my mother," he says. "She only likes Kwaśniewski because he's more refined than Wałęsa." He goes on to tell me that when pollsters asked Polish women why they had voted for Kwaśniewski, many of them reportedly said, "Because he's good-looking."

"It's not a question of good looks," Anna says, bristling at her son. "It's a question of manners, of savoir faire." To illustrate her point, she tells me of a TV debate between Wałęsa and Kwaśniewski, during which Kwaśniewski offered his hand in a handshake. "And would you believe it—" she looks at me intently "—a head of state saying—on TV—I'm willing to give you my foot if you like!" She looks indignant, her gray eyes flashing, but breaks into an abrupt smile when Janusz says, "If at least his socks were not so smelly, right?"

"No, seriously—" she turns back to me "—things are better for some, worse for others—that's the long and the short of it."

"You see how it is," says Janusz. "In Communist days there was no unemployment, but nobody really worked. The attitude was: you can always sleep on the job, right? Now everyone wants to work, but there's not enough employment."

When I echo Stefan's point of view in Warsaw—that many so-called unemployed Poles work under the table—Janusz concedes it's difficult to be sure of numbers. There are certainly those who are unofficially employed, but on the other hand, the government's optimistic figures are equally unreliable: Kwaśniewski has started a new policy of taking names off official unemployment lists once people's benefits have run out. "Half of what we hear on TV is just Kwaśniewski's propaganda," he says, and then they are off again, arguing across the table.

Paweł, the quietest of them, smiles at me with arched eyebrows. "You know what they say around here: two Poles meet on the street and immediately you have three political parties." I will hear this joke many times in Poland, for Poles love to laugh at themselves, even more perhaps than at the strangers in their midst. Eventually, the talk turns to Polish minorities, which still exist despite Communist efforts to eradicate ethnic identity. Though many have been absorbed by the urban mainstream, there are pockets of well-established ethnic and religious minorities in several regions. I am amazed to learn that Poland has an ancient Muslim community in the northeast, its history going back all the way to the seventeenth century!

"My girlfriend belongs to yet another minority," Paweł informs me. "She's Lithuanian and—"

"And she still worships fire and snakes," Staszek interjects, teasing.

When I look mystified, Paweł explains that the Lithuanians were the last Europeans to embrace Christianity; that one still comes across practices originating in their pagan past.

"Not in the cities, of course," says Staszek, "but in the northeast— a village called Puńsk, for example, where they're all Lithuanian."

And so my education continues. I learn that the Lithuanians are not Slavs but a Baltic people speaking the most ancient of Indo-European languages. Also, that despite the commonwealth established through Jagiełło's marriage to Princess Jadwiga, there have always been tensions between Poles and Lithuanians, who apparently regard Poles as a big, overdominant sibling.

"That's how it is with minorities," says Janusz. "There's always friction of one kind or another; often xenophobia too." Over a thousand refugees arrive in Poland every year, mostly from Asia and Africa. Though most of them eventually go on to Germany or Sweden, many do end up settling here, to some Poles' dismay. In 1995, one in eight applications filed by refugees was granted by the state.

I say I have not run into any hostility toward Third World refugees but keep hearing about Ukrainians' and Belarussians' criminal leanings. Things are much worse across the border, Staszek—who has been to the Ukraine—states. To the Ukrainians and Belarussians, Poland is like America. He then remembers something he and Paweł heard on their way home today. They had hitchhiked back from the mountains, getting a ride with a Krakovian who had been robbed at a supermarket. A week later, his wallet was returned with all his ID's, along with an apology for the conditions that forced the thief to keep the stolen cash.

"We have lots of thieves in Poland," Paweł says, laughing, "but at least they are gentlemen."

I laugh too, enjoying the food and wine, the congenial company. I think of my own hitchhiking days in Europe, and of my teenage daughter who, I fervently hope, will not repeat her mother's folly. I ask Staszek and Paweł whether hitchhiking is safe in Poland, and they assure me it is. Regular hitchhikers can actually buy special coupon books and, on obtaining a lift, give the driver a coupon for the agreed-on distance. Drivers who collect the highest number of coupons are eligible for prizes. Anna worries that in a few years such things will no longer be possible in Poland.

We have finished our splendid dinner and sit eating pale, translucent gooseberries when the doorbell rings and Janusz says that must be Mateusz Klasa, their ethnographer friend. My questions about Gypsies are about to be answered, I'm told.

In 1763, a Hungarian pastor at the University of Leiden chanced to meet students from northern India and, listening to them talk, noted a striking similarity between their speech and that of Hungarian Gypsies. Though Gypsies themselves have always maintained their origins to be in Egypt (hence the name *Gypsy*), the pastor's astute observation led to extensive philological studies, which in due course convinced most scholars that India was in fact the Gypsies' country of origin. Because Gypsies have always borrowed from the language of their host country, their speech also offered important clues to their migratory route. It is now believed that they left India for Persia in the tenth century, arriving in Europe toward the beginning of the fourteenth.

I get this introduction from ethnographer Mateusz Klasa, who has arrived for tea carrying a book about Polish Gypsies. It is a marvelous work, rich in photographs, which Klasa illuminates with many a fascinating anecdote. Gypsies arrived in Europe claiming to be religious penitents and, having been granted safe conduct by the Pope, roamed freely for over half a century, immune not only to persecution but also to prevailing laws. Some eighty years after their appearance in Western Europe, however, this reprieve came to an abrupt end, the reputedly lawless Gypsies finding themselves henceforth unwelcome in much of Western Europe.

So began the melancholy saga of one of Europe's most persecuted minorities; a people universally shunned, forcibly sterilized, and murdered—400,000 of them by the Nazis. Europeans' hostility, commonly attributed to Gypsies' unscrupulous ways, was apparently compounded by rampant superstition. Klasa shows me photographs of various objects used in Gypsy magic: a hairy black cross, a miniature black devil in a hen's egg, a wax corpse in a glass of water. Reputed to be cannibals, sorcerers, and necromancers, Gypsies were as feared as they were reviled. They were also deeply resented, for unlike the oppressed peasantry, they were not bound to any landlord and, initially, were even free of all tax obligations. Though most Gypsies have given up the nomadic life, they are still shunned today for their allegedly criminal ways and, more rarely, envied for their acquired wealth.

Having seen countless Gypsy beggars on Warsaw and Kraków streets, I am surprised by the last bit of information, but Klasa insists that some local Gypsies have in fact grown immensely rich. There have always been rumors of Gypsies secreting away ill-gotten gold, but in recent years, their wealth has become evident in Poland. Having migrated to Germany and Switzerland as guest workers, some Gypsies have apparently managed to save and invest their earnings, and today there are those among them who own villas, luxury cars, yachts. Most of these Gypsies belong to the Kalderashi tribe, which has gradually come to dominate other, less successful ones.

The Kalderashi are thought to be the most vital and enterprising of Poland's Gypsies and, having traveled widely, maintain a fiercely con-descending attitude toward their less adventurous brethren. Lowest in the Polish hierarchy are the Carpathian Gypsies, scorned for their abysmal poverty but also for having been the first to relinquish the nomadic life. Though social and technological realities eventually forced most Gypsies to abandon their traditional pursuits, they gener-ally remain associated with the trade for which their particular clan happened to be known. For women, the options were limited to fortune-telling and potion selling, but men were in great demand as musicians, blacksmiths, tinsmiths, and coppersmiths; many worked as tinkers, ani-mal trainers, or livestock traders. The latter often included horse theft, an occupation for which Gypsies had an inordinate respect, requiring as it did great skill and daring. I am surprised to hear that Gypsies were also known as gifted rat catchers, sought after in plague-infested Europe and, more recently, World War II's aftermath, when urban ruins had become infested with starving rodents.

"Gypsies maintain that rats are hypnotized by certain tunes," says Klasa, a fact documented in the following May 27, 1946 article pub-lished in a Warsaw daily, and cited by Jerzy Ficowski in *The Gypsies in Poland*.

> Last night, late by-passers on Pańska Street were able to witness a strange sight. An elderly man in a hat, the broad brim of which concealed most of

his face, was walking down the middle of the street, and beside him walked two small boys wearing the same kind of headgear. The older man was playing on a pipe, and the two boys were beating on little drums. . . Not far behind this strange procession ran a band of rats. There may have been several hundred of them. At the corner of Pańska and Chłodna Streets, there was a small lorry with a ramp. The musicians went up this ramp into the lorry and then sat on the roof of the cab, playing all the time. The band of rats stopped at first in hesitation on the pavement, but lured on by the never-ceasing tones of the strange rhythmical melody, reminiscent of the humming of enormous hornets, began at first singly, and then en masse, to enter the lorry. When all the rats were inside, several men standing nearby slammed the door shut and covered the top with a wooden lid.

And I thought *The Pied Piper* was just a fairy tale!

The next day, I make the trip to the Tarnów museum where Klasa has arranged for me to meet Adam Bartosz, director of Tarnów's Regional Museum and the man responsible for the creation of the Gypsy wing—the only exhibit in the world to deal with Gypsy history and culture. To my delight, I also find the English translation of Ficowski's book, a work that, together with Isabel Fonseca's *Bury Me Standing*, will go a long way toward satisfying my curiosity about Gypsies. I ask Adam Bartosz how many of them there are today, but the question turns out to be problematic, since Gypsies have traditionally been left out of European countries' censuses. Most Gypsiologists believe the world population to be approximately twelve million, he tells me, but all statistics pertaining to Gypsies are finally unreliable. It is not known, for example, what percentage of Gypsies remain nomadic, though they are probably a minority these days, and more likely to travel in cars, trucks, or trailers than the traditional caravans.

Having roamed as far as Australia and the Americas, Gypsies speak a multiplicity of dialects (sixty in Europe alone) but share a basic vocabulary rooted in Sanskrit. The Gypsies refer to themselves as Roma and to their language as Romany—from *Rom* for "man" or "husband." (The name is in no way connected with Romania, though Gypsies have lived in that country in large numbers for several centuries.) Romany, states Fonseca, is an exceptionally poetic language, in which "I love you," for example, is conveyed through expressions like

"I lick your tiny heart" or "I drink your face" and a sexual orgasm as the plucking out of one's own eyes. There is a Gypsy legend about the Romany language, in which the full moon is said to have been drawn down to earth by the sheer intensity and witchery of Romany.

Gypsy lore is rich in such legends, one of which attempts to explain the age-old Gypsy custom of taking on the religion of their host country. When God was giving out different religions, they say, theirs happened to be written on fresh cabbage leaves, all eventually ending up in a hungry donkey's stomach!

Whatever their officially adopted religion, Gypsies have always maintained their own set of religious beliefs and practices, with many tribal variations. The Kalderashi, for example, greet the new moon in hopes of ensuring good luck in their wanderings. They take off their hat to it, bow, and pray for protection and guidance. Interestingly, says Adam Bartosz, while Gypsies secretly scorn gullible outsiders' faith in their own powers, they are themselves intensely superstitious, given to perpetual interpretation of good and bad omens. They have a morbid fear of snakes, which they believe like to suck nursing mothers' milk, and of owls, whom they sometimes subject to verbal abuse in city zoos. Like many Europeans, Gypsies interpret a sighted lizard as a good omen; the disappearance of lice, on the other hand, fills them with peculiar terror.

"Death shows up, louse vanishes," they say, having evidently observed that lice invariably abandon a corpse as it starts getting cold. This was why, subjected to delousing treatments at Auschwitz, Gypsies often made desperate attempts to hold on to at least one louse, certain that its disappearance would bring on inevitable death.

Only twenty thousand Polish Gypsies managed to survive the war, and most of those were soon back on the trail, living in caravans, dancing around campfires, celebrating births, holidays, weddings. Contrary to popular belief, says Bartosz, Gypsies have very close family ties, with carefully regulated social and sexual mores. I ask about the position of women in Gypsy culture, and Bartosz tells me they are considered indisputably inferior to men and, except in old age, are virtually powerless. Though polygamy is no longer practiced, Gypsy men are still free to commit adultery, while a woman may find herself branded if caught in the act. Far from being the wanton seductresses of popular imagination, Gypsy women are in fact exceedingly prudish, as in some respects are the men. Believed to possess dark and mysterious powers, all sexually active women are thought to be innately polluted and thus capable of contaminating any man. They may defile one simply by throwing their skirts over his head, or just threatening to!

Despite such blatant risks, Gypsies are generally eager to marry and to procreate. They marry in their early teens, with or without family consent. Bride abduction, in fact, is a fairly common practice among Gypsies, for once virginity has been compromised, a traditional wedding inevitably follows. The marriage ceremony calls for an elder to tie the couple's hands together, reciting, "I throw the key into the water so that none shall find it and nothing shall be opened with it, and so nothing shall divide you."

In fact, tradition itself divides them for, until she reaches menopause, a woman's place is apart from the men's, with children and other women. "Lots of children, lots of luck," say the Gypsies and seem to cherish theirs. Gypsy mothers routinely nurse their young until they are three or four, with five- and six-year-olds still getting an occasional treat of mother's milk. Scandalous as this may seem to non-Gypsy observers, the custom may have served to ensure adequate nourishment for young children in frequently straitened circumstances.

What do most Gypsies eat? These days, pretty much what Poles do, though Gypsies have had to be as adaptable in matters of diet as in every other sphere. Bartosz tells me about nettle soup, for example—a once-common Gypsy dish—and roast hedgehog, which many Gypsies have long considered a special delicacy. The custom was to cook the hedgehog, prickles and all, in fresh clay, placing it on live embers. Gradually, the clay would harden, and once it cracked, the hedgehog would be removed, roasted to perfection, its prickles lodged in the dry clay.

But Gypsy customs, like their traditional occupations, are quickly disappearing as more and more Gypsies are assimilated into the general population. In Eastern European countries especially, Gypsies have fallen victim to Communist governments' concerted efforts to achieve social homogeneity. Forced in the 1950s to give up their nomadic lifestyle, many Gypsies found it impossible to adapt to what came to be known among them as the Great Halt. There were subsequent cases of reported suicide and of many psychiatric confinements.

"Life is too short for a Gypsy to work," some told government officials pressing them to conform. Though Gypsies have always worked, the new unskilled, poorly paid, and physically demanding jobs did not appeal to them. Alas, the subsidized housing offered by the government was contingent on regular, lawful employment. And so the Gypsies went to their menial jobs, thousands of them to the notorious Lenin steelworks and "anthills" of Nowa Huta. The rent-free apartments, Mateusz Klasa told me in Nowy Sącz, presented other, unforeseen, problems. Gypsy men, for example, could not abide having women live above them in high-rise blocks and sometimes insisted on having an entire top floor, where they led their extended-family lives, working at the foundry, cooking on home fires. At dinnertime, smoke would be observed by their Polish neighbors, billowing out of every window on the Gypsies' floor.

This life, however, remained utterly intolerable for some. Now and then, entire clans would pick up and settle in the forest. The concrete blocks made them feel like prisoners, they complained to officials. What Polish authorities often had to contend with was a seasonal shift in Gypsy attitude. The Gypsies would eagerly accept accommodation and employment in autumn but vanish without a word as soon as springtime came.

All the same, Adam Bartosz tells me, by the midseventies, the Communist government's campaign had reached its official goal, with Gypsies routinely taking on Polish names, sending their children to school, and, inevitably perhaps, intermarrying. In recent decades, Gypsies have been more kindly regarded by urban Poles, only to have old hostilities flare up after 1989. The change in attitude has accompanied the sudden influx of Gypsies from Romania, where they currently number at least two million and where, in recent years, they have been subject to lynchings and mob violence. Bartosz confirms that both Poles and established Gypsies resent the invasion of these destitute foreigners—the former because of increased vagrancy and crime, the latter because the newcomers' conduct is turning public opinion against Gypsies in general. When the Communist regime fell, says Bartosz, Gypsies became the first victims of widespread unemployment. In some areas, entire villages became abruptly idle, children stopped attending school, and many turned to begging. "Only 50 percent of

Gypsies are officially employed at full-time jobs," says Bartosz. They work in road or building construction; as drivers, salesclerks, and itinerant merchants. "There are, of course, the wheeler-dealers among them. They trade in gold or foreign currency; others in stolen cars."

Gypsies, I have been told, love cars as passionately as they once loved horses, and it's not difficult to guess why. When Bartosz tells me that there are many Gypsies who still dream of someday resuming the nomadic life, I remember a long-ago summer in Spain where, hitch-hiking with a friend, I stood on the roadside, watching a Gypsy caravan roll by. The Gypsies did not stop, but the children called out to us in Spanish, the women waved their tarot cards inquiringly, and the men sat there, intense and silent, watching us with their glowing eyes.

I know, of course, that Gypsy life has been highly romanticized, but I confess to experiencing a certain nostalgia for the Spanish Gypsies, especially after being ushered outdoors to look at some old caravans. It is early afternoon and, after a brief shower, the sun has come out and is quickly drying up small, shining puddles. There is an intense fragrance of wet earth, intermingled with that of black lilac blossoms. Bees buzz, and white butterflies flutter, and birds sing up in the trees, under whose branches several richly ornamented Gypsy caravans stand empty, idle. I think of the Nowa Huta Gypsies cooped up in the gray concrete blocks and remember how, all through my childhood, the arrival of spring would transform me from a bookish, housebound child into one so wildly restless that there was no keeping me indoors after school. Standing on the grounds of the Tarnów museum, and having spent two nights in Nowa Huta, I know one thing: I would have been among those who stealthily drove off into the spring night, notwithstanding lurking owls or snakes, just bowing to the moon and praying for a lizard.

CHAPTER 5

I HAVE BEEN WARNED against sitting alone in train compartments, particularly in isolated rural areas where passengers are often few and far between. On the way to Krynica, I find myself not only alone in my compartment but in the entire car. I have the uncomfortable feeling of being the only passenger left on the train and am thinking of checking out the adjacent cars when a scruffy, luggageless man tramps by; then, having registered my presence, backtracks and is about to enter my compartment just as the conductor approaches. The stranger must have seen him through the glass door, for he all at once freezes, wheels about, and sprints down the corridor in the opposite direction. A moment later, I see him through the window, running across the rail tracks toward an open field.

"He has jumped off the moving train, in the middle of nowhere!" I tell the conductor, but he only shrugs and says that's how things are. He warns me not to fall asleep while traveling by train. I ask where I can get some food, only to be told the train doesn't even have a snack bar. This has never happened before, but I know by now that not all Polish trains are created alike. They run the full gamut from the upscale Inter-City with air conditioning and dining cars to ancient, grimy ones with hard seats, broken toilets, and nothing by way of food or beverage. On most trains, even functioning bathrooms seldom have soap or tissues or paper towels; some may not even have a toilet, let alone a water fountain.

The train to Krynica may leave something to be desired, but the trip itself turns out to be one of the most exciting rail experiences I am to have all summer. Southern Poland is said to be the country's most scenic region, its topography defined by the formidable Carpathians, the highest and largest mountain chain in Central and Eastern Europe. Made up of several mountain ranges, the Carpathians link the Alps with the Balkans, providing breathtaking vistas straight across the south.

The rail route between Nowy Sącz and Krynica runs through a sparsely populated, largely unspoiled landscape. This was once Lemk and Boyk country, and though the Lemks and Boyks are mostly gone, their old villages continue to dot the hills, showing off a wide array of extraordinary timber churches. Known as *cerkwie*, these churches represent some of the finest examples of Polish rural architecture, the oldest of them (in Powroźnia) dating back to 1643. The *cerkwie* were built by the Russian Orthodox Church, or by the Uniates, but after World War II all were taken over by the Roman Catholic Church.

The train goes across the Beskid Sądecki range, through deep valleys and mountain gorges, past rivers and forests and small country huts straight from a child's drawing pad. Rural trains still have openable windows, sending my way heady whiffs of pine resin and mountain herbs, hay and ripe fruit and manure—an ongoing olfactory adventure that makes me forget both hunger and thirst. Outside the window, there are rye and wheat and potato fields, and cows chewing their cud in immense green pastures. Now and then, I see farmers at work, and they pause to wave at the passing train, screening their eyes from the sun.

In Rytro, two of them get on the train and come to share my compartment—an elderly, toothless couple carrying several plastic and rough cotton bags. The woman wears a kerchief tied under the chin and has a large hair-sprouting mole beside her mouth. A *baba-jaga* straight out of my childhood fairy tales but a surprisingly amiable one, with a child's unclouded blue eyes staring at me with open curiosity. She keeps trying to make conversation, but I can barely understand the dialect she speaks. She understands me perfectly, though, and makes an effort to improve her diction. They are, she and her husband, on their way to another village, where their youngest son is about to have a new field blessed by the priest. I ask how many children they have, and the woman says fifteen.

"I wanted to have two or three, but God decided otherwise." She smiles.

They share some wild strawberries with me—tiny and misshapen but exceptionally sweet—and seem delighted to try my Canadian chocolate. They get off soon afterward, bowing slightly in farewell and telling me to be sure and try the Krynica water. They wave at me from the platform, shouting their goodbyes.

Krynica is to the Poles what Bath is to the English, Baden-Baden to the Germans, and Spa to the Belgians. They have all had their day of international fame, the sixteenth-century Belgian town's name having become generic. But there are many other cities—including ancient Troy—that have been founded and developed to exploit existing mineral springs. Krynica is one of them, though it is not nearly as well known as its Western European counterparts. This is probably because its development as a health resort took place relatively late—in the nineteenth century—by which time the international spa craze was on the wane. All the same, Krynica's springs are said to be among the best in Europe and have been known as such for hundreds of years. In the interwar period, the town did briefly become a fashionable watering hole, attracting the Polish aristocracy and intelligentsia, as well as international celebrities such as Queen Wilhelmina of the Netherlands, and opera star Jan Kiepura.

Never having been to a spa before, I am somewhat baffled by the strong sense of déjà vu I experience on arriving in Krynica. The town, or at least its fashionable center, has a fin de siècle Central European atmosphere whose stately formality seems so uncannily familiar that I can't help wondering whether I had not, as a small child, visited the place with my parents. Set in a green valley, surrounded by wooded hills, Krynica has elegant avenues and villas, and brooding two-hundred-year-old sanatoria overlooking a broad promenade. Its center teems with tourists, walking up and down at a leisurely pace, serenaded by violinists. Suddenly, I know why the place looks familiar. It has something to do with an old black-and-white film: Alain Resnais' *Last Year at Marienbad*. I saw it years ago and remember nothing but its cool, stylized elegance and Delphine Seyrig's memorable face.

A spa cure traditionally entails bathing in, and drinking, mineral-rich water; occasionally, long immersion in mud baths. There are those who believe, however, that the main benefit is incurred through enforced rest and relaxation. After World War II, the Communist government accordingly took steps to provide these, along with medical care, to the Polish proletariat. It built large, functional hotels known as "holiday homes" and therapeutic centers treating a wide range of common ailments, from diabetes to gynecological disorders. Feeling in fine health, I bypass the treatment centers and mud-bath houses, heading for the main pump room to try some of the celebrated water.

There are twenty mineral springs in Krynica, about half of which are channeled into the public pump rooms, each with its own name: Karol, Jan, Józef, and so on. The name appears on a board accompanying each tap, along with the spring's chemical composition. The heaviest and most commonly recommended is the Zuber, which contains almost an ounce of soluble solid components per quart—a European record, I gather. Having brought a collapsible cup for the purpose, I line up gamely for the Zuber tap, watching my cup fill with a purplish brown liquid. It smells indescribably foul, however, and I hastily pour it out, then go for a less concentrated brew, which I proceed to sip along with hundreds of tourists, most of them Poles and Germans.

It is as I walk past one of the many statues Poland has put up in honor of Adam Mickiewicz that I see a little fair-haired boy, no more than three or four, walking alone downhill, chewing on a wafer. He looks a little lost, but there are people about, some of them on park benches, and when I ask him where his parents are, he points to one of them with utter confidence. And so I move on, walking backward slowly, my eye on the child. The boy drops the wrapper on the pavement. He skips past the poet's statue, pauses, looks right and left, takes a few more steps, then stops abruptly and breaks into a heart-wrenching wail. At once, several strangers pause and surround the boy, asking questions but getting barely intelligible answers. Suddenly, a pregnant woman comes running downhill, calling the boy's name, offering muddled explanations to no one in particular. The boy races up to his mother, throws his arms around her knees, but goes on sobbing on finding himself rebuked.

This is when I remember an incident from my own childhood; a day that started with a mundane trip to a Łódź butcher shop but ended in parental fear and humiliation. I was three and a half and had walked away from my mother and out of the shop, following a baby carriage.

I was soon lost, my tears too attracting a solicitous crowd. Eventually—it seemed hours later—my father arrived on the scene, only to be told emphatically, "This is not a Jewish child!" He was a dark, unmistakably Jewish man, and I was fair and flaxen haired, with eyes the color of dusty olives. When he tried to get through to me, my father was roughed up by the hostile crowd, ending up with a bloodied mouth. The incident ended with the arrival of a local policeman who had to be handsomely bribed: he had wanted to take my father down to the station and charge him.

"What for?" I asked my father on hearing this many years later, "for not supervising your child?"

"Don't be dense," he said. "He didn't need a reason. I was Jewish—that was quite enough."

This is one of my very first Polish memories.

I have stopped at a small Krynica restaurant to read my guidebook and have lunch. I study the menu and then order *bigos*, having read that Adam Mickiewicz so longed for it while in exile in Paris that he included the recipe as part of his epic poem "Pan Tadeusz." It turns out to be a Polish version of *choucroute garnie*, though this one is exceptionally aromatic, including wild mushrooms in addition to the usual cabbage and garlic sausage. Typical peasant fare but delicious, served with boiled, parsleyed potatoes and black Russian bread. As for my guidebook, it tells me that, among other things, Krynica offers gas- and air-baths. I have no idea what these might be but, eventually passing the Old Spa House, decide to go in, hoping for a chatty receptionist.

I find myself alone in a cool, empty lobby with cathedral ceilings, as spacious and hushed as an abandoned church. The place is immense, with several vinyl sofas and chairs, and flourishing plants at the windows. There is an intense medicinal smell in the air, the sound of running water. But no voices or footsteps or even ringing phones. Silence. I have never been to a morgue but, walking toward the exit, reflect that this is what a morgue might be like. As I approach the front door, however, a man comes out of nowhere and, not paying the slightest attention to me, brushes hastily past and goes through the door, coughing all the while. He looks like a workman going off duty rather than a patient, but I suddenly remember *The Magic Mountain* and think of tuberculosis, while a childish voice echoes inside my head: Curiosity killed the cat!

And so I give up on the sanatorium and go instead into the local museum, which contains the paintings of a famous naive artist known as Nikifor. A local Lemk, Nikifor was born in 1895, a poor, illegitimate deafmute. He was an adult before he learned how to read and write, but from a young age drew and painted ceaselessly on any available surface. He was of course shunned, pitied, and taunted—until 1930 when he was suddenly discovered, living to enjoy his growing reputation for another thirty-eight years. Today, Nikifor is considered one of Poland's most important painters, his oeuvre including numerous vivid, splendidly intricate paintings portraying every facet of changing Polish life. Unfortunately, the museum has run out of brochures, and so has the well-hidden tourist office. The clerk, who speaks only Polish, explains that they have been ordered but delayed—who can tell why.

Walking away from the tourist office, I see a state hygiene inspection van that bears the following quotation by someone name Marek Kotański: "The best cure for AIDS is fidelity." I walk into a nearby shop and ask who this Kotański might be. There is not much more for me to do in Krynica, and it suddenly occurs to me that I have heard nothing about AIDS in Poland.

The owner, who has been idling at the door, sits down and motions me to a chair. Kotański, he informs me, is a well-known psychologist; the first Pole to establish centers for drug addicts and AIDS victims.

"People thought he was crazy—why would an educated man want to work with that type of individual?" The merchant shrugs, noncommittal. Poles are changing, he says. They are becoming more socially aware and responsible, shaped as in all things by the views of the West. He is a balding, heavyset man somewhere in his sixties; old enough, at any rate, to remember Nikifor shuffling through Krynica, and Jan Kiepura coming out onto the Nowy Dom balcony to sing to an adoring crowd.

This information is accompanied by a nostalgic sigh; an unmistakably reminiscent look, which fades into a frown when I return to the subject of AIDS. No, there is no treatment center for AIDS in Krynica, he says, answering my question. He doesn't think there are many cases in Poland, but their number is said to be growing. Later, when I look into it, I find that there have been 4,100 registered cases of HIV infection in Poland, but the actual number is probably much higher. So far, 300 have died of AIDS (Poland's population is about 39 million), but the number is indeed rising. I learn too that a Western sex-education textbook promoting the use of condoms has recently been translated by the Ministry of Health but that the Ministry of Education has failed to approve it for its schools, knowing the Church was bound to block the book's distribution.

But Pan* Wolny, the Krynica merchant, is understandably less interested in AIDS than the state of his own deteriorating health. Poles are given to public discussions of their health. They sit on trains and buses, comparing blood pressure and digestive problems (and exchanging medication with the ease of housewives swapping recipes). Their lack of reserve is surprising because, in most ways, Poles are far more decorous than their Western counterparts. One of their most frequent criticisms is "He's uncivilized." ("Don't be uncivilized," my parents would say if ever I interrupted an adult conversation or failed to respond politely.) A middle-class Pole finding himself in North America is often astonished at how widespread "uncivilized" can be: an eminent doctor sitting in the medical library with feet on the table; an affluent lawyer and his wife showing up for dinner empty-handed; an elegant female executive eating lunch while talking on the phone. These are things that seem boorish to most Poles, and it was only when I got to Poland that I realized how Polish—or perhaps just European—I still am in some respects.

By the time I meet Pan Wolny, I am not as astonished as I might have been last month to see him pull up his pant leg to show me the scar from his bypass operation. He has had circulation problems in recent years and also some cardiac irregularities. He tells me about all this at length, and having posed so many unwelcome questions, I feel honor bound to stay and listen. Interestingly, having unburdened himself, Pan Wolny grows considerably friendlier. He leans across his desk and asks where I live in Canada, and how I come to speak Polish. And then he smiles at me, showing a sparkling gold tooth or two. "Is Canada really

---

*Pan is Polish for Mr.; Pani for Mrs.

Canada?" he asks.

❀

"It seems to me," says one of the narrators in Bram Stoker's *Dracula*, "that the further east you go, the more unpunctual are the trains." This, I gather, is as true today as it was in 1897 when the book was published. Krynica may be in the south of Poland, but the train I am waiting for is due from the east and will be over an hour late. I am still somewhat mystified by the workings of the Polish rail system, though I know by now that there are slow trains, and so-called express trains, and the superexpress Inter-City trains. Sometimes, I have discovered, it is more practical to take a roundabout route, or zigzag across the country, in order to save travel time. A geographically sensible itinerary is in any case all but impossible, given my various contacts' summer vacation plans. I had hoped to straighten it all out in Tarnów, but was discouraged by a long queue and a snappish ticket clerk. In Krynica, however, it is early evening and rather quiet, and so I decide to give it another try while waiting for the delayed train. When the ticket clerk understands the extent of my inquiry, she suggests I go to the back and ask for the "information clerk." He turns out to be an elderly semiretired Krynician who looks up with some surprise when I appear—he is actually there for phone inquiries—but tells me to take a seat anyway. He listens carefully to my questions, pores over half a dozen tomes, and offers advice in a low, measured voice. When I propose taking a night train to save time, he counsels against it. There have been rumors of robber gangs all over Poland, injecting sleeping gas through the ventilation system, putting to sleep entire compartments.

"You are a woman traveling alone," he says. "It's better to go slow and safe."

He tells me which trains are to be avoided, and which have dining cars, and points out ones likely to be overcrowded. He does all this unsmilingly but with an oddly touching dignity, his clouded eyes intently fixed on my face. He is seventy years old, he eventually tells me, and has been with the railroad for over forty years. When I thank him for spending so much time with me, he shrugs it away, saying, "There's only one thing I have too much of and that's time, dear lady."

"Well," I say, "There's still thirty-five minutes before the train is due—may I ask you some other questions?"

"Of course," he says. "Of course." He is a singularly grave man whose surname means cabbage in Polish: Kapusta. His face is gaunt and wrinkled, but must have been exceptionally handsome in his youth. He is somewhat feeble now, and hoarse voiced, but his hands are long and beautifully expressive, like the hands in Rodin's *La Cathédrale*; his manner is deliberate, thoughtful.

"I'm a simple man," he says humbly, "with little education, but I know one thing: capitalism has no use for the likes of me." A childless widower, he has been retired for nine years but works part-time to help pass the hours. To listen to the politicians on TV, he says, the country is flourishing, but the sad truth is that the new system is designed only for the healthy, the capable and ambitious. As for the sick and elderly, or just simple folk lacking initiative, they are bound to be trampled by others, more nimble and aggressive.

"People like to put down the Communists these days, and it wasn't a perfect regime, mind you—I don't say it was—but under Communism, the individual counted, you see. Now you're a zero, a total zero, unless you know how to hustle."

Pan Kapusta says all this in a strikingly neutral tone, without a trace of self-pity. His parents were farm laborers, he tells me, and if he could only show me the wretched poverty of peasants before World War II, I would surely understand what Communism was all about. "I'm a simple man," he repeats, "but since you've asked for my opinion, I think it's a government's job to ensure that people's basic needs are provided for—everybody's needs in society. There shouldn't be all these jobless and homeless people, and patients in hospitals getting less to eat than criminals in state prisons."

I must look somewhat skeptical, for he assures me this is a fact. His sister, who lives in a small town near Lublin, had an operation and was told to bring her own pillowcase, needles, even painkillers; her children had to supplement the meager meals she got.

When I ask whether there is anything about the new system he does approve of, he says it's good to be able to say what one wants and to travel freely. "People should be free to go where they want, say what they want, and capitalism gives us that, but if you ask me, it doesn't develop a man intellectually or spiritually, does it?" He urges me to consider what is happening in America—a truly sick, Godless society that Poles seem determined to emulate. "Look at all the dirt we get from them: the sex shops, AIDS, drug addiction. Do you have children?" he asks with sudden interest. It is the first personal question he has asked. When I tell him I have a daughter, he gives a heavy sigh. In recent months, he has read in the paper that Polish children are routinely approached at school by dealers with free drug samples. "Children!" he says and looks at me intently. "We didn't have that before, you can be sure of that."

The drug problem is so serious, he tells me, that the government has had to ban poppy cultivation in hopes of arresting production of opium and heroin. "You probably know Poles use a lot of poppy seeds in their baking. . .well, we're now in the absurd position of having to import them from the Czech Republic!"

When I ask why Poles have one of the highest alcohol consumptions in the world, he says it's obvious: people are poor and desperate these days, many of them anyway, and vodka is cheap and helps them forget their sorrows. When I venture to point out that alcohol was a problem under Communism too, he makes a vaguely dismissive gesture and says Communism never really took in Poland. "You know what Stalin said—" He looks at me for the first time with a glimmer of amusement. "He said, back in '44, that trying to set up Communism in Poland was like fitting a saddle onto a cow."

I smile at that and refrain from comment. It is, in any case, almost time to go. The windows are dark by now, and somewhere in the distance, a dog has begun to bark. I feel a sudden heaviness in my chest, leaving this old man in his dingy office, with nothing whatever to look forward to. I write down his name and address and console myself with the thought of sending him a gift for Christmas. And then I shake hands and thank him once again, and he gives me a rare, melancholy smile.

"Goodbye," he says; then, "remember not to walk alone after dark."

CHAPTER **6**

HIS NAME WAS Juraj Janosik, but he came to be known as the Polish Robin Hood—an antifeudal bandit leader who roamed the Polish highlands, robbing the rich and giving to the poor. A Slovak by birth, he lived in southern Poland's Podhale region in the early eighteenth century. In 1713, aged twenty-five, he was captured and hanged by the authorities, having been betrayed, like Samson, by his own woman. A short bus ride out of the town of Zakopane, in the lovely Kościeliska Valley, there are limestone cliffs with much-visited caves. These, legend has it, were once the haunts of Janosik and his band of outlaws.

The caves are in a heavily forested national park, and I have just arrived at its entrance when it begins to rain. I have a small umbrella, but the rain is coming down like bullets, obscuring the green valley. I take refuge in a chalet restaurant named Harnaś—the Bandit Leader. It is a spacious, upscale eatery aimed at the tourist trade, and the Polish hikers caught in the rain know better than to come inside. They huddle outside under the awnings, while a few privileged foreigners—including me—sit in the chalet's rustic warmth, listening to taped ballads about the local brigands and studying the menu.

It is a little early for lunch but, having risen at six, I decide to eat anyway. The menu is elegantly printed and offers picturesquely named dishes: the bandits' pot (a goulashlike stew) and mountain shepherd's pierogi. I opt for the latter, and they turn out to be a complete surprise. Pierogi are normally the size and shape of a human ear. The mountain shepherd's pierogi have been made of the usual white dough, and boiled, but they are the size and shape of a large cupcake, stuffed with ground meat and fragrant with mountain herbs.

The idle waiter—a tall, fair-haired young man with a single gold earring—answers my questions about Janosik, but advises me not to go to the caves in this weather. It has been raining on and off for the past five days, and the park is bound to be very muddy. On the other hand, if I insist on going, his grandfather owns one of the horse-drawn carriages outside and can take me there for about 80 złoty. This is the equivalent of $40 and, by Polish standards, an outrageous price.

"That's tourism," says Andrzej Klimczak. "The Germans and Dutch have deep pockets these days."

Andrzej is twenty-one years old, one of the new generation of Górale, the renowned Polish highlanders who once made their living as shepherds in the Tatra Mountains. Zakopane, the Podhale region's main town, was "discovered" in the 1870s by a Polish doctor whose consumptive patients flocked here in search of pure mountain air. They were soon followed by various artists and intellectuals who, in the final decades of the Austro-Hungarian Empire, established a fashionable colony in the village. Sometimes referred to as the Polish Chamonix, Zakopane nestles at the foot of the Tatras (part of the Carpathian chain), attracting some three million tourists a year, mostly for its superb skiing and hiking. It is a town of some thirty thousand inhabitants but feels more like a village; a lively and picturesque one, surrounded by craggy snow-capped mountains and a landscape rich in alpine pastures, waterfalls, and deep glacial lakes. I visit a spectacular one called Morskie Oko (Eye of the Sea), a craterlike, emerald green lake that, despite the poor weather, is overrun with tourists. The weather has complicated my own sight-seeing plans, but Andrzej Klimczak makes up for it by telling me about the region.

The Górale are an intensely proud people with a strong sense of their own identity: they refer to themselves as Górale rather than Poles. Renowned for their fierceness and their distinctive woodcraft, they live in quaint wooden villages, in one of the few areas of Poland to have escaped high-rise development. It is one of Poles' favorite vacation spots, a place which draws backpacking teenagers along with Polish celebrities. When the Swedish Academy called Wisława Szymborska to inform her of her Nobel Price, it was to Zakopane that they finally traced her, only to be told that the elderly poet was having lunch and could not be disturbed.

Andrzej Klimczak can't possibly know this (it is only July at this point) but having learned that I am planning a book on Poland, seems intent on impressing me with the region's exceptional prestige. In the Chochołowska Valley, for example, there is a chalet where, in the 1980s, a clandestine meeting took place between the Pope and Wałęsa. There is a plaque commemorating this event, he hastens to assure me. There are also many famous people buried in Zakopane. His grandfather personally knew the family of Helena Marusarzówna, a local skier who was tortured and executed by the Nazis for her resistance activities. The famously defiant Górale were brutally punished by the Nazis for their underground activities and Allied Intelligence connections. Andrzej tells me I can learn more about it at the Tatra Museum, but when I try, the following day, I find it closed.

This is when I learn that all Polish museums are closed on Monday; some, it turns out, on Tuesday too—or the day following a national holiday. All are closed after three o'clock, and what with occasional renovations and other unexpected events (a Shakespeare play staged, of all places, at Gdańsk's Gothic Prison Tower!), I keep running into closed doors.

But Zakopane's setting, together with its distinctive architecture, are well worth the visit, despite inclement weather. Traditionally constructed of pine logs, Zakopane houses have a steeply sloping roof, and gables carved in various folk motifs. Though recently constructed houses are actually made of bricks, with only wooden siding to keep up the Zakopane facade, woodwork remains an important tradition in the region: everything from carved garden swings to mailboxes is seen on a walk through town. In the cemetery, the extraordinary grave markers are carved tree trunks with little black roofs to protect the inscription and relief sculptures. They make me think of extended birdhouses, though some of the inscribed names are indeed widely known.

One of the most celebrated artists associated with Zakopane is Stanisław Ignacy Witkiewicz (1885-1939), known locally as Witkacy. Son of an eminent painter and art historian,* he was a prolific painter, philosopher, novelist, and playwright. He is said to have written in the

---

*Confusingly, his name too was Stanisław Witkiewicz, though the father is known above all for having popularized Zakopane architecture.

Absurd tradition long before Ionesco made it famous, though Witkiewicz's plays, too, were eventually produced on the international stage. Though initially baffled by Witkiewicz's work, Poles eventually became intrigued by his plays and paintings, many of which were executed under the influence of narcotics. Witkiewicz carried out his drug experiments with an almost scientific dedication, indicating in the corner of each canvas the name of the drug he had been taking. When the Nazis invaded Poland in 1939, Witkiewicz fled east but, on learning about the Russo-German Pact, committed suicide. "A nation is a people and its graves," says the inscription on the Zakopane cemetery gate.

Walking away from the cemetery, I run into a Górale funeral. A young choirboy walks ahead of the procession, carrying a carved wooden cross. He is followed by a priest, then a creaky horse-drawn hearse. The hearse is bedecked with flowers, surrounded by Górale men who walk solemnly, wearing traditional brown felt pants and vests and black plumed hats. The women come last, all dressed in black, though many of them wear a brightly flowered shawl around their shoulders. Suddenly, I spot the owner of the pension where I have been staying—a wispy-haired woman in late middle age, also named Irena. Since she was chatty and high-spirited only yesterday, I assume the deceased is neither family nor friend. All the same, she looks suitably somber, clutching her floral shawl as the distant church bells begin their melancholy toll. The road leads to the Sanctuary of Our Lady of Fatima, one of several rustic churches. There are tourists who, like me, have paused to watch the procession, and shopkeepers wiping their hands in doorways. The sky has been clear all morning, but the mountain air still smells sweetly of rain and wet evergreens. Pani Irena disappears from sight.

It was almost ten p.m. the Sunday I arrived at Pani Irena's pension. I had reached Zakopane around eight, to find the railway station jammed with hundreds of backpacking teenagers, waiting out the rainstorm. The kids looked grim and exhausted, staring bleakly at the falling rain. It was coming down in sheets that evening and the teenagers—some no older than my daughter—were parked in the waiting room and outside, under the station's awnings. There was a time when you could tell kids from Eastern Europe anywhere in the West, at least for a month or so after their arrival. They were invariably neater in appearance, and better behaved than their Western counterparts. These Polish teens, however, were indistinguishable from the kids back in Montreal. Their jeans were fashionably frayed, their hair was unkempt, their conduct uninhibited. They were sprawled on the ground, sleeping, eating, singing, or listening to their Walkmans. Some stood changing their wet clothes in the crowd, or lay necking in each other's arms. A few waited for the public phone.

There were two of them but one was out of order, the second taking cards but not tokens. There are two types of public phone in Poland, and the one you find is usually not the one you happen to be prepared for. On the rare occasions when you do have both tokens and a card, one of several things is likely to happen: the card may expire in mid-conversation (after which you can never get the line again), the phone will swallow up your token, or it will simply be out of order. It did not take me long to understand Stefan's response in Warsaw, when I first inquired about public phones.

Making a phone call in Poland is complicated by the scarcity of public telephones. In one or two cities I found the occasional public booth on the street, but usually, the only place to call from was the post office, the railway or bus stations.

At the Zakopane railway station, there was a long queue in front of the only functioning phone, and having purchased a card from the local kiosk, I eventually found myself before it. I had two Zakopane hotel numbers, which I had tried to reach from Nowy Sącz without success. In Poland, I was often forced to choose between spending a good part of the day getting a phone connection, or simply giving up and counting on my good luck.

In Zakopane, it seemed to be running out. One of the hotels was not answering (which probably meant it was full); the other had had its number changed. Alas, there was no number for Information, and dialing zero failed to get me the hoped-for operator. Surprisingly, no one seemed to know the Information number, not even several railway officials whose help I vainly tried to enlist.

The rain went on falling, lashing against the waiting room windows with spiteful ferocity. An hour and a half after my arrival, cold and exhausted and hungry, I still had no idea where I would spend the night. Eventually spotting a stopping taxi, I ran over and asked the driver whether he knew of any pensions that might still have a room at that late hour. This is how I came to meet Pani Irena, a Górale woman who peered at me a little suspiciously before letting me in. She was a bony, gray-haired woman who, perhaps because of the weather, put me in mind of a furled umbrella. But she was friendly enough, once she'd completed her inspection, even agreeing, for a small fee, to give me a cold supper. She had a quaint way of saying "Please accept" whenever she handed me anything: a cup of tea, a towel, the keys to my room.

The room she gave me could not have been bigger than six by twelve feet but, miraculously, had its own tiny bathroom. There were no windows in the room, but there was a skylight and I went to sleep with the lulling sound of rain pounding on the glass. In the middle of the night, however, I was wakened by sudden discomfort at my feet: it had been raining so hard that water had begun to drip from the skylight and onto the narrow bed. Fortunately, Pani Irena had left me some extra blankets and there happened to be a pail in the bathroom. Now and then, there was a flash of lightning, a terrible clap of thunder. The rain dripped and dripped into the metal bucket.

In the morning, the sun came out for a few hours and Pani Irena, looking horrified at the news of the dripping skylight ("We just had it built this spring, barely three months ago!") seemed determined to make it up to me. She gave me, on the house, an early-morning breakfast that resembled last night's supper: cheese and ham and bread, with sliced cucumbers and tomatoes, accompanied by a pot of blueberry-flavored tea. She offered me another room for my second night and, perhaps thinking I might still go elsewhere, tried to charm me. She told me amusing stories about her various family members: her husband, who worked for the mountain rescue service; her daughter, who had got married last year; her two sons, one of whom was a well-known local fiddler, the other a salesclerk. She spoke one of the Podhale's dialects, which Poles usually listen to with a tender, indulgent air. I did not understand everything she said, and sensing it, she would frown and press her hand to her brow, groping for another way to convey her meaning. She had fine communication skills, Pani Irena, and a good deal of native cunning. When she sensed that my interest was flagging, she quickly reached for a white photo album, sliding it toward me.

"Please be so kind as to look at these."

The album was taken up with photos of Pani Irena's daughter's wedding, which, as is the local custom, took place in church and at the fire station. There were photos of the wedding party approaching the church, the bride in one horse-drawn carriage, the groom in another, the Górale band accompanying their entry into the church. Music plays a crucial role in Górale culture, and the string band featured in most of the photos at the fire station, where the wedding guests feasted and danced their polkas, waltzes, mazurkas. "None of your modern American jerking to and fro," Pani Irena stated.

Her elder son was the first violinist in a group made up of three violins and a cello. He was a beefy, mustachioed man who, like his colleagues, was dressed in tight felt pants, a wide, abdomen-hugging leather belt, and an embroidered vest. There were also hats decorated with cowrie shells, and I at once recognized the costume from the televised concert I watched in Danuta's apartment. Pani Irena's daughter—a bright-eyed nineteen-year-old-girl—reminded me of Hogarth's *Shrimp Girl*. She was wearing a white cotton dress with floral embroidery, chunky red beads, and laced-up brown shoes over white stockings. In the early pictures, there was a garland on her fair head, but a later photo showed it replaced by a kerchief. The ceremony is one of the highlights of the wedding, symbolizing as it does the passage from maidenhood to mature womanhood. The bride looked remarkably solemn in this photograph, but her usual gamine self while dancing with the groom. The young man was slight and earnest-looking and, I was told, extremely hard-working. His father owned the grocery where Pani Irena's son worked. It was, apparently, a particularly gratifying match, though I sensed that Pani Irena thought her son-in-law a bit of a stick.

Zakopane having an unusually vibrant night life, the grocery sold liquor all night, though transactions took place through a small wicket. Nonetheless, there was an attempted holdup at the wicket one night and Pani Irena's future son-in-law ("an easily flustered type") lost his wits and nearly his life as well.

Zakopane, like all Polish vacation spots, has a rising crime rate, a fact that made Pani Irena give one of her deepest sighs. I refrained from pointing out that the region seemed to take a certain pride in its old brigandic tradition, as was evident from the photographs of Górale men doing the traditional Robbers' Dance. The photographer had captured them in a costumed circle, wielding small axes, looking fierce and proud. Later, reading up on the Górale, I would come across the following quotation from a nineteenth-century Górale musician: "To hang on a gibbet is an honorable thing. They don't just hang anybody, only real men!"

The weather is still capricious on my last morning in Zakopane, but I spend it poking about town, shopping for postcards and souvenirs for my parents. I still remember, when I was about five, the two of them going for a weekend in Zakopane, leaving my brother and me with the maid but coming back with a costumed doll and a carved flute. Around noon, having little time to spare, I line up near the central bus depot for a barbecue chicken drumstick, only to be told that the power has just gone off and that, since the scale is electric, they have temporarily stopped all chicken sales. I suggest to the clerk that, since they sell hundreds of drumsticks a day, she must have an idea of what the price might be.

"I have an idea," she says, "but if I overcharge you, you'll be mad at me and if I undercharge you, the boss will."

"Is the boss here?" I ask. I am curious to know whether a businessman could possibly have chosen to relinquish all profit rather than run the risk of losing a few złoty.

"He's on the phone, talking to Warsaw."

I tell her to go ahead and charge me the maximum she has ever charged for a drumstick and she looks skeptical. "You're sure you don't mind?" she asks.

I sit at the depot and eat my chicken and bun, then buy a box of raspberries from a nearby stall. I walk toward Krupówki Street, circling around giant puddles as I eat the berries.

Zakopane's main drag is a trendy street full of art galleries, restaurants, souvenir stores, billiard halls—and, of course, sex shops. It is a crowded street (Zakopane is more crowded than any place I visit in Poland), bustling with tourists, street performers, itinerant merchants, beggars. The tourists are overwhelmingly young, many wearing cheap plastic raincoats in a bright array of colors. The raincoats are sold on every corner, along with umbrellas and toys, all made in Hong Kong. Halfway up the hill stands a white human statue on stilts, resembling a Roman emperor on a pedestal. A few feet away, a young man sings an Elton John song, and I instantly recognize him, having heard him sing the same song in Kraków. There is also the inevitable Gypsy duo, playing the violin and accordion, and a young couple with a boa constrictor that they rent out for Polaroid snapshots.

My shopping done, I head toward the post office for stamps, bemused by the red-and-white sign affixed to all government buildings. It depicts a white eagle—Poland's national symbol—which, under the Communists, was divested of its royal crown, but now once again wears it.

Having stood in a long queue for the stamps, I sit outdoors at a wonderfully fragrant café to write postcards, have coffee, watch the world go by. I have written two when a Gypsy woman stops under the green awning and asks permission to read my palm. Amused, I indicate the empty chair beside me, and she sits down, poring over my hand.

She is a good-looking woman of indeterminate age, with flecked light brown eyes and one charmingly crooked front tooth. She wears a floral headscarf and a long, striped skirt that must have once been purple. It is a faded violet now and clashes with her bright orange sweater. Answering my question, she tells me she was born in the Podhale region; she is not one of those thieving beggars from Romania. She knows by now that I am a foreigner but doesn't say, as I expect her to, that I have come from afar.

"You have a very complicated hand," she says, speaking Polish. "Very complicated. You are an artist, I'm sure of that—perhaps a poet or painter. Am I right?" she asks.

I give her a neutral smile.

"See all these tiny crisscrossing lines everywhere? You have so many of them and they mean frustrations. No big tragedies, but lots of obstacles, lots of rivers you've had to cross."

I look down at my palm in silence. I remind myself I don't believe in palmistry.

The Gypsy frowns. "You have a child," she says, "a son or a daughter, I'm not sure, but you have no husband."

Well, I say to myself, I wear no wedding ring—but how would she know I have only one child?

And so it goes. She tells me a few more facts, which are more or less right, but saves her trump card for the last.

"You've been working hard and you're going to gain great recognition," she says, smiling, "but not until the age of eighty-one."

"Eighty-one?!" I mock-frown at her, thinking it's better than posthumous anyway.

"Yes," she says, "you'll have to be very patient." She charges me 20 złoty ($10) and leaves me to comfort myself with the thought that no one will ever be able to accuse me of having been spoiled by early success.

Hours later, on the train heading for Bielsko-Biała, I reach into my bag for my pocket agenda and find it gone—gone! I sit there for a few minutes, trying to think where I might have left it but fail to come up with anything plausible. And then, going over the day's events, I suddenly remember the Gypsy. My bag had been hanging on my chair, and seeing me momentarily captivated, she might have reached into it and pulled out the small pocket agenda. Going in blind, she must have mistaken its vinyl cover for a wallet, which I was savvy enough not to carry in Poland. I had a money belt on, well concealed under my bulky sweater. The agenda had nothing of great importance, and I sigh with relief, thinking of the Gypsy's rage on finding herself outwitted.

Only then do I remember my daughter's photograph, slipped into the agenda's inner cover. It is a photograph of Ranya on a Greek beach, where she goes every summer to spend time with her father. It is, I remind myself, only a photograph. I do not believe in Gypsy spells. And yet, and yet. . .I can't quite rid myself of the vague unease accompanying the mental picture of the Gypsy, still seething with disappointment, poring over my child's picture as she had over my hand. Holding the snapshot in her cool, dry hands, then tearing it up with an angry curse.

Though I am dismayed to have lost the photograph, I am even more distressed by the evidence of my own irrational feelings. Has Poland made me suddenly superstitious? Vexed with myself, I cast the whole thing aside—for about five minutes. I resolve to call my daughter the moment the train gets in.

CHAPTER 7

Cieszyn is an ancient town divided by the Olza River—not an unusual geographical phenomenon but for the fact that half of Cieszyn lies in Poland, the other in the Czech Republic. It is not one of Poland's celebrated towns, but it happens to exemplify the ephemerality of Eastern European borders, and the frequent impossibility of finding satisfactory solutions to its conflicts. Founded at the end of the eighth century, this attractive town was once part of the Duchy of Cieszyn, which controlled much of the traffic between the Black Sea and Bavaria. In 1920, following the collapse of the Hapsburg Empire, it was claimed by both Czechoslovakia and Poland, and was subsequently divided: the western half was given to the Czechs, the eastern to the Poles. In 1938, with the Germans invading Czechoslovakia, Poland managed to capture Cieszyn's western half and keep it until 1945, when the town was once more brutally cut, with no regard for the mingling populations.

There is a Gothic tower in eastern Cieszyn, offering a superb view of the divided town, with the Beskidy Mountains in the distance and, closer up, the bridge marked with the frontier line. Standing atop the fourteenth-century tower, one can see the brisk flow of a two-way traffic across the bridge. The Czechs come to Poland in search of clothing and household items; the Poles cross over to obtain beer and other alcohol. Czech beer is thought to be superior to the Polish and is certainly cheaper. There is a set limit on the amount of alcohol importable on each crossing but none on the frequency of border crossings. This loophole has generated a lively trade, with Polish importers, locally known as "ants," crossing back and forth several times a day.

I had never so much as heard of Cieszyn until two weeks before my departure for Poland when my neighbors asked whether I might be in a position to take a gift to an elderly relative. Having already planned to be in nearby Bielsko-Biała, I agreed to oblige (this is how I came to be given the Warsaw number of Stefan Kryński, a nephew on the husband's side). I was already in Poland, and unreachable, when it was learned that the Cieszyn relative—an elderly woman living alone in a nearby hamlet—had recently passed away.

It is almost noon when I finally arrive from Bielsko-Biała and learn the news from a neighbor whose geese seem bent on attacking me. Pani Gwiazda died in early June, aged seventy-nine, but I am not altogether out of luck, says the neighbor: Piotr Gwiazda, the deceased's grandson, is visiting with his wife and will likely be back shortly. I am invited to wait in Pani Śpiewak's kitchen while she serves me tea and goes about making dinner.

The Śpiewaks' home, which seemed like a dollhouse from outside, turns out to have two floors and a kitchen spacious enough for a daybed and table, as well as an old wood stove. Pani Śpiewak—an elderly, pink-faced woman with large bones and swollen legs—chats as she cooks *czernina,* a black soup made with fresh duck blood, bones, and giblets. She talks for a while about her deceased neighbor—"a saintly woman; she even saved Jews in the war"—and then, answering my questions, of life in this rural community. Both her family and her husband's have been farmers for generations, but her children have turned their backs on agriculture, and who can blame them? It's backbreaking work with little future these days. Ever since the Russians stopped buying Polish produce, local farmers have been in dire straits. Many have gone into heavy debt; others would have starved if it weren't for parcels from America. Pani Śpiewak scoffs at the widely circulated view that most Polish farmers lack the expertise and resourcefulness to cope with new economic conditions. "The rules, they keep changing all the time," she says, "changing every year. Who knows what it'll be like when we join the European Union?"

Though Poland fervently hopes to achieve membership by 2002, there are many who share Pani Śpiewak's concern. It is feared that rural unemployment will rise sharply, inflating the already dense ranks of farmers and agricultural workers idle since the dismantling of collective farms.

I ask Pani Śpiewak whether things were better under Communism, and she says they certainly were—for most farmers. Her own husband, however, ran into trouble with the authorities for refusing to use chemical fertilizers. Determined to modernize Polish agriculture, the Communists levied fines on farmers who insisted on using natural fertilizers.

"They kept saying it was backward of us," says Pani Śpiewak, "that we were stupid and primitive, but it turns out that people raised in such backward areas are much healthier than others."

Asked how she knows this, Pani Śpiewak says there was a report on television. This is how they learned about the growing trend toward organic farming in Poland. There is an official organization promoting it now, she tells me with evident satisfaction: her husband has finally been vindicated by Polish scientists and agricultural experts.

Unfortunately, too late. Tired of paying fines and squabbling with the authorities, and having become eligible for old-age pensions, the Śpiewaks decided to sell much of their land. They bought some chickens and geese, and today manage on that, as well as a few fruit trees. They grow their own vegetables and sell eggs, apples, and plums in the farmers' market. Since the Śpiewaks' house seems fairly comfortable and well maintained, I assume that they are also helped by their sons; and perhaps they are, in part. When Piotr and Hania Gwiazda return, however, they tell me that Pani Śpiewak's husband has been engaged for years in the illegal production of potent plum vodka (70 percent proof as compared with the usual 40 percent).

But this will take place several hours later. Meanwhile, having finished the soup, Pani Śpiewak joins me at the table and tells me about her children who, thank God, were smart enough to get a good education. The Śpiewaks have two sons, one a director in the local Fiat plant, the other a textile engineer. The surrounding hills have always provided abundant sheep wool, ensuring a thriving textile industry in the Bielsko-Biała province. "Thank God none of us is dependent on American charity!"

It is while Pani Śpiewak shows me photographs of her family that I am reminded of the vague unease I have felt ever since yesterday's discovery of the lost agenda. As soon as I arrived in Bielsko-Biała, I tried to phone my daughter in Greece. I kept trying all evening, and also early this morning, unable to get an answer. I spoke to Ranya only a few days ago, and she made no mention of any plans that would explain the silence. I have, on many occasions, had trouble getting a connection to Lesbos, but never an answer. I have been telling myself that they no doubt took an unexpected trip, or perhaps the phone was out of order? Still, I can't shake the unease of knowing that in an emergency, no one would be able to reach me now. I am about to ask whether anyone in the hamlet has a telephone when Pan Śpiewak arrives, pulling off his muddy rubber boots and blinking at me in surprise.

He is a shriveled-looking man with nicotine-stained fingers and a voice made hoarse by excessive smoking. At once, he offers me some plum vodka, looking somewhat offended when I decline. I quickly explain that I never drink during the day, but just this once will take a sip or two. Mollified, Pan Śpiewak pours me a glass, looking gratified to see me gasp after a tiny swallow.

"That's how we like it in this part of the world," he says. "Nice and strong, especially in winter when the temperature, if you'll excuse me—"

"That's enough!" his wife interjects, clucking her tongue in open disapproval. "What will foreigners think, listening to your language?"

Pan Śpiewak grins, pleased with himself, and proceeds to satisfy his curiosity about me. When he is done, I ask how *he* feels about the changes since 1989, and he takes another swig of vodka before he answers.

"I'll tell you," he says, "there was more work under the Communists, I can't deny that, but it was a corrupt system—people forget it sometimes, but it was." He looks at me intently, as if waiting for a rebuttal, then goes on to complain that, alas, many ex-Communists are still living off their shady deals and their crimes. They are as rich and powerful as ever, he says, and, since Kwaśniewski's election, have gained new legitimacy. This point of view is common enough in Poland, but not among farmers.

"What she wants to know is, is life better or worse these days," Pani Śpiewak puts in.

"Better or worse? Ach, the devil knows." Pan Śpiewak makes a vaguely dismissive gesture, then offers another popular saying: "Under the Communists, whether you stood up or you lay, you got your paycheck anyway."

"And now?"

"Now we must work to get paid, but at least we're allowed to complain, right?" He looks pleased to see me laughing and, perhaps encouraged, decides to tell me an old joke—a clean Polish joke, he assures his quibbling wife. An American farmer comes to Poland and visits a local farmer. The Polish farmer shows the American his farm, pointing out its parameters with his finger. "This is my farm," he says, "and how big is yours?" "Well," says the American, "I get up in the morning and I drive and drive and drive, and in the afternoon, I reach its outer limit." "Ah yes," says the Pole, chuckling, "cars like this we have in Poland too."

Pan Śpiewak guffaws in delight and pours himself another drink, asking his wife for something to eat—perhaps the guest too is hungry? The guest isn't, though Pani Śpiewak has already made it clear I am to share their dinner if the Gwiazdas fail to show up in time. She repeats this to her husband, who seems satisfied—but only for a moment. He looks balefully at my glass and, perhaps miffed at finding it almost full, decides to challenge me. What do I think about the way the world is going, he asks; where will it all end, would I please tell him.

"I don't know," I confess sadly. "I really don't know."

"You see!" he says, turning to his wife at the kitchen sink. "She doesn't know either." He has, I gather, asked his sons the same question and failed to get an answer. "What's the good of all that education if you can't answer an important question like that?" he asks.

"It's a good question," I say, reminded suddenly of Kazantzakis' Zorba asking the intellectual writer, "Why do the young die? Why does anyone die? Tell me!" When the writer concedes he can't answer that, Zorba gets worked up. "What's the use of all your damn books?" he shouts. "If they don't tell you that, what the hell do they tell you?"

"They tell me," replies the helpless writer, "about the agony of men who can't answer questions like yours."

But I am somewhat luckier. Before the full brunt of Pan Śpiewak's disappointment can be unleashed, there is the sound of car wheels on nearby gravel, a suddenly slamming car door. Pani Śpiewak turns away from her bubbling pots.

"I think they are back," she says.

It is almost dusk when we set out for an aimless walk—Piotr, Hania, and I. A heavy mist hangs over the southern hamlet, lending the houses, with their small, lit-up windows, the evanescent quality of some dimly remembered place; a place you think you remember, though it may have figured only in some forgotten dream. We walk down a long dirt road with two rows of rustling poplars, led on by Piotr's young golden retriever. He takes us through a country lane overgrown with raspberries, pausing to wait while we pick some berries, then sprinting back to tug on Piotr's pant leg with his teeth. We laugh and eat fistfuls of berries, and make our way down to a nearby pond with its lone, mist-shrouded weeping willow. For somewhat mysterious reasons, I feel positively blissful. Something about the mist, and the mingling scents of grass and earth and evening primroses. The silence too, perhaps. There is nothing but the distant sound of a bleating sheep, the desultory clucking of cooped-up hens. But then it comes to me that there is something else: I have finally managed to get hold of my former in-laws, who assured me that my daughter was safe and sound, having indeed gone on an excursion to a nearby island.

The call was made from the post office in Cieszyn, where Piotr, Hania, and I spent the afternoon, sight-seeing and walking by the river. They are here on their summer holidays, fixing up Piotr's grandmother's house, which they plan to keep as a family getaway. Like most Poles I have met, Piotr and Hania saw it as their immediate duty to show me the sights and to keep feeding me. Having already shared their dinner with me, they brought me back in the early evening, to sit in the grandmother's garden, eating one uncle's spicy, homemade sausage, another uncle's smoked cheese, and Hania's Russian salad, made with cooked carrots, potatoes, beets, and pickles, all diced and laced with sauerkraut and sunflower oil. It was a perfect accompaniment to the somewhat bitter beer from nearby Żywiec, a beer that, under Communism, was more easily found in a British or American supermarket than a Polish one.

I have been invited to spend the night and have by now learned to accept such spontaneous hospitality graciously. I am, in any case, rather curious about Piotr and Hania, who have much to divide them but who, despite a good deal of arguing, seem genuinely devoted. Piotr is Roman Catholic by birth, Hania Jewish. They have been married for almost three years but, except for long weekends and summer holidays, are forced to live apart for the time being. Piotr works for the Ministry of Agriculture; Hania is a special education teacher, working with handicapped children in Bielsko-Biała. She has applied for a transfer to Warsaw but must wait for a post to become available.

"And my mother wants to know why we don't have a baby!" Hania laughs, showing two exquisite dimples. Contrary to stereotype, she is blue-eyed and fair, with short, honey-colored hair, while Piotr is dark and has a long narrow face with pensive eyes and a distinctly non-Slavic nose. To look at him, one would say, Greek or Armenian, or Gypsy. The truth is, so many foreigners have passed through Poland that it is futile to try to guess a person's origins.

Hania is not particularly keen on moving to the capital, but Piotr's career is thriving in Warsaw and there seems to be little choice. Piotr has a master's degree in economics and agriculture and is involved in government efforts to improve the efficiency and quality of agricultural production, with an eye on that fiercely coveted membership in the European Union. I tell him about Pani Śpiewak's apprehensions, and he says they are not groundless. The terms and conditions of joining the Union are not all known as yet, but some of the consequences seem inevitable. Economists predict an increasing liquidation of unprofitable farms and heavy migration to urban centers. Moreover, there is likely to be a sharp increase in the importation of agricultural products, simply because Union subsidies will make it more cost-effective to import some products than to produce them locally. Other economists, however, believe that membership in the Union will actually bring about an expansion of agricultural exports and higher returns for farmers, as well as access to a free flow of capital and financial aid. What all agree on is that Union membership must entail intensive restructuring of the agricultural sector, with emphasis on the improvement of modern production technology. It is also agreed that a solution must be found to the growing unemployment in the agricultural sector, and that this is perhaps the greatest challenge facing the Polish economy.

As for Hania, she decided to study special education mostly because one of her sisters was born with cerebral palsy. She tells me this as we arrive at the pond, speaking feelingly of her sister's suffering, and the growing awareness in Poland of the rights and needs of the handicapped. There are more than five million disabled in Poland, but they are rarely seen because current conditions make mobility extremely difficult. In recent years, however, the government has initiated new programs to encourage the hiring of disabled workers. Employers who hire at least 7 percent disabled workers get substantial tax breaks.

"It's not altruism, that's for sure," says Hania, "but open any newspaper in the country these days and you'll see Disabled Wanted ads."

The changes taking place in Poland have made Hania's work more meaningful because she knows most of her pupils have a future now. Many of the kids come from single-parent homes, abandoned by fathers who couldn't cope with the birth of a handicapped child. "We have a long way to go," she says, "but we're on the right path, I think. Our parents' generation made so many mistakes, in so many areas."

Hania is twenty-six and Piotr twenty-eight. They are both articulate, idealistic Poles, members of an environmental pressure group responsible for many of the antipollution measures taking place in Poland. Here too, Piotr reiterates, there is a long way to go. Pollution from urban factories has been seeping into the adjacent countryside. It's estimated that 80 percent of the land has acidic soil, with several areas recording dangerous levels of heavy-metal contamination.

"Places like this may seem pastoral," he says, "but the truth is half our wells have water unfit for human consumption, that we still have sewage problems, and so on." Piotr runs a hand nervously through his hair. Because of limited facilities for the disposal of waste, villagers often use ditches or forests as untreated dumps. "What can I tell you?" he says. "We have our work cut out for years—decades—to come." He sighs.

It is dark by now, and we are on our way back home, accompanied by a chorus of shrilling crickets and swarms of fireflies whirling before our faces. We take a short cut through a fragrant apple orchard, arousing a chained German shepherd. Apples, and apple juice, are at the top of Poland's list of agricultural exports, but Piotr tells me these are not quite ripe as yet. A pity, because, like wild mushrooms, the Polish apples of my childhood are more vividly delicious in my memory than the loveliest specimen purchased in Canadian markets. I tell Hania and Piotr about the joy of eating mountain mushrooms in Nowy Sącz, and they at once suggest mushroom hunting tomorrow.

"I can make some Swedish pierogi with them," Hania volunteers. "Would you like that?"

I have no idea what Swedish pierogi might be but would, I say, be delighted to find out. On the other hand, I would be equally pleased to take the two of them out to dinner—perhaps some place they might not normally think of going to?

"Out of the question," Piotr says in a categorical voice. "What would my grandmother say?" he adds in a moment. "You come all the way from Canada to eat in restaurants?" He scowls at me in the moonlight.

"It's too bad you couldn't meet Piotr's grandmother," says Hania. "She was a very strong, very interesting woman."

I am about to ask whether it's true that she saved Jews during the war, but just then we become aware of a group of men standing outside an open gate, smoking in the dark. Piotr's golden retriever starts to bark, and one of the men detaches himself from the group and moves toward us, reeling drunkenly. He bends down—to pick up a stone?— and falls flat on his face. The dog barks and barks, while a second man moves to offer help, stumbling in the dark. The moon drifts in and out of the clouds while Piotr helps up the cursing drunk. He winds his arms around his buddies' shoulders and tells them to take him home.

"Do you know why the Russians kept vodka so cheap?" he asks after we have walked some distance. When I shake my head, he gives me the answer, speaking in a tone of suppressed fury. "So they could keep peasants in just the state you've seen—millions of them, under their bloody thumb!"

"The truth," says Piotr the following day, "is my grandmother was an antisemite—quite a fervent one."

"So," I say, "it isn't true that she saved some Jews?"

"Oh, it's true, it's true. She hid at least four, two of them in the forest and two in the barn, though my grandfather was none too pleased about it."

Piotr's paternal grandfather was a forestry supervisor whose job was to analyze soil conditions, check the trees' growth rate, and look for disease. There was a hut in the forest where equipment was kept, and that was where Piotr's grandmother made her husband hide them. She also persuaded him to put up a false wall in the barn, one concealed by a mountain of hay. The Jewish couple didn't stay long in the barn, though. They managed to obtain Aryan papers and left for Kraków, only to be betrayed and shipped to Auschwitz.

"But the others survived?" I ask.

"One of them died of pneumonia right after the war," says Piotr. "The other one—as far as we know—still lives in the States."

This conversation takes place in the afternoon, while we finish eating Hania's Swedish pierogi. These pierogi are somewhat like small baguettes, stuffed with mushrooms and onions and baked in the oven. Hania's are utterly delicious, though made with purchased mushrooms. The morning having been rainy, we did not go mushroom picking as planned. But Piotr had an errand to run, and when he came back, it was with a bag of wild mushrooms bought in the farmers' market.

"Not quite like picking your own, but these aren't bad." He grinned at me, clearly delighted to have found them, together with a box of miniature *mille-feuilles*, which the Poles call Napoleons. Having finished the delectable meal, we sit in Piotr's grandmother's dining room and sip percolated coffee imported from Germany. The room is a long, somewhat shabby one, with peeling paint and an old hand-hewn pine table. This house has two floors as well, but the rooms are tiny, with low ceilings and rotting pine floors. Piotr plans to renovate it in his spare time; he wants his children to be able to play in wheat fields and fruit orchards.

We can't see a wheat field or an orchard from the dining room, but the window overlooks a wonderfully overgrown garden. Poles don't seem to go for the manicured lawn and neat flower beds favored by North Americans. They plant fruit trees and ivy and a profusion of flowers that receive a minimum of attention yet look as beguiling as a spring meadow. The Gwiazdas' garden has an apricot and a cherry tree and an old picnic table under a chestnut tree. At some point during dinner, the weather began to clear, but I hardly noticed, absorbed as I was in the story of Pani Gwiazda's life. What Piotr tells me over dessert is that though his grandmother was an antisemite, she was also a devout Christian and, quite simply, saw it as her moral duty to save persecuted human beings.

"She didn't see any particular contradiction," he tells me with a shrug. "She personally did not like Jews, but she also thought killing them was a sin."

"Why didn't she like Jews?" I ask at length.

"Why?" echoes Piotr. "Let's say it was. . .politically correct to dislike Jews in those days. They were said to be Poland's political and economic enemies, but—"

"Have you heard of ŻEGOTA?" Hania interjects, refilling our coffee cups.

ŻEGOTA was a clandestine Polish organization dedicated to saving Jews during the war.

"There were many antisemites in ŻEGOTA," says Hania. "Even the co-founder* was well known for her antipathy." And yet, Hania's father spent the war years in Warsaw, living with ŻEGOTA's help outside the Jewish ghetto; her mother was sheltered in a Catholic convent.

"The interesting thing," says Piotr, "is that my grandfather, who was not in the least antisemitic, was against getting involved with the Jews. He felt, my father says, a lot of pity for them but thought it was a mistake to risk your own life, and your children's, for the sake of others."

"And I agree with that," says Hania, looking defiant. "I wouldn't do it myself, especially if I had children. After all, why should a stranger's life be more precious than my own?"

"Well," I say, "heroes are, by definition, a tiny minority."

"Exactly," says Hania. "That's why I think it's wrong of Jews to hold it against the Poles that they didn't manage to save more of them. Would most Jews stick out their necks for the sake of some Gypsy, or an African refugee? Would you?" she asks, looking me in the eye.

"Probably not," I say.

---

*Zofia Kossak-Szczucka, a leading prewar writer.

"Actually," says Piotr, "at least three thousand Poles were put to death for helping Jews in the war; thousands more were sent to prison or concentration camps, but you don't hear much about them, do you— the nuns and priests and peasants who risked their own lives?"

The truth is that only a small minority of Poles ever murdered Jews, and another minority risked their own lives for them. In postwar polemics, however, each minority has been pushed forward as representative of the entire Polish nation. It is interesting to note in this regard that Simon Wiesenthal, whose life was saved by Poles, is quoted by his biographer as saying, "No Jew who survived in Poland during the war could have done so without at least some small measure of assistance from a Pole."

"The strange thing was," says Piotr, "that having done her bit to save the Jews, my grandmother apparently began to feel more kindly disposed toward them. That's what my father says anyway. After the war, she began to say it was all propaganda, the negative things said about the Jews."

"But then she changed her mind again," interpolates Hania. "Tell her," she urges Piotr when he seems to hesitate. "Why shouldn't you tell her?"

This is when I learn that his grandmother's lone survivor—a beautiful young woman who ended up in the States, married to a button manufacturer—wrote a card to tell them she was getting married and never wrote again—not once, in all those long, difficult postwar years.

"Piotr doesn't like to talk about it," says Hania, "because it makes it sound as if his family had *expectations*, you know—as if they had done what they did because they hoped to have some kind of eventual reward."

"It's not at all a question of reward but of gratitude," explains Piotr. "Some acknowledgment of the enormous risks my grandmother chose to take. After all," he adds, "it couldn't have been very difficult to send some Christmas trinkets for the children or something, could it? Well, there was nothing, not even a Christmas card. All my grandmother ever got from America was a button."*

---

*Piotr is playing on words here, using the American husband's occupation and a Polish expression in which a button is synonymous with zero.

This elicits a deep sigh from Hania. "You can imagine how it must have felt," she says, glancing towards me. "But, after all, there are all kinds of people in any nation, why not the Jews?" She turns to look at Piotr. "Just because your grandmother saved this woman was not automatically going to change her character, was it?"

"That's true," says Piotr. "But you can't blame my grandmother for being bitter about it, can you?" When his wife fails to answer, he addresses me. "What Hania says is true, though. After a while, my grandmother began to feel vindicated in her former antisemitism. Even in her old age, she would sometimes say, 'I never asked for their charity—never—but, after all, there is such a thing as common decency, isn't there?'"

Though I am old enough to know that the concept of decency is nothing if not elastic, I find myself compelled to suggest the possibility of mitigating circumstances. For all they know, I want to say, something tragic happened to this woman: she might have been mugged in New York, might have got killed in a car accident. And maybe she did. What stops me from voicing these thoughts is a somewhat similar incident recounted in a book titled ŻEGOTA—a more extreme case of ingratitude encountered by a Pole whose husband was suffering from cancer and needed therapy. Having come to the States, the Pole wrote the Jewish woman whose daughter she had saved, hoping for help from the family, or perhaps some Jewish organization. The Jewish mother wrote back to say their life was fraught with problems; her daughter, however, was sending her best wishes.

I sit mulling all this over while I drink my coffee, as silent as my two companions. When, at length, I ask how Piotr's parents felt about his marrying a Jew, he and Hania exchange glances.

"To tell the truth, they were not very happy about it, but—" he touches Hania's hair fondly "—they changed their minds once they got to know her."

"You have to understand," says Hania. "Piotr's parents never met a Jew, that they could remember, but Jews have always been the bogeymen in Poland. And, well, I think they imagined someone, you know... alien, someone who would have strange habits and all that."

"She's right," says Piotr. "The first thing they said to me, after they met Hania, was 'But she looks so Polish!'" They both laugh, and I think of the novelist Louis de Bernières saying that nationalism does nothing but cause wars and prevent marriages. It hasn't prevented this one, though I sense that Piotr and Hania have not quite laid to rest the question of Polish-Jewish relations.

I ask Hania how *her* family felt about the marriage, and she shrugs, saying there was little hope of her marrying a Jew. There are so few to choose from and very few who maintain Jewish traditions. Most Polish Jews still don't acknowledge their Jewishness, she tells me.* Hania herself did not know she was Jewish until she turned fifteen. Her parents decided to put off telling her because a neighbor's son had committed suicide, having been taunted at school for being openly Jewish.

"Of course, he may have had other, adolescent problems, but when kids want to pick on you they'll seize on anything."

"Adults too," says Piotr. "If my family hadn't liked you, they would have thought it was because you were Jewish. Since they took to you, it didn't seem to matter." He turns back to me. "As you know, during Communism, ethnicity was supposed to be irrelevant and—well, the whole question of antisemitism was swept under the rug. Now—turn on the radio or the TV, or open the newspaper: the Jewish Question is discussed all the time."

"The good thing," says Hania, "is that antisemitism is no longer respectable in Poland. It's condemned in the media every day." This, she is quick to add, does not mean, of course, that there is no antisemitism in Poland. "But to tell the truth, I am not at all sure that Poland was ever more antisemitic than other nations." She points out that there were far more Jews living in Poland than in other countries— and perhaps, therefore, more frequent reports of open hostility? "Did you know," she asks, "that Warsaw alone had more Jews before the war than all of France, for example?"

"That's perfectly true," I say. There were 350,000 in the capital; about three million in all of Poland (roughly 10 percent of the population, though there were many places where the population was more or less divided between Jews and Poles, and some where Jews were in the majority).

---

*All this is quickly changing as the small Jewish community regains its vitality. Secular Jews have begun to take up old traditions, send their children to a Jewish school, etc. Enrollment at the school has jumped from thirty in 1996 to ninety-two in 1998.

At this point, having finished his coffee, Piotr leans back from the dining table. The sun is shining now, he points out with a smile; would I like to see how things look in broad daylight before we say goodbye?

And so we go for another walk, past vegetable gardens with picture-book scarecrows and giant sunflowers looming behind picket fences. There are cats sunning themselves on doorsteps, and mourning doves cooing within the trees. But there are people too: hanging out laundry, picking fruit, chatting at the gate. They return our greetings as we go by but look at me with silent disapproval. Or so it seems to me. Certainly, these are the most unfriendly faces I have seen so far, and I find myself considering my own appearance. Perhaps jeans are not appropriate in such places? Is it perhaps my lipstick? Whatever the reason, xenophobia is plainly writ on these peasant faces. They are the kind of faces that always frighten me—whether in Poland, Quebec, or the Deep South—and perhaps Hania too. Soon after, as we discuss my itinerary, she quietly suggests I might want to keep my semi-Jewish identity to myself.

"You're traveling to all these remote places—you never know what kind of people you'll run up against."

I acknowledge the truth of this but feel compelled to add that so far I have encountered nothing but kindness on my way. Some of my hosts have been strangers but could not do enough to help me.

"And did they know that your father is Jewish?" Hania asks.

"Yes," I say. "Of course."

"Well," she says, "there's a certain kind of educated Pole who'll do anything to show there's absolutely no truth to claims of Polish anti-semitism."

"That's not fair!" cries Piotr. "If Irena told you they *didn't* know she was Jewish, you'd have said they were decent only because they didn't know."

"That's true." Hania gives him a sheepish grin, but Piotr looks back, baleful. "You see how it is." Hania turns back to me. "After all these years, it's still impossible for Jews and Poles to have a. . .how shall I put this. . .a natural—an unburdened—relationship. There are many, many people of good will in Poland, but the past. . .well, it just keeps getting in the way."

CHAPTER 8

My own Polish past revolved around *ulica* Narutowicza—a long, elegant street in the center of a city whose spectacular growth began with Poland's Industrial Revolution. At the beginning of the nineteenth century, Łódź was still an obscure village, with a population of about two hundred. By 1840, it had become Poland's second-largest city, a flourishing textile center with an ever-growing population of Poles, Germans, and Jews. The Germans were mostly entrepreneurs, and it was their well-established presence that eventually led the Nazis to incorporate Łódź into the Third Reich, where it was promptly renamed Litzmanstadt.

Having escaped major damage, postwar Łódź began to attract thousands of migrants in search of livelihood, many of them Holocaust survivors. There had been a quarter of a million Jews in prewar Łódź; in the late 1940s, there were approximately thirty-eight thousand. Arriving in Poland with his new family, my father too gravitated toward Łódź, the city where we would live for the next four and a half years, and that would shape most of my early-childhood memories.

After Orenburg, our Narutowicza Street flat seemed positively palatial. My father had obtained it through the usual channels—by bribing a municipal official—but postwar Łódź suffered from a severe housing shortage, so the large flat had to be shared with at least one family. That was how we came to live with my father's Jewish partner and his wife—a taciturn, melancholy couple named Simon and Hannah Blum.

Our new Polish home had three bedrooms with high, ornate ceilings, and double doors with panels of beveled glass, and a bell in my parents' room to summon the maid. Wanda, who slept in my room, was a Polish country girl from a Mazovian village. She was related to the concierge in our building, a widow rumored to have consorted with German officers and then with their Soviet counterparts. She had lived on Narutowicza before the war and was likely the one who told Wanda about our prewar predecessors. It was through Wanda that my mother eventually learned that a Jewish family named Silverberg had occupied our flat in the prewar years and that everything in it had belonged to them. Once she found out, she began to hate living in the haunted flat. Every time she picked up a monogrammed spoon or pillowcase, she was to tell me in later years, she would think of the hapless family of five murdered at Treblinka.

To make matters worse, the Blums were Auschwitz survivors still looking for a lost daughter. They had, facing wartime deportation, left her in the care of a Polish couple living in a nearby village. When the war was over, having somehow survived, they went back for their child and found her gone—where to, no one seemed to know. It was rumored that a neighbor with a grudge had reported the child to German author-ities; that the guardians, having been warned, had fled in the night to some other village. The Blums were undaunted. They took up the search from their base in Łódź, following an uncertain trail across Poland. Eventually, they would trace the guardians to a remote northeastern vil-lage, only to learn that the girl had died of diphtheria back in 1944.

Since my parents moved in mostly Jewish circles, everyone they knew had lost relatives in the war and all felt intensely vulnerable as news of antisemitic aggressions became commonplace. All over Poland, Jews were reportedly being murdered for their jewelry or money; for their homes, their shops, for no apparent reason. One day, when I was about five, there was great turmoil in our Narutowicza building. A friend of my parents'—a textile manufacturer who had lost his entire family at Auschwitz—had been murdered in his sleep, pre-sumably for his money. The assault took place barely two blocks away and profoundly shook my parents, all the more when a police search uncovered a hit list of Jewish names, the textile manufacturer's among them. Though unrelated to us, the manufacturer had shared my own family's surname, a fact that made the hit list seem doubly ominous. It was after this event that my father decided to emigrate to Israel, a move undertaken when I was about six and a half and my brother Władysław three. If my Polish childhood was fraught with tension, it was also the only time in my life when I felt truly pampered. There was a luxurious white rabbit fur coat at the age of four, a gold locket with my Russian grandparents' photo, my first piano lesson. My father's jewelry and watch-repair business was apparently flourishing, but out on the street, there were war veterans on crutches, and Gypsy beggars, and countless blue-collar Poles barely able to eke out a living. Just outside our neighborhood park stood a gaunt-looking man selling sugar buns. Sometimes he had his daughter with him—a girl my own age, blind in one eye. The good eye was black and, next to the sealed, inanimate lid, seemed particularly luminous.

One day, my mother bought herself a pair of high-heeled shoes and a black felt hat with an audacious white feather. She bought me some ice cream and we were walking home, past the park, when I spotted the sugar bun vendor's daughter. She stood there, following us with her one good eye: my mother with her clicking heels and me in my soft white fur, holding her hand while I ate my treat, looking back over my shoulder. *Privilege* was a word I did not yet know, but the blind girl's lingering look was beginning to define its meaning.

These are some of the things I remember about Łódź. They are not necessarily remarkable things, but they are what I find myself dwelling on as I travel to Łódź. What does strike me as remarkable is the fact that until I arrived in Poland, I felt no desire whatever to revisit Łódź. It was only the awakened smells and sounds of my childhood—the scent of a dense forest, the sound of a young mother's Polish endearment—that generated a sudden curiosity, almost a longing, to see Łódź again.

There is a scene in *Schindler's List* in which a Jewish family is being evicted from their Kraków home—one of many heart-wrenching scenes and, for me, a uniquely startling one: the Jewish family's elegant residence was much like our own postwar home in Łódź. The Narutowicza flat is a place I have often thought about, occasionally dreamed about, and have used as a setting for several recent stories. It is as real to me as any of the flats I have occupied as an adult and, approaching Łódź for the first time in over forty years, I fervently hope it is still standing. I have no doubt that I will recognize every nook and cranny: the spot on the bedroom floor where my mother forgot a burning iron; the closet in which, fearful of burglars, I hid my precious locket. All of it, if only it has not been demolished.

Narutowicza Street is a five-minute walk from the train station and I arrive there on a Sunday midafternoon, clutching a note with a scribbled address: 152 Narutowicza, fourth floor, Łódź. Named after Poland's first constitutionally elected president (assassinated two days after his inauguration), the street is lined with the nineteenth-century homes of the former haute bourgeoisie. Having been in Poland for two weeks, I am not at all surprised by the decaying facades, but I am soon distressed to realize that the street numbers have apparently been changed. Many of the Neoclassical buildings on the street look vaguely familiar but, having walked past 152 several times, I begin to think I have come in vain. The apartment building bearing the address I have obtained from my father has a scratched, peeling metal door next to a small grocery. The locked door looks like the entrance to some abandoned warehouse; the grocery has a Coca-Cola sign, its door plastered with advertising stickers: Gauloises, Tetley, Kraft. It's a small convenience store bearing no resemblance to the neighborhood grocery I remember; a shop in which herring and pickle and sauerkraut barrels stood by the entrance, their smells mingling with that of bread, smoked fish, and salami chains suspended from the ceiling.

The convenience store is closed, but as I stand, undecided, on the street corner, an elderly man comes by and asks whether I am lost. He seems eager to help but, having glanced at the note in my hand, stuns me by saying the street numbers have not been changed, certainly not since the war. He has lived in the neighborhood all his life, he says, and this—he points up to the street number—is the building I am looking for.

"Impossible!" I say. I look into his clouded eyes, his heavily lined features. He is very old.

"No," he says and sighs. "This is it, madam."

"But where is the entrance?" I ask, feeling my chest constrict. "This is all locked and barred and—"

"It's in the back," he says. "That *has* changed in recent decades. It's off the courtyard now."

The courtyard I remember is a leafy, cobblestone one, with a pale lilac tree where, one summer morning, a neighbor's twin girls were photographed, their arms around each other. Dressed in communion white, with floral wreaths on their heads, they looked to my child's eye like fair-haired angels; an aloof, dazzling pair whose brief appearance began my unwelcome acquaintance with the sixth deadly sin.

There was also the dairyman, stopping in the courtyard with his giant tin bins, calling out "Milk! Milk" in a cracking voice. He would stand by his cart, ladling the milk into the housewives' vessels, while out on the street other hawkers announced farm-fresh eggs, chickens, sometimes vegetables.

The courtyard is no longer there. It has been paved over and turned into a driveway where a Fiat and a Polonez are parked the Sunday I arrive. There are two entrances, each with a row of ancient bells, and the usual faded name tags. The entrances are unspeakably shabby; more so than any of the Polish blocks I have visited so far and possibly even more than most Montreal slum dwellings.

I have come here on sheer impulse, expecting to go up to the fourth floor, ring a bell or two, and explain my purpose. Instead, I find myself faced with two locked identical entrance doors and no choice but to ring bells at random. I start at the top but get no answer to my first three rings. Are the bells working? I try the fourth bell, beginning to regret having come to Łódź, when I finally get an answer. An old woman listens to my spiel on the intercom and says she'll be right down. She could buzz me in but evidently wants to look me over. Incredibly, she turns out to be the only person in the building who has lived here since the end of the war, when she moved into her parents' flat with her young husband and her two-year-old son. She does not remember my family but, after a few inquiries, says it's the second entrance we must have lived at. She tells me most of the flats have been subdivided and goes over to help me identify the fourth-floor bells.

Failing to get an answer, Pani Michta takes me up to her own flat, introducing me to her visiting daughter-in-law and two teenage grandsons. She invites me to sit at the dining table in a room full of art deco furniture, plants, several bookcases. There are pots of African violets at the windows and splendid prewar hand-crocheted curtains. It is a crowded, somewhat shabby room in which recent smells of baking and roasting linger. Have I eaten, Pani Michta asks and, satisfied that I have, offers the usual tea and cake.

The building, she tells me, began to change in the 1950s, when the flats were cut up and offered to villagers flocking to the city in search of employment. They brought their relatives and their animals, constructing chicken coops in the lobby, stealing chandeliers and mirrors for sale. One of her neighbors had a goat at home, as well as chickens on the ground floor. There was no one to complain to because the authorities were invariably on the side of the Proletariat.

"The rougher your family background, the better the Party liked you," Pani Michta says. It was different when she had first moved in. Most of the tenants then were respectable Jews, keeping up the immaculate flats abandoned by the Germans fleeing west after the Allied victory. Pani Michta's father was a pharmacist, and she is delighted to hear that I still remember the neighborhood pharmacy, a shop with a hushed, serene atmosphere, redolent of medicinal preparations. The pharmacy had once belonged to a German, and when I tell Pani Michta about my mother finding a copy of *Mein Kampf* in one of our closets, she sighs deeply and says Poles are too quick to forgive and forget. "The Nazis ruined Poland. They devastated our country. Now—" she shrugs "—they're suddenly our best allies."

Elżbieta Michta, who has been washing dishes in the kitchen, joins us at the dining table, saying history has never been an impediment to commercial interests. Right now, all Poland cares about is the road to Europe. If I look around Łódź, I'll soon see why. They may be in the heart of Europe, but Poland is said to have the same standard of living as Turkey. Cities like Łódź are in urgent need of foreign capital, but investors are often reluctant to put up the money because of Poland's outdated industry. Still, they are making progress. Just the other day she learned that a group of French investors are planning to turn an 1852 factory—the biggest in Łódź—into a major hotel and business complex, with casinos, restaurants, modern offices. "Come back in five or ten years and you'll find Łódź changed more than it has since you left Poland."

At this point, I ask permission to use the bathroom, unprepared to find it looking so familiar. The Michtas' bathroom has the original sink and an old, capacious bathtub with brass lion-claw feet. I remember our

Łódź bathtub particularly well because it was here that my mother discovered the pleasures of long immersion. She had been accustomed, back in Russia, to bathe in a round wooden tub taken out once a week and filled by the kitchen stove. She couldn't understand why Hannah Blum did not like to have baths, until one day she happened to overhear a conversation between the Blums. "I can't!" she heard Mrs. Blum cry on being urged by her husband to have a bath. "I just can't, Simon! The thought of *them* soaking in that tub, the thought of *their*—" And then she began to sob.

Though I did not yet know about the lost child, I knew there was something odd about Mrs. Blum. I was fascinated by the blue number etched into her arm's flesh, but no one would explain it to me. "When you grow up, you'll understand" was the standard answer to most of my questions. One day, slicing bread, Mrs. Blum cut her finger in the kitchen, where we found her clutching her hand, shrieking, "Blood! Blood!" Though I too had a horror of blood, there was greater horror in the spectacle of an adult's apparent disintegration: the childlike sucking on the bleeding finger, the frantic sobs behind the bedroom door. When, years later, I was deemed old enough to learn of the Holocaust, Mrs. Blum's echoing sobs provided the soundtrack to that first glimpse of hell.

Soon after I reenter the dining room, Pani Michta's son arrives from a workout. A bearded, middle-aged man, he shakes my hand and, hearing that I lived here right after the war, asks whether I happen to be a "Litzmanstadter." He looks disappointed to hear that I am not. "There are so few Poles," he explains, "born here in those five Litzmanstadt years."

When I tell him I was actually born in the Urals, and that my father is a Polish Jew, he is visibly surprised but quickly recovers, saying that two of Łódź's most famous sons happened to be Jewish: Artur Rubinstein, the celebrated pianist, and Julian Tuwim, the poet.

"And Jerzy Kosiński, of course."

"Ach, Kosiński I'd rather not think about," says Roman Michta.

"You don't like his work?"

"The work's as depraved as its author—all those bestial, sadistic obsessions of his." Michta waves his hand. "Americans love to be shocked," he adds.

Though I happen to agree with the observation, I feel compelled to point out that Kosiński might have written more sanguine novels if he hadn't experienced so much wartime brutality. After all—

"But he *didn't* experience any of it!" interjects Michta. "All those gruesome events in *The Painted Bird* are a pack of lies. Didn't you know that?" He looks at me for a long moment while I search my memory, vaguely recalling doubts about Kosiński's authorship, but nothing about the book's contents. Though many years have gone by since I read *The Painted Bird*, I still remember the unspeakable abuse inflicted on the child by Polish peasants. The thought comes to me that Michta is quite simply in a typical state of denial.

Eventually, however, back home in Montreal, I will pick up James Parker Sloan's new biography of Kosiński and learn that Roman Michta was perfectly right. Though Jerzy Kosiński's first book was presented to his publisher as nonfiction, and despite its heavy promotion as one of the most significant contributions to Holocaust literature, *The Painted Bird* is, for the most part, a figment of the author's imagination. In fact, Kosiński spent the war years with both his parents, living in exceptional luxury in the Polish countryside. The family was widely known to be Jewish, and though there is no question that perpetual fear left its mark on Jerzy, the villagers neither abused nor betrayed the family, on occasion even taking heroic steps to shelter them from the Germans.

Though this discovery is still in the future for me, I am surprised to hear Michta say that his personal views notwithstanding, Kosiński's last book signing in Poland was attended by hundreds of Polish admirers. I suppose this must have something to do with Poles' growing interest in Jewish culture. In recent years, Polish bookstores have begun to stock Judaica, Kraków has an annual festival featuring Jewish music and kosher cooking classes. For the young, Judaism seems to be a new form of chic, a trendy, exotic pursuit with vaguely intellectual associations. These days, Michta tells me, Poles flock to Warsaw's Yiddish theater; they buy records of Yiddish songs; some are learning Hebrew. "There are, of course, people who will tell you that all Poland's troubles are due to Jews, Freemasons, and Communists," he says, "but they're a tiny minority these days."

Perhaps to prove his point, he tells me about Warsaw's Contemporary Art Museum, where a recent exhibit of Jewish photographs proved to be a spectacular success. Michta, a film cameraman, happened to be there on opening night and tells me some four thousand guests clamored for admission to the museum.

The exhibit is over by the time I visit Poland, but I am just as interested in Roman Michta's connection to the Polish film industry. Łódź may be Poland's Manchester to some, but many others regard it as the Polish Hollywood, made famous by the presence of the Łódź Film School. True, the city lacks any trace of American glamour, but the school has produced an impressive number of celebrated film directors: Wajda, Polański, Holland, Kieślewski, etc. In Bielsko-Biała, I met a man named Stanisław Janicki, a well-known broadcaster and film critic, who told me that the school's heyday has long since passed. It continues to attract a good number of foreign students, but this is mostly due to its past reputation. The truth is that the entire Polish film industry has been in steady decline since 1989.

Like every other sector in Poland, the film industry is undergoing profound and unsettling changes. The end of state censorship has liberated Polish filmmakers, but it has also brought about new competition from widely distributed foreign films. The competition from the West has been especially hard on Poles because, for the first time in decades, local filmmakers find themselves without the state funding they had come to rely on.

Poland has traditionally produced about thirty films a year, but most of these, according to Stanisław Janicki, have nothing original to offer these days. Kieślewski is dead, Holland works abroad, Wajda's foreign films are inferior to those produced in Poland. This bleak view, it turns out, is entirely shared by Michta. He has recently attended the annual film festival in Międzyzdroje and tells me about the endless sessions with film stars, businessmen, and politicians discussing the fate of the Polish film industry.

"It does not look good," he concedes sadly. For one thing, only the young flock to the cinema these days, and given the general mood in the country, they are happy to see Hollywood imitations. "What are the film directors to do?" asks Michta rhetorically. "They can't make films without financial backing and can't get the backing unless they compromise." He looks at me steadily for a moment. "And so they do, they go on working, but most produce films they are privately ashamed of."

In Bielsko-Biała, Janicki told me that the film industry had no option but to undertake coproduction with TV networks. This step has provided partial funding, as well as a committed home audience. Roman Michta says that television may have helped the film industry's finances, but it has done little to raise its artistic standards. There are several new TV stations in Poland, some of them private, and competition is fierce among them.

"What's wrong with competition?" I wonder out loud.

"What's wrong is the quality of the films you get. Everyone's in such a rush to beat out the next guy that the films are seldom what they used to be." He hates to say it but, more often than not, the films are downright shoddy, like anything produced in a hurry. Saying all this, Michta looks increasingly downcast, but his wife assures me he is actually delighted to have found such a receptive ear. She herself is a social worker and has grown a little tired listening to their various friends' grievances.

"Did you know," she says, abruptly changing the subject, "that in 1995, thirty thousand Polish children were made state wards—mostly because their families couldn't afford to keep them? That's the kind of problem that really gets to me. As for the rest—" She makes a vague, dismissive, gesture, eliciting a hopeless sigh from her husband.

There is a prolonged silence, which I finally break by saying that having talked to various people connected with the arts, I can't help feeling that, despite state censorship, the arts in Poland actually fared better under the Communists.

"I'm not even sure you should be saying *despite*," Michta answers sadly. "If you ask me, people found greater satisfaction in their work before 1989 and—this may sound strange to you—but believe me, getting around the censor had a lot to do with it."

I never get to see the flat I used to live in. I walk around the neighborhood park where I played and rode my first tricycle, then along elegant Piotrkowska Street, where Rubinstein once lived, and where my mother bought most of her clothes and, one autumn day, a hideous fox neckpiece with a sharp brown face and small glassy eyes. When I think of Łódź, I invariably think of this fox piece, and of the bun vendor's daughter over by the park—three eyes that have followed me year after year, season after season. But in my thoughts of Łódź, it is most often autumn, horse-drawn carriages are rolling down the gray streets, and the sidewalks are littered with yellow leaves, and ripe chestnuts whose fragrance still lingers in my nostrils and will likely do so till the day I die. One of the revelations of my trip to Poland is the tenacity of the prototypes originating in childhood. I was only six when I left Poland, but a Polish fall is quintessential autumn, as is a Polish forest, village, and so on. It seems extraordinary that four and half years of one's life should have a more persistent hold over one's psyche than all the years, all the places that follow—than the place itself, for that matter, under adult scrutiny.

It is evening when I go back to Narutowicza Street, but there is still no answer in the fourth-floor flats. Elżbieta and Roman Michta, who have come out for the walk, say that the fourth-floor tenants are probably on vacation, and so I give up at last, half relieved at being spared the ultimate confrontation with my distant past. Metaphorically, of course, it is altogether appropriate: the past, however assiduously pursued, is bound to remain somewhat elusive. Before I leave, however, I stand out on the sidewalk and look up to the fourth-floor window from which Mrs. Blum leaped to her death one spring morning, when everyone was away from the flat. Her dark features are blurred in my memory now, but not my sense of having been surrounded, those few postwar years in Łódź, by variously wounded survivors. Looking up at the dark windows on Narutowicza, I can easily understand the inner state of a surviving bereaved mother seeking her own death while lilacs bloomed all over the city. Perhaps, as T. S. Eliot wrote, April really is the cruelest month; it must have seemed so to many Holocaust survivors, in those first postwar years in Poland. Today, however, what engages my greater interest is the more complex despair of people who have unexpectedly lost the adversary that gave their life much of its former meaning. The old Communists are gone, but I am beginning to see that Polish farmers and old pensioners are not necessarily the only ones nostalgic for their presence.

And now, what's to become of us without barbarians?
These people were some sort of a solution. *

---

*Constantine Cavafis, "Waiting for the Barbarians," in *Modern Greek Poetry*, Kimon Friar, ed. (Athens: P. Efstathiadis and Sons, 1982.)

CHAPTER 9

THEY CAME CHARGING out of the steppes of Central Asia, an indomitable tribe of small but ferocious men, sweeping on their horses through villages and towns, slaying, burning, and laying waste to everything in their way. The year was 1241 and, not for the last time, the Tatars had arrived in Poland. Lightly armed—they carried only spear and saber, and a short dagger—they had been legendary even among the formidable Mongols. It was only because the latter could not subdue the Tatars that they invited them to join the alliance established by Genghis Khan.

The Tatars had made their first appearance among northeastern Mongolia's nomadic tribes around the fifth century. Unlike the Mongols, they spoke a Turkic language, ate raw meat, and drank horse milk mixed with blood. Having joined the Mongols, they were eventually absorbed by the Golden Horde, so called because of the gorgeous tents used by all Batu Khan's followers. In time, the name Tatar (or Tartar) came to designate to Eastern Europeans any invader of nomadic Oriental origin. It remained most closely associated, though, with the Golden Horde empire that had fused Mongol and Tatar elements, undergoing conversion to Islam in the fourteenth century. The empire went on to control most of Russia until the late fifteenth century, when internal divisions, the expansion of Moscow, and invasions by Tamerlane and the Ottoman Turks brought about the disintegration of the Golden Horde. By the middle of the sixteenth century, most Tatars had settled down in the Crimea and Siberia regions, where they devoted themselves to agriculture and various crafts. They were no longer a threat to Poland; indeed, some of them had become the country's new allies, helping Poland triumph over its latest enemy, the aggressively expansionist Teutonic Knights.

After the famous 1410 battle at Grunwald, Tatars began to settle in Poland, and to participate regularly in the defense of their adopted country. It was not until the late seventeenth century, however, that the Tatars were officially granted land of their own by a Polish king.

Jan Sobieski is one of the few Polish historical figures known to the outside world. Despite many political failures, he is remembered as the Polish king who, against all odds, saved Christendom from the Turkish Infidel.* By the late seventeenth century, the Turks had gained control of the Danube and, having triumphed over Budapest, were on their way to Vienna. They seemed likely to conquer all of Europe and so, having defeated the Turks at three earlier battles, King Sobieski was called on to save Europe at the eleventh hour. "Without Sobieski and his hussars we have no hope," Emperor Leopold of Austria was told. It was one of history's most momentous battles, won after a two-month siege to fortified Vienna. Sobieski, heading a united European army, won the fierce battle, promptly sending a message to the Pope: "Venimus, vidimus, Deus vicit" (We came, we saw, God conquered). The grateful Pope sent Sobieski the regalia of the Knights of the Order of the Holy Ghost, today on exhibit at Kraków's Wawel Castle, next to Sobieski's glittering trophies from Vienna.

It was after this celebrated battle that, wishing to demonstrate his gratitude for the contribution of a Tatar contingent, King Sobieski bestowed on the Tatars a small territory close to the eastern border, where they founded new settlements, building mosques and devoting themselves to horticulture, tanning, and carting.

The mosques in the old villages of Kruszyniany and Bohoniki still stand today, but most of the Tatars have been dispersed all over Poland. There are some five thousand in the country, and many of them still flock to Kruszyniany and Bohoniki on Muslim holidays. Until my trip to Poland, I did not now that there were any Tatars living in Poland but, having learned that their original settlements are quickly dying out, decided to pay a visit.

The large, white-haired, white-bearded man on the train to Białystok is surprised to learn that I am on my way to visit Kruszyniany

---

*Jan Sobieski's granddaughter, Clementina Sobieska (1702–1735) eventually married James Edward Stuart and so helped found an extraordinary line of British pretenders, the Sobieski-Stuarts.

and Bohoniki, but when I tell him why, informs me that he himself is half Tatar. I am delighted by what seems like an extraordinary bit of luck, but Stanisław Marciniak tells me there are about two thousand Tatars living in Białystok, so it is not so extraordinary after all that I should find myself sharing a compartment with one of them.

He proves to be an intense and loquacious man, eager to tell me about his life and much else besides. Marciniak is a bioenergy healer, working in a field that is quickly gaining ground in Poland. There are some five thousand practicing bioenergy healers in the country, though Marciniak says fewer than fifty are fully qualified. Poles are beginning to file lawsuits against healers making false promises, but celebrated healers like Clive Harris and Father Tardiffe continue to attract enormous crowds; bigger than Michael Jackson's on his recent trip to Poland. Marciniak tells me of a TV program in which a Warsaw healer puts his hands over the camera, in hopes of transmitting his energy to the viewers. Would I by any chance like to try *his* skills? I let Marciniak know that I am far more interested in his Tatar upbringing, and eventually he tells me that he was raised speaking Tatar to his mother, Polish to his father. His father was a Communist government employee working as an itinerant book salesman. Marciniak himself had always been attracted to natural healing, an apparent legacy from his mother, whose services had been sought by Tatars and Poles alike.

As a child, Marciniak was often caught between Tatar and Polish sensibilities. By way of example, he tells me of an occasion when he came home crying because he had been beaten up by classmates. His father took him in his arms and tenderly tried to console him. But then his mother came home and, seeing his tears, spanked him soundly for having failed to defend himself.

"There are no women tougher than Tatar women," Marciniak says with grudging admiration. It was they who drove their men to ever greater exploits, heaping scorn on them if ever they came home empty-handed. "You're no warrior to return without booty," Tatar women would reportedly say to their men.

Marciniak heard of such things from his mother, who was herself typically fierce toward those she loved. "She would put up with almost anything," says Marciniak, "except a show of weakness."

When Marciniak reached adolescence, the family moved to the city, and it was several decades before he went back to visit the place of his birth. He was by then well into middle age and, appearing unannounced in the village, encountered elderly villagers who began to shriek his dead grandfather's name, taking Stanisław Marciniak for a ghost.

I ask Marciniak how Tatars' lifestyle today compares with the Poles', and he tells me that Tatars drink very little and regard Polish drunkenness with intense disapproval. All the same, most Tatars have gradually been integrated into Polish society, some having converted to Catholicism. Marciniak looks somewhat offended when I ask whether Muslim Tatars are polygamous. It seems they never were, the Koran notwithstanding. They have always maintained a few uniquely Tatar customs, some of which were still in practice at the turn of the century. For example, a young man wishing to marry a particular girl was forced by Tatar tradition to face a line of veiled girls and choose one at random.

"As you can imagine, there were all sorts of agreed-on signals to avoid choosing the wrong bride, but that was the tradition," says Marciniak. There is an indulgent note to his voice, a hint of nostalgia that fades abruptly when the conversation shifts to Catholic traditions. Marciniak himself is a born Catholic but one fiercely opposed to the Church's position on divorce. Though he seems a little vague, I gather he is separated from his lawful wife and living with another.

"Thirty percent of Poles attend church," he tells me, "but can't receive communion because they are divorced. In this day and age— imagine!"

Whatever the subject under discussion, Marciniak is singularly passionate in the expression of his views. Speaking a little later of Kwaśniewski, he says, "I think of him and the Tatar in me jumps out." He is by far the most intense opponent I have met of the current president who, he says, is an obvious charlatan. Marciniak points to the fact that Kwaśniewski lied to the people about his educational background, and to his failure to write his master's thesis as proof of the president's inherent laziness.

"And this is the man chosen to govern us? Cholera gets me, thinking of him!" Marciniak fumes.

He is not alone in criticizing the president for his prolonged visit to the recent Atlanta Olympics. Marciniak accuses Kwaśniewski of caring above all about his private pleasures. "Doesn't he have responsibilities at home?" he asks, echoing many others.

What worries Marciniak is the possibility that Polish disillusionment will sooner or later lead to total anarchy. He too points to the high unemployment rate, the thousands of malnourished Poles in rural regions.

"And this is a country determined to join the European Union!" he rages. To my surprise, he then quotes Philip V of France, who reportedly declared, "Every man must have a chicken in his pot!"

"That's how it is," says Marciniak. "That's what Kwaśniewski should be aiming for." He looks at me for a moment with his fierce black eyes. "Mark my words," he says. "Poland's troubles are not over yet."

After more than four decades of Communist rule, most Poles like to think of themselves as fervent democrats, and perhaps they are. Paradoxically, however, despite forty-three years of Soviet indoctrination, Poland remains an intensely class-conscious society. It must have something to do with Poles' famous attachment to their traditions, but no doubt even more with the prominent place aristocrats have occupied throughout Poland's beleaguered history. Traveling through Poland, one becomes aware of a certain reverence for the names of Poland's great families. Among country people—the peasants who once toiled on these families' estates—there is a tenacious, respectful attachment to the memory of their former masters.

Traditionally, the two basic criteria for Polish nobility were high birth and military prowess, but other factors contributed to the gradual stratification of the aristocracy, land being one of them. Though not all landowners were noble, and noblemen were not necessarily landowners, the two were often interrelated. Top-ranking aristocrats often owned hundreds of thousands of acres, whereas a petty nobleman belonging to the class known as the *szlachta* might own two or three. There was only a score of the former, but the latter included 800,000 noblemen of varying means. There were those who owned serfs and those who didn't, and those who, despite a family coat of arms, possessed neither land nor serfs. In the eighteenth century, there were cases where circumstances forced some noble families into serfdom, but interestingly, even as serfs, they did not lose their exalted status. They might have had to live in a small, thatched cottage, but their coat of arms was invariably displayed over their porch for all the world to see.

Toward the end of the seventeenth century, Polish society saw the emergence of an increasingly powerful class of aristocrats who were known as "magnates" and who, in addition to owning vast estates and serfs, maintained their personal troops. Sometimes wealthier than the king, the magnates formed the highest estate in Poland, wielding disproportionate power and influence. They not only ruled their own provinces but participated with their troops in fighting Poland's battles. In peacetime, they established themselves as patrons of the arts, engaging the best architects and artists in building their cities and their palaces, inviting renowned scholars, and generally devoting themselves to the promotion of Polish culture. Soon, the magnates were holding Poland's most prominent positions, playing pivotal roles in the development of its political, social, and economic policies.

One of Poland's most celebrated magnates was an eighteenth-century aristocrat named Jan Klemens Branicki. A landowner with vast estates, including the yet-undeveloped town of Białystok, he had distinguished himself as the commander of the armed forces and was for a time a contender for the Polish crown. Ever since the sixteenth century, Polish kings had to be elected, and when Branicki's hopes in the capital were dashed, he left the court and took up residence in Białystok, where he went about building a palace to rival the king's.

Though destroyed by the retreating Nazis, the Branicki palace still stands in the northeastern city of Białystok, albeit in carefully reconstructed glory. It is a vast late-Baroque palace often referred to as the Versailles of the North. Certainly, it once saw great splendor and lavish entertainment, with Branicki playing host to countless Polish and foreign performers; on one occasion, an entire corps de ballet. Today, the palace is the seat of the Polish Academy of Medicine and, looking at its gleaming white facade, I find it difficult not to muse on the vagaries of Time. I am, I suppose, in a contemplative mood, strolling alone through the English park, with its bridges and weeping willows, its mallards and black swans gliding in canal water. Resting on a park bench across from the palace, I find myself thinking of Anna Branicka-Wolska—Jan

Branicki's direct descendant—about whom I first read in Eva Hoffman's *Exit into History*.

The story of Branicka-Wolska, whom Hoffman interviewed, is typical of the privileged class to which she belonged. Though some aristocratic families had become impoverished as far back as the Polish Partitions, the Branicki family's hardships began during World War II.

Polish aristocrats were among the most active members of the resistance movement and as such suffered exceptionally high losses. The Branickis, having been imprisoned and freed by the Germans, found themselves at war's end arrested again by the Communists and shipped to an infamous Russian prison, and then a labor camp. There, the Branickis spent several arduous years, but their story is memorable less for its litany of suffering (which Branicka-Wolska determinedly plays down) than the manifest pride in their survival skills; the ability not only to withstand hardship but to do so with an unvanquished spirit.

Eventually, the Branickis returned to Poland but, like all land-owning aristocrats, were forbidden to live anywhere in the vicinity of their former homes. Branicka-Wolska's father was jailed by Polish Communist authorities and is poignantly quoted as saying, "I can survive in a German jail, I can stand a Russian labor camp. But I can't bear to be imprisoned in Poland." He died soon afterward, leaving behind an impoverished wife and daughter struggling for survival.

As class enemies, the children of such families, and many lesser ones, were not only deprived of land and influence but also of a future. They were often denied employment and admission to university, while the children of the peasants once employed in their parents' estates found themselves enjoying undreamed-of opportunities. Some aristocrats went so far as to change their illustrious names, in the humble hope of avoiding persecution. It was only after 1989 that aristocrats great and small began to come out of hiding, some making attempts to regain their ancestral homes. There must be bitter ones among them, but Branicka-Wolska is certainly not one of them. "People who never experienced [hardship], who were never down and out, seem to me somehow unfinished, unripe, don't you think?" she says.

My eleventh-edition *Encyclopaedia Britannica* (published in 1911) says that Białystok is a Russian city, which it was between 1807 and

1921. It also says that three-quarters of its population is Jewish, which explains why Białystok figures so prominently in Yiddish literature. Having been founded in 1310, the city began to develop only after Branicki's return in the mid-eighteenth century. Soon, Jewish entrepreneurs began to flock here, thriving alongside Poles, Russians, White Russians, and Germans. The city grew by leaps and bounds, gaining a reputation for the quality of its leather and its textile industries. In World War II, however, Białystok lost its Jewish population and not a few of its Polish citizens. It was one of the cities devastated by the Germans, so there isn't a great deal to see here, other than the Branicki palace and some onion-domed Orthodox churches. If I am in Białystok, it is only because the bus to Kruszyniany leaves from here and I have come too late to make the trip today. Walking away from the Branicki palace, I find my way to a public toilet, which, like all such facilities in restaurants, railroad stations, and so on, has a caretaker sitting at the entrance, giving out carefully measured bits of gray toilet paper in exchange for a small fee. The Białystok caretaker is a hefty woman sitting at a tiny, oilcloth-covered table with a plastic red rose in a Pepsi bottle. She is, as I walk in, frowning with the effort of understanding a couple of foreign women who stubbornly keep trying to communicate with her in German. The two look flustered by their failure, and a little indignant too. Fortunately, they speak English and I am able to act as interpreter. It appears that one of the tourists has lost a ring and wonders whether the caretaker might have found it a little earlier. The caretaker hasn't, and when the women leave, she looks after them with evident aversion. I assume this is because she feels herself under suspicion, or perhaps because of the tourists' insistence on speaking to her in German, but as I wash my hands, she finally unleashes her fury, telling me that when the Germans came in an hour or so earlier they had demanded half a toilet roll between them.

"Half a roll," she says. "I kid you not, madam, *almost* half a roll, with prices going up all the time these days and everything. I tell you—" she shakes her head "—I saw them come in again, and I said to myself, I said, Here they are, coming back to use the second half of the roll! Can you imagine?" she says and hands me a paper towel. "It's a good thing we don't get too many of those around here."

There are few Western tourists in Białystok, but many Belarussians, who cross the border for short holidays. Though the city has a shabby, distinctly Eastern feel, it offers inexpensive hotels and bars, a few nightclubs and Western restaurants, a few sex and porno shops. I know by now that the sex industry is flourishing in Poland but all the same was taken by surprise one day, coming across two classified pages in *Warsaw Life,* with ads racy enough to make the Church fathers lapse into despair. "A married woman—discreet relationship;" "a pregnant masseuse for your pleasure;" "an 18-year-old student will grant you all you've ever dreamed of. . ."

Ever since Danuta's surprising exclamation about sex shops in Kraków, I have been wondering what kind of Pole frequents the many such places in Poland. In Białystok, having some time on my hands, I buy an ice-cream cone next to one such shop and sit on a nearby bench to observe the entrance. I sit in the afternoon sun for about forty minutes, during which two burly Belarussians go in, running their hands through their thinning hair. Next are three adolescent boys, laughing and teasing each other; coming out, red faced, a few minutes later. Finally, there is a woman with a great deal of eye makeup, tottering along in golden high-heeled sandals. She is somewhere in her late forties but wears an electric green miniskirt and a deeply décolleté blouse. Her dark hair is so long, and so extravagantly teased, that her head seems to take up half of her petite frame. She may or may not be a hooker, but her appearance inspires what I hope is an interesting idea; more interesting, certainly, than the prospect of spending the evening alone in a Białystok hotel room.

"I'll tell you something a Polish filmmaker said on TV recently. He said that the Church, having lost its Communist enemy, is obviously looking for a new one now—in people's pants and under their skirts." Beata Zegar smiles, blowing rings of smoke. She definitely is a member of the world's oldest profession, but a high-class one, working out of the bar of an upscale downtown hotel. I have been directed to this hotel by the sex shop owner, who told me to say that Kasia sent me. We are in the bar now, Beata and I, having a tête-à-tête at a dim corner table like a couple of old friends. This in itself is interesting: there are so many things I find myself doing in Poland that I have never done back home.

Białystok is Beata Zegar's home; has been for the past twenty years. She is twenty-eight and the mother of a four-year-old child. It was having a child that got her where she is today, she tells me, though without bitterness. She was married when she gave birth, but the baby boy was sickly and spent his first few months crying incessantly.

"Finally, my husband got fed up. I was always exhausted, I couldn't stand to have him touch me, and Janek never seemed to sleep, never."

And so one day he got up in the morning and left the two of them without a word. Where he went Beata doesn't know, and no longer cares.

"He was a bastard anyway," she says in an odd, expressionless voice. "He never wrote, never sent a złoty. But the strange thing was, as soon as he was gone—almost from one day to the next—Janek stopped crying. The first time he slept through the night, I was horrified; I was sure he'd died!" Beata smiles, showing me a snapshot of a pretty blond child clutching a teddy bear. Beata is also fair-haired and pretty; she looks like a somewhat plumper version of a Barbie doll, with her carefully coiffed hair and long scarlet nails. She is well dressed in high heels and a pale summer dress but wears too much jewelry. What is surprising is the quality of her attention. She has a keen, unflinching gaze and a purposeful, no-nonsense demeanor.

I ask Beata to tell me about her family, and she says she is virtually alone. She has a sister in Warsaw, but her parents have been dead for years. She had, before giving birth, worked as a cosmetician, but the job was gone by the time her husband took off, and anyway, she had no one with whom to leave her son. One day, she ran into an old classmate who had two children and was working out of this hotel bar. The two women took a flat together, working alternate nights, but always in the clients' rooms. Beata's johns are mostly businessmen, some foreign, many from Belarus and, she says, if she doesn't like the look of one, she simply says no. She is much in demand, I gather, and can afford to be choosy.

I ask how much she earns and, for the first time, Beata looks a little smug. "Often more than 3,000 złoty a month," she says (about $1,500). "Triple the average Polish salary." What pleases Beata most is her ability to do so well on a part-time basis; a run-of-the-mill prostitute would have to work twice as hard for that kind of money. According to

Beata, a quickie with the average streetwalker generally goes for about 50 złoty; a good night might bring in close to 200.

"Are Poles good lovers?" I ask the question remembering Xaviera Hollander's assertion that Greeks are the world's best lovers, a statement that subjected me to friends' occasional teasing when it was learned I was to marry a Greek. As for Poles, my investigations have failed to cover this particular area, so I am interested to hear Beata say that Westerners are usually better. She tells me about a recent survey conducted by a condom manufacturer, one indicating that Poles are more concerned with quantity than quality in their sex lives. Also, that the nation is obsessed with fear of pregnancy. This, claims Beata, is mostly the fault of the Catholic Church, meddling as it does in people's private lives. It was Church pressure that has led to the recent banning of several contraceptives, and she fears that condoms will be the next to go. Already, an anti-AIDS poster campaign promoting the use of condoms has had to be scrapped.

Interestingly, these conservative measures are taking place in a country whose laws, in some ways, are more liberal than many in the West. The age of consent, for example, is fifteen in Poland, regardless of sexual orientation, with gays enjoying greater legislative freedom than many of their Western counterparts. Of course, all this may change in the future, if the Church succeeds in its current pressure tactics.

I ask Beata what she thinks of the recent pornography boycott movement in Białystok—a campaign gaining force in other parts of Poland—and she makes a scoffing sound. She is all for keeping porno publications out of children's way, she says, but as for banning them altogether, that will never succeed "because sex and making money are all most men really care about," she states.

What does appall Beata is the recent news about widespread pedophile operations. In western Poland, just before the summer holidays, maps of Berlin were posted outside Polish schools, indicating spots frequented by pedophiles. "And so, many boys—poor boys who want their Adidas and their Walkmans, just like everyone else—end up going to Germany and offering their services, competing with equally desperate Romanian kids." This elicits Beata's only sigh. "My son is only four," she says, "but I already worry about the world he is growing up in."

What worries Beata most? Any fool knows it's a sick world out there, full of drugs and perverts and vicious, corrupt men. Her ex-husband, for example, has a brother in the local police force. The things he used to tell them: policemen taking bribes and beating up innocent people, even raping and committing occasional armed robberies. Disbelief must be written on my face, for Beata hastens to tell me this was actually in the paper, in an article that said the situation has gotten so bad that the police are setting up an internal body to fight corruption within its own ranks.

"I don't know how much good this will do," says Beata, looking skeptical. She is among a growing number of Poles who are for the establishment of citizens' self-defense groups, independent of the police. Recently, a Łódź businessman's pregnant wife was kidnapped by the man's former partner, drawing public attention to this increasingly common crime. Eventually, I will look into it and find that there are about 145 annual abductions in Poland, most of them of children involved in custody battles, but some sex-related, and recently a few involving ransom. There have been cases of wealthy Poles having their children kidnapped. "This sort of thing never used to happen in Poland before," says Beata.

We talk about this and that and, not surprisingly, Beata comes down hard on men whatever the subject. When I ask how she feels about feminism, she looks no less scornful.

"I hate feminists. I'd rather share a flat with a criminal than a feminist," says Beata. Asked to explain, she says that feminists, at least Polish feminists, are all arrogant, privileged women who have no understanding of the plight of ordinary Polish women. "Of course I think women are entitled to the same rights and all that. It goes without saying. As for the rest—" She waves it all away.

Beata has agreed to give me two hours, meeting me at seven in the evening in order not to interfere with her nocturnal schedule. I have offered to pay the usual hourly rate but she has declined it, saying it's not every day she gets to talk to a foreign writer. When our two hours are almost up, I ask whether she has any particular dreams for the future.

"Who doesn't?" she says, and shrugs.

"Would you like to get married again someday?" I prod.

"If I happen to meet a really decent guy," says Beata. "A one-in-a-million guy, ideally a foreigner who'll take me away to some place like Canada." She grins, blowing smoke sideways.

"Otherwise. . .?"

"Otherwise I'll go on saving money and eventually open a sex shop like Kasia did. That's when I'll really be on easy street," says Beata.

❁

The next day, I find myself doing something equally improbable, this time in Kruszyniany. Having taken an early-morning bus from Białystok, I end up in a dusty, gloomy, unknown frontier village, pushing an old Tatar in an ancient wheelchair toward the local mosque. The old man and his wife are the Kruszyniany mosque's caretakers, and since she was busy, I have been asked to wheel him over, a rusty key in his shaky hands.

It was my British guidebook that directed me to the caretakers' house, where I found the old man sitting morosely in an overgrown garden while his wife peeled potatoes into a tin bucket. They looked decidedly grim, the woman in her apron and babushka, her much older husband huddled in his wheelchair. He said he would take me to the mosque—it was his job after all—but he went on looking disgruntled, ordering me to start wheeling. He must have been close to eighty, perhaps older, wearing an embroidered cap and oversize black jacket. His face was as wrinkled as a prune, his mouth toothless, his eyes surprisingly blue. He kept turning his head and spitting, muttering to himself. "Turn to your right!" he barked.

The early-eighteenth-century mosque stands off a cobblestone road, surrounded by linden trees. It is made of pine, and despite the Islamic crescent over its entrance, rather resembles the old timber churches I have seen along the way. The village has old houses, also made of timber, but looks forlorn and shabby rather than picturesque. Unlatching the mosque's creaky gate, we find three Polish tourists who are delighted to see us, having unsuccessfully tried to look into the mosque through the garden windows.

We take off our shoes and enter a cool interior divided into two sections: a small one for the women, and the main men's hall, off limits to

Muslim women. The main hall is much larger, and carpeted, its walls covered with printed Koran texts imported from Mecca. There is the usual recess pointing in the direction of Mecca, and a pulpit from which the imam traditionally leads the congregation in prayer. It is Friday, the Muslim Sabbath, but there is no imam and no congregation. Why? I ask the caretaker.

And so the bitter litany begins. There has not been an imam here for over twenty years, except during Ramadan, when city Tatars come for the holiday. There were originally three thousand Tatar inhabitants in the village, but now there are only seven; the rest are all Poles and Belarussians.

"Seven!" I hear myself exclaim. I knew the Tatar communities were dying out, but had no idea the end was so imminent.

"Seven," the old man echoes, "and we won't be here much longer either." He coughs, then goes on to speak with rancor about young Tatars, his children included, who have abandoned the village to pursue new ways in the city. He has four grandchildren and three great-grand-children but doesn't see any of them very often.

"That's how it is," he says, "when people are old and poor, even their children have no use for them."

"Oh, don't say that. I'm sure it's not true," the Polish woman says, exchanging looks with her husband. I am not sure what's behind their look, but my own pity has gradually become tinged with unmistakable disappointment: that this—this frail, irritable, whiny old man—is a descendant of the legendary Tatars, whose very approach made their neighbors quake. Throughout my childhood, my mother, speaking of a brother-in-law or old neighbor, would say, "Ah, s/he was a real Tatar!" This let me know that the person in question was bold, strong willed, domineering, hard.

The old man has meanwhile shifted gears and is giving us a brief history of Poland's Tatars. He is barely intelligible, speaking as he does in a low, monotonous voice, very rapidly. When he pauses for breath, one of the Poles ventures to ask a question, but the Tatar goes on as if he hasn't heard. It is clear that he has memorized the entire text; one he has quite likely been repeating for many years. Though he told me there are very few tourists who come this way, the visitors' book has a long list of Arab diplomats who, I gather, have made regular contributions to the mosque's maintenance.

We, too, are expected to give some baksheesh, which the old man makes clear by holding out a brass platter as we turn to go. One of the Poles wheels him back home, then the four of us head toward the Tatar cemetery.

The cemetery has been here, at Kruszyniany, since King Sobieski's time. The earliest burials took place in the seventeenth century, and some of the tumbled-down gravestones we find are so old that the writing on them is illegible; on some it is totally effaced. We keep having to pull aside stubborn weeds and grass, finding a few graves inscribed in Russian, others in Arabic and Polish. The names we read are intriguing, for they are typically Muslim names with Polish endings, like Ibrahimowicz, Ismailowicz.

But there are recent graves too, and this is the first time I come across plastic flowers in a cemetery, presumably left by all those delinquent children who can't come often enough from the city. We make our way toward the exit, laughing to see a shiny granite sarcophagus with an incomplete inscription. It states the name and the date of birth, but the date of death is temporarily blank, for the future occupant is still among the living, grandly awaiting his own burial. I imagine him lurking somewhere near the fence, watching with satisfaction as visitors pause to read the elegant inscription: "Beloved husband and father. . ." I am reminded of Fellini's *Satyricon*, in which the middle-aged protagonist stages his own funeral, gratified in his coffin to the point of tears by the mourners' grief.

Walking away from the cemetery, we come upon a memorial erected in 1979, commemorating the three-hundredth anniversary of Sobieski's land gift to the Tatars. We stand reading the inscription.

"Just think," I say, "if it weren't for Sobieski, you might all be living in a Muslim country today."

"Exactly." The three Poles chuckle, and Teresa, the only woman among them, says Poles like to think they have actually saved Europe three times: from the Tatars, the Turks, and the Bolsheviks whose post-World War II advance was stopped in Warsaw by the forces of Józef Piłsudski, a military hero who finally realized the Poles' fervent dream of national independence.

As for the visit to Kruszyniany, after all the time and effort spent getting here, I feel somewhat let down by the apparent fact that we have seen all there is to see. My new Polish companions—a couple from Białystok and a younger visiting cousin—are amazed that I have come all this way alone.

"Weren't you afraid?" Teresa Antosiak asks. She is a pale, broad-shouldered woman with chestnut brown hair pulled into a chignon. She makes me think of a librarian—the way librarians looked once upon a time.

I admit I was somewhat uneasy, mostly because someone had told me of a young Dutch girl who had had a dog unleashed on her by some irascible Tatar. This might have stopped me had it not been for the additional information that the tourist had come wearing shorts and a sleeveless T-shirt.

But the four of us are appropriately clad and determined to give Bohoniki a try. Teresa and her husband, Bogdan, have offered me a ride, a bit of good luck that will save me hours, because of the poor bus connection between the two villages. The Poles are amused by the fact that I, a foreigner with a foreign guidebook, know exactly where to go in Bohoniki, as I did in Kruszyniany. They have a Polish book, but it offers no addresses, and so they are as glad to have run into me as I into them.

Bohoniki, however, does not have anything new to offer, though the mosque's caretaker here is a youngish, chatty woman who proudly tells us she is a direct descendant of Tatars settled here in 1697. An apron around her waist, she unlocks the mosque, happily answering all our questions.

In Bohoniki, five holidays are regularly celebrated. Once a year, they slaughter a lamb or bull, each according to his means. This ritual is supposed to help sinning souls get to heaven, having to travel first through hell and purgatory. Bogdan's cousin, Robert, asks how often she prays, and she admits she doesn't.

"Only sinners have to pray—that's my personal point of view," she states. All the same, she considers it important to maintain Tatar traditions. In Communist days, Tatar children were unable to learn how to read and write in their own language unless their parents taught them at home, and who had the time? Now that religion is once more being taught in Polish schools, all minorities have an opportunity to study their own language and traditions.

And so, of course, the caretaker is happy with recent events in Poland. She is altogether an upbeat, almost jolly, person whose views contrast sharply with the old man's in Kruszyniany. She says everyone's relatives come to visit on a regular basis; they all have enough to eat, thank God, and their relations with their Christian neighbors are very good. They all farm and raise families and try to improve their children's lives.

"We each have our ways but respect the other's. We rest on Friday, they do on Sunday, but we let each other be."

Locking up the mosque, she offers to sell us "merchandise from across the border." Alcohol and cigarettes, she tells us and, learning that none of us smokes or drinks much, urges us to buy some to sell in the city.

"The price is so good you'll still make a nice profit," she says with a smile.

We decline again and, sorry to let her down, I ask whether by any chance she has caviar for sale. She doesn't but informs me it is 75 percent cheaper in Białystok than in Warsaw. Bogdan, however, is quick to point out that it is illegal to take caviar out of Poland. Privately, he later tells me that imported vodka has been known to cause blindness in Poland, due to chemicals.

But the caretaker is the sort of person who does not seem to believe in the possibility of calamity. Saying goodbye, she shakes our hands warmly, pointing to a low-flying stork, its matchstick legs thrust downward, its wings a fluttering black cape against the cloudy sky. It flies directly over our heads, toward a nearby nest.

"Good luck is coming your way," states the Tatar.

There are about six million Tatars in the world today, most of them in Tatarstan (Russia), a million and a half in the Urals where I was born and where my mother's family has lived for generations. My mother has high cheekbones and hooded, somewhat slanted eyes, and so does my brother. When he was a small child, people would often exclaim in surprise, for he had straight, pale hair but a distinctly Oriental cast to his face. There are no baby pictures of my mother, but now that she is in her midseventies, her face is that of an elderly Oriental matron—perhaps a Tatar? Knowing what I do now, it is difficult not to think of those ferocious horsemen galloping through the Urals, burning and looting and no doubt siring countless unwanted children.

The reason I find myself thinking in Białystok of my mother has to do with Teresa's own elderly mother. Like mine, she is afflicted with Alzheimer's, though hers is at a more advanced stage. Having given me a ride back to Białystok, Bogdan and Teresa have invited me up for tea, along with Robert, who is in Białystok for the weekend. They live in a recently built high rise, in a flat adjacent to Teresa's parents'. Her father, a retired industrial designer, takes care of his wife, occasionally relieved by his daughter. He had an errand to run after we arrived, so the old woman was brought to Teresa's flat and placed in front of the television. And so there she sits, along with millions of Poles, watching the Atlanta Olympics.

The Poles are intensely proud of their athletes, who have won one silver and four gold medals in the first three days and who will win seventeen by the time the games are over. Teresa's mother is not capable of following the events but seems content to sit in a large armchair, her eyes fixed on a Polish athlete receiving a gold medal in the fifty-kilometer walk. The athlete kneels down dramatically and kisses the track, dedicating the medal to his young daughter.

"Ah yes," says Bogdan, "we Poles love theatrical gestures, don't you think?" He smiles at me, tugging at his graying beard. He is a tall, restless-looking man with a grave, gaunt face, like Abraham Lincoln's. Having pulled up a chair, he sits beside his mother-in-law with a plate and feeds her poppy-seed cake. He does it matter-of-factly while Robert makes a phone call and Teresa prepares tea in the kitchen. He watches the screen and chats with me, occasionally addressing his mother-in-law as one would an infant. Unlike my own mother, who is confused and disoriented but still reasonably functional and responsive, Teresa's mother never utters a word, though she looks oddly peaceful in the red plush chair, opening her mouth at regular intervals to receive more cake. We are seated in the living room, facing a sideboard with a collection of family photographs. There is one—a faded, sepia photo taken just before the Germans invaded Poland—of Teresa's parents on the day of their engagement. They are an attractive, somber-looking couple whose youthful, hopeful faces bring a familiar ache to the vicinity of my heart.

My mother too was very lovely once—lively, flirtatious, and highly competent. Also, though she herself would not have acknowledged this, as willful and domineering as any Tatar woman. She is still willful but in a mulish sort of way, and still gregarious, stopping strangers in the street, flirting with young men on store escalators. But she does not recognize my voice on the telephone and once, running into me and Ranya on the street, she failed to recognize us altogether. The woman who once shopped for the best clothes on Łódź's Piotrkowska Street now dresses like a bag lady, sporting hideous wigs and dollar-store jewelry. She has, in recent years, become increasingly parsimonious, though she was all her life a spendthrift, generous to a fault. Oddly, the habit of generosity has not died out, though these days it expresses itself in heartbreaking gestures: a roll of pink toilet paper, a half-eaten bunch of grapes, a transparent plastic rain hat for my teenage daughter. I am touched by the Antosiaks' casual kindness; by the mere fact that the old lady is allowed to sit here in company, occasionally making an odd gurgling sound, but eliciting only sad, tolerant smiles.

Teresa has come with the tea and a large tray full of cake, cookies, cheese, and fruit. I have taken my shoes off at the entrance, and noting my bare feet, Teresa brings me a pair of slippers, then urges me to eat. Not for the first time, I am reminded of my own mother's former hospitality; the compulsive mothering of guests, the often excessive gesture. In Białystok, with Teresa's mother beside us, all this calls up a vivid vision of my irrevocably lost mother. It makes me feel, for the first time in my life, like a grown-up orphan.

Then Robert comes back from the hallway, having reached his Tatar girlfriend on the phone. She lives in Gdańsk, where he met her on a recent holiday, and it is because of her that he was curious to see the Tatar villages. Robert lives in Hajnówka, working as a vet in the Białowieża National Park, south of Białystok. There are twenty-three national parks in Poland, scattered throughout the country, in addition to ninety-eight picturesque landscape parks. Mostly state owned, the parks are highly diverse in their topography and shelter a bounty of sometimes rare flora and fauna. Białowieża is the oldest national park in Poland. It has a primeval forest and, Robert tells me, the only free-roaming bison in Europe. The forest was once the exclusive hunting ground of Polish kings and later, of Russian czars. During World War I, hungry soldiers killed virtually all the bison in the area, but the stock was eventually replenished with donations from zoos. The park also breeds tarpans, a small, stumpy breed of ponies believed to be ancestors of today's horse. Poland's tarpans are cousins to the wild horses that once populated the Ukrainian steppes but became extinct in the nineteenth century. They are the product of select breeding in the 1930s, and theirs is one of many success stories associated with the Polish Academy of Science, which breeds various species of animals in its northern Poland reserve.

It is from Robert that I first learn about tarpans and a good deal more about the Białowieża National Park. He has been working there for five years and is intensely grateful for his luck in being able to spend much of his time close to nature. The trees in Białowieża, he tells me, are eighty feet high; some are so old that they have been designated Monuments of Nature and given the names of Polish kings.

"Polish kings!" I echo over my steaming tea.

"Yes," says Robert. "Poles worship nature and royalty in about equal measure." He grins, telling me I must come and see the park for myself. "Walking through the Białowieża forest is like walking in a great green cathedral," he states.

And so, as often on this journey, I am forced to decline a tempting invitation because of time constraints. This is not a trip during which I will see much of Poland's nature, but I have seen and heard enough to know that the country suffers from underexposure, and that I will have to come here again, to see all I have missed.

Meanwhile, I am happy to sit in this pleasant home, chatting with Teresa, who is a dentist, and her land-surveyor husband. They are both in their early forties and have two teenage daughters who are visiting Bogdan's parents in the country. Bogdan is half Belarussian, half Polish, and has many contacts in both rural communities. This background is partly responsible for his success, he tells me, but mostly it is due to the fact that land, especially in the countryside, is continually being handed down and split up among heirs, growing smaller with every generation. I have been reading about Polish royalty in recent days and can't help thinking of Bolesław Krzywousty (Bolesław the Wrymouthed) who, for political reasons, divided the country among his sons. They in turn left lands to their own heirs, further subdividing each region. The small, newly created duchies soon succumbed to the influence of their neighbors, undermining the Polish state which Bolesław the Brave, Poland's first king, had so assiduously built in the tenth century.

Bogdan and Teresa live on the fourth floor of a cement tower but, like many Poles, belong to a cooperative that entitles them to a small plot of land where they grow their own vegetables. Poles spend about 40 percent of their income on food, and though one sees attractive markets with fresh fruit and vegetables, they are often prohibitively expensive. But many urban Poles have their roots in the countryside, and it may well be that even if cheaper produce were available, they would derive satisfaction from cultivating their own plots of land. Teresa and Bogdan assure me it is one of their favorite activities and, when I express surprise that they find the time, tell me they all take turns. Though there are several of them, I find myself bemused by what is a bit of a mystery to me. How is it, I ask myself, that we in the West, with our various labor-saving devices, seem to have less free time than Poles, most of whom do not have dryers, dishwashers, food processors, and the like. Not only that, but many of them work longer hours, have no access to convenience foods, live in cramped quarters. And yet, they find time for aging parents and stray foreigners, for ironing bedsheets and underwear, for baking cakes and making jam and pickling vegetables.

Perhaps, Robert speculates, they watch less television than North Americans? It's possible, though I think it's more likely that Poles simply go on with their domestic chores while watching television. "That's quite true," Teresa confirms, thoughtful. "We usually do at least two things at the same time." She laughs. "Not necessarily all that well, mind you."

Bogdan repeats what I have heard elsewhere—many people have more than one job—but he adds a new twist. Some of those with a second job are actually exceptionally well off. One way or another, they have made a good deal of money under the table and are now forced to work at a second job to justify their excessive income.

I ask for examples of moneymaking opportunities in Poland and am told that many people have grown rich importing computer parts. Teresa's own brothers caused the family much chagrin when they dropped out of university some years ago in order to start importing parts from Southeast Asia. Within five years, the two became so successful that they bought homes in Warsaw and European cars.

"Now they come to visit and poke fun at my father and me, both of us university graduates making a pittance in comparison." Teresa shrugs.

I ask Bogdan whether he has any siblings and he tells me about his sister who married a Communist Party official and has lived to regret it. Despite her fiancé's reluctance, she had insisted on a church wedding, and finally the young man relented, only to find himself in subsequent years repeatedly passed over at promotion time.

"Of course he blames it all on poor Maria. Even his alcoholism is now her fault." Bogdan gives a sigh. His sister puts up with it, he says, because she too feels it is probably her fault and also because she is categorically against divorce.

"It's really very sad," says Teresa, "and actually there's no way of knowing how much the church wedding had to do with it. There was another factor—the sudden death of an old apparatchik who had been my brother-in-law's mentor."

"Well, it was probably both," says Bogdan. "You may have heard the old Polish riddle," he says to me: "What's the worst sentence you can get for a criminal offense?" When I shrug, he smiles wryly. "Three years in Poland without any pull."

Laughing, I ask whether pull is still crucial in today's Poland. Robert begins to answer, saying it's less important than it used to be, except at the very top. "For example," he says, only to be interrupted by a sudden, anguished exclamation from Teresa's mother. Since there is nothing on television but a commercial for a new fruit juice, it is not clear what the cause might be. Teresa goes over and crouches beside her mother and, placing her hand on the creased forehead, tries to determine what is ailing her. The old woman goes on making a sound so distressed it makes my eyes begin to sting. It is a sound my own mother has never made, but it somehow suggests a lifetime's cumulative fear and anguish. Sometimes I think it is not Alzheimer's that has claimed my mother but a willful refusal to confront the brutal fact of a life approaching its end—a life it is too late to change.

CHAPTER 10

SHE WAS NOT MUCH of a reader, yet some of the
warmest memories I have of my young mother revolve around books—
Polish children's books, which she bought for us with almost as much
enthusiasm as she did elegant hats or shoes. By the time I was six and
my brother three, we had stacks of them, mostly fairy tales, and the
spell cast by my mother's reading has hardly diminished with time. All
of which explains, I suppose, the childish thrill I feel on finding myself
in Poland's Suwałszczyzna region. For this—this remote northeastern
corner tucked against the Lithuanian border—is without a doubt
Brothers Grimm country.* The forest that Little Red Riding Hood had
to cross, the one where Hansel and Gretel got lost, is the famous
Augustów forest—or so I'd be willing to swear. A remnant of the vast
primeval forest that once covered much of this borderland, it now
encompasses more than 386 square miles of dense woods teeming with
birds and wildlife: deer, wild boar, wolves, elk, beavers. The forest is
divided by the spectacular Czarna Hańcza River and has fifty-five
lakes, formed—like all lakes in northern Poland—by the retreating
Scandinavian glacier that once covered the entire region. In all, there
are two hundred lakes in Suwałszczyzna, smaller but deeper than the
adjacent Mazurians, and considerably less known.

Despite its natural beauty, Suwałszczyzna is still terra incognita for
most Poles, who think of it as a wild, barely inhabited region with long,
icy winters—their own unexplored Siberia. In recent years, however,
the new concept of ecotourism has caught on in Poland, with an

*The region became part of Prussia in 1795, when the Grimm brothers were about ten years old.

increasing number of nature lovers venturing to little-known areas like Suwałszczyzna. Despite the long-established presence of two towns (Augustów and Suwałki), the vast region remains largely unspoiled, offering limitless opportunities for outdoor activities, from hiking to ice boating. There are "photo safaris" and geological expeditions, and programs combining ecotourism with agritourism, the latter promoting accommodation in peasant farmers' homes. Since Suwałszczyzna has a national park, two landscape parks, and ninety nature reserves, it is not difficult to imagine its imminent invasion. The entire region, however, has been designated "Poland's green lungs" and as such is subject to strict environmental controls.

Ironically, it is the region's economic insignificance that has ensured its pristine condition. The original inhabitants—a tribe known as Jacwingians—were wiped out by the Teutonic Knights in the thirteenth century, after which Suwałszczyzna remained uninhabited until the sixteenth century. The region continued to pass from one occupier to another, a fact that considerably slowed down its development. Early in the nineteenth century, with the lower Vistula in Prussian hands, work was begun on the ambitious Augustów canal. The project was to provide an alternative route to the Baltic, but it remained uncompleted after the region fell into Russian hands. The dense woods around the canal were soon sheltering anticzarist insurrectionists, much as they later did World War II partisans. In late 1944, the region became a battleground for clashing Russian and German armies, a two-month struggle that left 70 percent of Augustów in utter ruin.

Augustów is named after a sixteenth-century Polish king, Zygmunt August, who had his heart set on founding a town in this spectacular region. The spot he chose lay at the edge of a vast forest, on an isthmus separating three lovely lakes. Today's Augustów, alas, is a small, undistinguished town of some thirty thousand. Its postwar facade is utterly utilitarian, but given its exquisite setting, it is difficult not to think of what might have been.

I arrive in Augustów on Saturday afternoon, hoping to make it on Sunday to an obscure little village called Gabowe Grądy. I have no contacts here, or hotel reservations, but find my way to a tourist office in hopes of a good pension. It has not taken me very long to discover that staying in hotels seldom yields much by way of information or insight, and that most towns in Poland have a tourist office with a list of families in search of lodgers.

"But is it a family?" I ask the young clerk at the tourist office. I raise the question because she has a Pan Kielak on hold and because I have learned to be cautious. She assures me there is a family, and that the house, though far from the center, is on the lake. I am not very happy to pay for a room sight unseen, but there is no time to check it: the office is about to close for the day. It is a hot, humid afternoon, and having traveled for days, I have a vision of a restful overnight stay on a placid lake—maybe a view of the water? "I'll take it," I tell the clerk. I ask her to let the landlord know I won't be coming immediately. I want to make inquiries about Gabowe Grądy and to have lunch in town. I promise to call again in about three hours.

"Everything is in order." Having confirmed arrangements with Pan Kielak, the clerk gives me the suburban address and a cash receipt. She tells me how to get there but knows nothing about the church choir at Gabowe Grądy. She doesn't even know how to get there.

The fact is, most of the so-called Polish tourist offices are actually privately owned travel agencies sustained by small commissions. Their clerks are not as a rule well informed, nor do they have much interest in helping travelers in unprofitable directions. The Augustów clerk has never been asked about Gabowe Grądy but is at least able to direct me to a nearby Russian Orthodox church. It has occurred to me that since Gabowe Grądy is an Old Believer village, an Orthodox priest is bound to know about its Sunday service, and the best route to the village.

The Old Believers are a Russian Orthodox splinter group whose seventeenth-century adherents turned their backs on liturgical reforms introduced by the Russian Orthodox Church. Insisting on their right to practice the old rites, they were persecuted by the Church, as well as czarist forces. Failing to find safety and peace at home, they began to migrate toward Europe, many of them settling in the Suwałszczyzna and Mazurian lake regions. There are about two thousand of them in Poland, and a sizable community in nearby Lithuania, where many fled during World War II. An obscure Polish minority, today's Old Believers speak a strange hybrid of archaic Russian and rural Polish, but their religious practices remain fairly uncompromised.

There are three centers of Old Believer worship in Poland, one of them in the forest village of Gabowe Grądy where, I have heard, there is a women's choir not to be missed. I had assumed that once I was in Augustów, it would be easy to obtain information, but the Orthodox Church office in Augustów is closed, and I can find no one to answer my questions. The line to the bus information bureau is busy as usual, so I decide to go and have lunch, and then call the Kielaks. Perhaps they will be able to help?

I can't put my finger on what it is about Kielak that makes me uneasy. He is a courteous enough man with a competent air; a little reserved perhaps but certainly not unfriendly. I guess him to be in his midfifties, a rather beefy man with a large, ruddy face. The impression of stamina and strength utterly belies the fact that he has apparently had three heart attacks in the past nine years. He tells me this soon after we meet, explaining the necessity of early retirement. He had worked for years as a provincial bureaucrat in charge of what used to be called "holiday homes." I learn all this in the car, Kielak having offered to come pick me up when I telephoned. I thought that was very kind of him, but I have grown accustomed to people's kindness, and it is only now that we are on our way that I find myself growing uneasy.

It turns out there is no family, at least not in Augustów, but my discomfort begins before I learn that Kielak in fact lives alone. It is possibly not his fault that I was misled at the agency, but who knows? Travelers, particularly lone women, quickly develop sharp intuitions, and mine suddenly remind me of Hania Gwiazda's advice in Cieszyn to keep my identity to myself. "You're traveling to all these remote places. You never know what kind of people you'll run into."

And so I tell Kielak I am a Canadian of Greek origin—I have my ex-husband's name, thank God—but that my husband is Polish. This is supposed to explain my flawed knowledge of the language, tell him I am married, and ward off questions about my Polish background; questions that are bound to reveal my Jewish connection, though I can't for the life of me say why this should suddenly seem like such a threat. There have been times—in trains, buses, lobbies—when I have sat mutely, an English book in my hands, looking like a solitary, uncomprehending tourist, secretly alert. If I felt obscurely guilty on occasion, I would remind myself of the words of the celebrated American photographer Walker Evans: "Stare. It is the way to educate your eye, and more. Stare, pry, listen, eavesdrop. Die knowing something. You are not here long." In Augustów, however, I find myself actually lying about my identity and my Canadian self is frankly appalled. It is having some trouble comprehending the mysterious anxieties of its twin, the one whose earliest memories took shape in war's aftermath. After a while, I give up the struggle, to focus on practicalities: is there a restaurant or grocery near his home, I ask Kielak, or should I be getting something for my supper, breakfast?

"Don't worry, I'm about to take care of all that," he says. I am still puzzling this one out when he stops at a delicatessen, preparing to get out without another word.

"Perhaps I can come with you and pick up something if—"

"There's no need." He smiles. "Stay here and relax. We're going to settle everything later." I don't much like the way all this is going and consider getting out of the car while I still can. But before I can quite make up my mind, Kielak returns and places a paper bag in my hands. "Don't worry," he says, "you won't go hungry with me."

Do I worry too much? My daughter calls me a worrywart, so I suppose I must. This somewhat reluctant inner admission prompts me to cast all my doubts aside and, settling back in Kielak's car, try to make conversation.

The house turns out to be a good twenty minutes away from the lake, but it offers excellent accommodation. I had more or less made up my mind to look for another room in the neighborhood, and to hell with the lost payment. Worrywart or not, I decided I didn't like the idea of spending the night alone in a perfect stranger's house, particularly this stranger who had taken charge in a way I found disconcerting. Having arrived at Kielak's house, I am surprised to discover that I am actually to occupy a small cottage across the driveway from his own two-family dwelling. When he tells me he has a couple from Poznań staying at his house, I begin to relax at last. Kielak tells me he is expecting friends for supper at eight o'clock. Would I like to join them?

All this sounds so perfectly reasonable that I accept at once, attributing my nervousness to travel fatigue, hormones. I remind Kielak of his promise to find out about Gabowe Grądy, and he says he will do so at once.

"Don't worry," he says yet again. "By the time you come, I'll have an answer for you. I may even decide to take you there myself."

"Oh. . .thank you," I say, aware of an abruptly resurfacing unease. There may be wolves and wild boar in the Augustów woods, but I am more unnerved by the thought of being alone with this Viking-like stranger; with no one in the world knowing my whereabouts.

At the same time, I feel ashamed of myself. I think of women like Mary Morris, an intrepid American writer who, traveling through Central America, went galloping off into a remote Guatemalan jungle with a perfect stranger. Was Morris foolhardy? Am I really a coward? And can I hope to accomplish anything with such fearful anxiety?

The truth is that though I have never been a true adventurer, I seldom thought about my own safety before I had a child. My subsequent anxiety may be in the nature of things, or just my nature, but either way I find myself inwardly torn in Augustów. I have come quite a way to visit Gabowe Grądy, and since I have a Monday-morning appointment in Suwałki, it's tomorrow or never. Perhaps I can persuade Kielak's friends to come along for the ride?

With this thought, I go for an exploratory walk in the neighborhood. It is an undistinguished one, but there is something reassuring about Kielak's well-cultivated vegetable garden and small apple orchard, his well-washed laundry drying in the late-afternoon sun. The cottage I am to occupy has two spotless and comfortable rooms with a bath, immaculate bedding, a blue vase with fresh flowers.

The flowers are from Kielak's back garden, where I eventually go to rest, only to find it occupied by the Poznań guests. They are a striking-looking couple in their midthirties, Alicja and Adam Gutowski, both of them tall and fit and dressed with casual chic. Alicja has long, wheat-colored hair and bluish-gray eyes as placid as the region's lakes. But her husband's eyes are even more arresting, being an odd shade of yellow green, and slightly slanted—a wolf's eyes, made all the more memorable by his dark hair and beard.

The Gutowskis are here on their annual vacation. They are both outdoor enthusiasts and have come to Augustów with their car, canoe, and fishing gear, leaving their two children in Alicja's mother's care. They will have a family vacation later, after a week alone in the woods—fishing, canoeing, bird-watching. The lakes are crystal clear here, they say, speaking English, the river eighty-seven miles long. As for the air, it is said to be the purest in Europe. We sit chatting for a while about our respective interests, and eventually I ask whether they know about Gabowe Grądy.

I tell them about the Old Believer village and the women's choir, which, I have been led to believe, can be heard on Sunday mornings. If they like sacred music, I say, the hymns and chants are supposed to be hauntingly beautiful. Would they care to go?

"It sounds very interesting." The Gutowskis sit in Kielak's reclining lawn chairs, considering. They have made plans for the afternoon, but the morning looks free. What time? How far? When I admit I am not sure, Adam Gutowski goes and gets their map and comes back to study it in the waning sun. This is how, after all the obstacles and anxieties, I find myself at the last moment not only with the promise of a comfortable ride but with two congenial companions who will take me through the ancient Augustów woods, then drop me off after a pleasant lunch with an invitation to visit them in Poznań.

I can hear their voices through the open door. A woman laughs as I climb the stairs; a jovial male voice tells me to come in, come in. It is eight o'clock, but I can see at a glance that Kielak has been at the bottle for some time. His blue eyes are bright, his face is florid, and his manner—particularly in contrast with his former laconic self—disconcertingly boisterous. The entrance leads straight into the kitchen, and this is where I find him, sitting with four friends around a laden table. Kielak waves me over, calling me by my first name and instructing me to call him Ignacy. He introduces me to his friends, two men and two women, one of them his niece. The men seem rather reserved, but the women are instantly friendly, pulling out a chair and studying me with frank curiosity. Kielak fills my glass with vodka and asks whether all is well at the cottage. Everything is fine, I say, except for the hot-water tank, which I couldn't get to work. Kielak promises to show me later, then tells me he has found out how to get to Gabowe Grądy. "I'm going to take you there first thing in the morning."

"Well. . ." I take a deep breath, a sip of the Polish vodka, and explain I have already made plans to go with the Gutowskis.

"Why did you do that?" Kielak sits frowning, and continues to do so as I point out that he had not been at all definite about tomorrow. I wanted to be sure to get there, but if he would like to go, perhaps he could come along, I say, and at once regret it.

"No," he says, "I'm not interested. I just wanted to do you a favor." He looks momentarily dejected, and I feel a pang of guilt. Should I have consulted him first? Suddenly he says, "Are you really married?"

"I am." I blink at him for a moment. "What makes you ask?"

"You're not wearing a wedding ring," he points out accusingly.

"Oh." I explain that the ring is a little tight. When the weather's hot, it becomes uncomfortable. It has been unusually hot, hasn't it, I ask, hoping to change the subject.

"It's summer," says Kielak. He asks my husband's name, and one of the male guests inquires about his origins in Poland. The fair, somewhat obese man beside Kielak's niece is obviously shy, but Tomasz in the corner, the one asking questions, is quiet in an odd, speculative way; or so it seems to me as I sit there, fabricating answers.

"And what do you think of Poland?" asks the woman on my right. Her name is Lidia and she is a vivacious blonde with a sharp tongue, a sardonic laugh. She seems the brightest of the lot, and her presence, and that of gentle-faced Monika, helps me relax a little.

I tell Lidia it's an interesting country, though a bit difficult for a foreigner to figure out. It's far from clear, for example, whether the majority of Poles are happier now than they were before 1989. "People contradict each other all the time," I say.

"What you have to understand," says Lidia, "is that we Poles are contrary by nature." By way of example, she points to Poles' attitude toward the Catholic Church. When religion was forbidden by the state, everyone rallied to defend it; now that restrictions have been lifted, all you hear is criticism of the Church.

"Lidia's right," says Monika. "Take Wałęsa, for example. When—"

"Ach, forget about Wałęsa," interjects the one named Jurek. He is, I eventually learn, Monika's live-in companion. "Wałęsa's out of the game now. He had his chance and blew it. He alienated a lot of brilliant men and now—"

"What brilliant men?" Kielak suddenly booms on my left. "That bloody Michnik and his coterie? Did you read what Jankowski called him the other day—an invisible tumor attacking cells from within. That's Michnik for you!"

The controversial editor of Warsaw's *Gazeta Wyborcza* has—not for the first time—been attacked by an equally controversial figure: Father Henryk Jankowski, the Solidarity priest who made headlines around the world in 1995 with his antisemitic sermon. What outraged many people, including President Clinton, was Wałęsa's refusal to repudiate the Gdańsk priest. Jankowski was a friend and ally, but American pressure eventually forced Wałęsa to take action. Jankowski apologized and withdrew his comments but lately has been at it again. And so, for better or for worse, I suddenly find myself in the midst of one of those heated political arguments Poles seem to thrive on, vodka or no vodka.

"Oh, you and your obsession with Michnik," Lidia scoffs at Kielak. "I'd rather take Michnik any day than that hypocrite Jankowski."

I ask what makes him a hypocrite and Lidia gestures irritably. "A man of God," she says, "who lives like a maharajah—that's Jankowski. Jesus Christ rode a mule, but Jankowski needs a chauffeur-driven Mercedes. Some say he has two," she snaps.

Tomasz, the quiet one, smiles ironically. "And you said others are criticizing the Church unfairly."

Lidia turns to face him. "I didn't say *others*, I said *we*; and I didn't say *unfairly*. The point I was trying to make—"

Before she can complete her sentence, Kielak raises his voice. "Irena! You're not drinking!" he accuses.

"I am." I mutter something about not being able to sleep if I drink too much.

"Eat!" he commands. "And then you can drink all you want." There are numerous dishes on the table—sausage, smoked eel, headcheese, potato salad—a wonderful spread that remains virtually untouched. The others are apparently here to drink, and I have been too timid to go for it on my own. "Eat as much as you want," says Kielak, as if sensing my hesitation. He made it all himself, he tells me, and I say sincerely that it is all delicious. I can't remember the last time I had headcheese. I know it was years ago, before my mother became someone new, someone who hates to cook.

And so I eat and drink a little, and listen to the argument in progress on my right. Or try to, for suddenly Kielak says, "You have beautiful eyes, Irena—Polish eyes. Are you sure you're not Polish, not even a little bit?"

"Not that I know of," I say.

"And you speak Polish so well, so—"

"I've been married over twenty years; I once ran a language school."

"You don't look Greek to me," he says, staring into my eyes. "You look Polish to me and—"

"Take that as a compliment," Monika interjects. She winks at me. "Watch out, he's taken a shine to you."

Tomasz asks how I come to have a Polish first name, and I explain it is a variation on a Greek name. Irini means "peace" in Greek.

"And are you at peace, Irena, are you happy with your Polish husband?" This, once more, from Kielak, who is sitting on my left, a little too close for comfort. He seems intent on my face but, it turns out, has simultaneously been following the discussion between Lidia and Jurek, for suddenly he looks up and bellows in their direction.

"What're you saying, Lidia?" She had been saying, quoting someone on television, I think, "They promised us golden fish but they were smart enough to keep all the nets for themselves." Kielak says something I can't quite follow, but I do understand the conclusion: "At least Poland is finally going somewhere."

"Yes," says Lidia. She too is beginning to look rather flushed. "I'm not sure that's where I want to go, that's the problem."

"Your problem," says Kielak, "is you're critical of everything and everyone—that's just your way, isn't it?" He looks around the table, as if in search of consensus.

"I may be critical," says Lidia, "but at least I'm not blind. "I'd rather—"

"Oh, stop that, the two of you," says Monika, who is Lidia's friend. She turns to me, shaking her head in mock exasperation. "Don't pay any attention to those two—they're always bickering, have been for almost eighteen years." She then tells her uncle he had better start eating. "A hungry Pole is an angry Pole," she says, smiling at me; then, when Kielak goes on arguing, adds, "*Eat,* Uncle, you'll feel much better." Apart from me, she is the only one nursing her drink, with Lidia and Kielak downing their vodka at a truly alarming speed.

"I feel fine!" Kielak bellows at his niece. He turns back to me, his hand on my arm. "The problem with Poland now is everybody says whatever comes into their heads. Like children—kids who've had to keep quiet in class; then, suddenly dismissed from school, talk nothing but nonsense." He takes a gulp of vodka. "The thing is, you can't really blame the people," he says. "It's the media's fault, above all that filthy Jew's *Gazeta Wyborcza* with its constant propaganda."

"Come on, Uncle," says Monika. She picks up a slice of sausage on a fork and shoves it toward Kielak. "Eat and relax or you'll have another heart attack right here, with a foreigner at the table."

"Well," he says, "she's a journalist. She probably knows it as well as anyone. The media—not just in Poland but everywhere, all over the world—the media's controlled by the Jews. Isn't it so?" he asks me.

Thankfully, before I can answer, Lidia speaks up again. "I don't know about the world," she says, "but what Michnik says in his editorials is usually persuasive. He—"

"Kwaśniewski too is persuasive!" roars Kielak. "All Jews have a silver tongue, didn't you know that?"

" I *don't* know that," says Lidia, looking stubborn. "I don't believe Kwaśniewski's Jewish anyway."

"As I live and breathe, he's a Jew!" says Kielak. "If he wasn't a Jew, I'd have voted for him."

"Don't be silly. That was just political maneuvering on Wałęsa's part." Jurek is referring to Wałęsa's election campaign, in which the former president planted the idea of Kwaśniewski's Jewishness in the minds of the electorate. "Did you see Kwaśniewski's mother's funeral on television?" asks Jurek. For the second time, I then hear of the three officiating priests, but Kielak is no longer listening.

"I'm a Pole heart and soul!" he says, slapping his chest. "And I'm telling you the Jews will be our downfall again; they'll ruin us all over again, mark my words!"

"Come, come, Ignacy," says Lidia in a suddenly subdued voice. "Let's change the subject. What will the world think of us, hearing you talk this way?"

This, I know by now, is a frequent preoccupation with Poles, some of whom feel the Jews have tarnished their image abroad. I'm amused to find myself representing the World, but Kielak is too far gone to care what I think, though he keeps touching me in a proprietary manner.

"Let them think whatever they want!" he spits out. "Who was responsible for World War II? Jews! Who ran Poland for the Bolsheviks? Jews! Who—"

But Lidia does not let him finish. "I don't know why you keep saying that. You're a happy capitalist now, but you did very well for yourself, working for the Bolsheviks," she says. "*Didn't* you?" She stares accusingly at Kielak, and this time he just glares at her, the red threads in his eyes swelling. It comes to me then that Kielak was quite likely one of the many Poles to benefit from the antisemitic measures taken by the Communist government in 1968. It was that year that most Jews left Poland, after the State Security Service began to circulate lists of Jews to Polish employers; lists going back several generations, often surprising Poles who didn't know that they had Jewish ancestors. Needless to say, there were many Poles who would never harm a Jew but who could hardly help rejoicing at the Jews' expulsion, opening up as it did thousands of new positions for ambitious Poles. Kielak would have been around thirty then. His bureaucratic career may well have taken off after the mass emigration of the Jews.

I sit thinking of all this, sorry to have come, glad to have come. It is the first unambiguously antisemitic outburst I have heard in Poland, and I have been caught somewhat unprepared. When Kielak finally asks me what I think of all this, I say I don't understand why he so fears the Jews. There aren't any to speak of, I gather, and nothing Kwaśniewski has done so far suggests—

But no one gets to finish a statement at this table, and the guest is no exception.

"You don't understand how cunning they all are, how insidious," Kielak insists. "Here we are, just beginning to get back on our own feet, and in the blink of an eye, they start flying back, coming to demand their due."

Kielak gives the last word an ugly emphasis, and I look into his hateful face, thinking, So this is what it's all about, the controversial issue of compensation for lost property. Some of the Polish Jews' property was seized by the Communists and now belongs to the state. Like Polish aristocrats, a few Jews have recently begun filing claims, but Kielak makes it sound as if the Jews were holding Poles responsible for losses inflicted by the Germans. "Didn't we too lose property to the Nazis?" he demands. "They just want whatever they can grab," he states. "Before you know it, they'll be demanding interest on top of everything!"

And so it goes for a while longer, until Tomasz picks up his pack of cigarettes and says he has to go. It is by now going on eleven and I take the opportunity to say that I too must be turning in.

"Stay," says Kielak, coaxing, "you've hardly drunk anything."

"I'm sorry—I'm really tired." When he insists, I explain I've been traveling for days and must get up early tomorrow. I'll probably be going directly to the station from Gabowe Grądy, I add, and since he's not likely to be up before seven, I'd like to pay whatever it is I owe him.

"Oh, Irena," he says, "you're such a lovely woman. Are you sure you wouldn't like me to—"

"Come on, Uncle, let her pay and go to sleep. She's a married woman."

"Yes," he snaps. "But why is she hopping all over the world by herself, then? That's what I—"

"Please," I say. "I really must go. How much do I owe you?"

"All right," he says, "all right. Give me 30 złoty if you insist, and that'll be that."

"Thirty złoty? For supper?"

"I came to pick you up, Irena." He looks at me with smiling reproach. "Have you forgotten already?"

"All right," I say. I don't point out he had offered to come and get me. Thirty złoty is after all only about $15, not worth arguing over. And so I take out my wallet without a further word and give the bills to Kielak, suddenly aware of the silence around me.

"You should be ashamed of yourself, Ignacy!" says Lidia and stomps off toward the bathroom.

Kielak looks at Monica. "What's the matter with her tonight?" he asks, blinking at his niece. "Is she showing off because there is a foreigner, or what?"

"Never mind now," says Monika, tight-lipped. She too is on her feet now and offers to show me how to use the water tank.

"Yes, be a good girl and show her," Kielak says, gesturing vaguely.

"He's really fallen for you," Monika says as we cross the driveway. It is then I learn he is separated from his wife, who lives in Chicago with his grown children. Monika says not to be offended by him; he's just lonely and has had too much to drink. It is as I stand unlocking the front door that it suddenly occurs to me that Kielak almost certainly has a second key. Monika seems both sober and solicitous and so I feel free to voice my concern, but she too tells me not to worry. He drinks all the time and has had countless tourists staying here with him. He is not so drunk that he doesn't know the agency will stop sending people if ever there is any trouble.

This reassures me somewhat, but all the same it takes me a long time to fall asleep that night. For what seems like hours, I keep hearing their voices across the driveway—above all, Kielak's own strident voice, turning my anxious dreams to nightmares.

It is a Sunday-morning scene more evocative of Tolstoy than the last decade of the twentieth century. A forest village, a graveyard with wooden crosses, a rural church in front of which stand some three dozen worshipers, among them an elderly priest in a black cassock. Like all the men in the congregation, the priest has a long flowing beard; the women are colorfully dressed and wear printed babushkas. They stand in small clusters, chatting, laughing, scolding rambunctious children, speaking a language we don't quite understand. What we— the Gutowskis and I—do understand is that we have come too late. It is nine o'clock, but the service has evidently ended. Not only that: it seems we are not at all welcome here, respectful attire notwithstanding. This is made clear by an elderly village woman who, going through the gate, turns on us in Polish, telling us to go back wherever it is we have come from. This is a private place of worship, not a museum; we were not invited by anyone, were we? We should just turn back and leave them in peace, the sooner the better.

I stand between Adam and Alicja Gutowski, stunned, considering the old parishioner's words. In truth, Gabowe Grądy looks a lot like a live museum, one reminiscent of Massachusetts' Old Sturbridge or Ontario's Upper Canada Village.

"Don't pay any attention—she's old and not very well these days." The speaker is a middle-aged woman in a paisley dress and matching kerchief. She has waited for the angry parishioner to turn the corner before addressing us, but now stands at the gate, waiting for her father and making conversation. She was born and raised in Gabowe Grądy but now lives in Augustów with her own family. It is her parents she has come to visit, as she does every Sunday. What can she do? They have no one else and refuse to move to the city. Alicja asks whether it would be all right for us to stroll through the village, and the woman, perhaps wishing to make up for our poor welcome, tells us to come along and have refreshments at her parents' house.

And so we walk through the village together, Pani E. and her elderly father, who runs a small grocery in the village. Though this community too is dying out, its demise is not as evident as that of the Tatar villages. There is an elementary school with sixty local children, a youth center with a library and dance hall; it's a small but apparently thriving rural community. The timber houses we pass may look shabby but there are flowers behind the picket fences, and fruit trees, and fields of sunflowers, beets, cabbages. There is the sound of chickens clucking in several yards, and curtains in the windows, and hand-loomed rugs drying in the sun. The village has not changed much in the past century or two, but there are several reminders of the twentieth: TV antennas, for one thing, and an occasional car and barbecue standing incongruously beside a draw-bar well. The barbecues, Pani E. tells us, are the gift of relatives from abroad; the cars belong to Augustów visitors. It is, she says, a very poor village and would not survive without outside help. True, they all have electricity now and a few of them own televisions, but on the other hand, some Polish Old Believers still have dirt floors in their hovels.

Walking down the main road, we see a fair-haired woman with an uncovered head, and Pani E. explains that though a married woman should have her head covered in public, not all do. The Old Believers are divided into two groups, the more conservative of the two shunning even tea and coffee. Even the less orthodox, however, don't drink or smoke, and in general frown on the ways of the Polish Catholics who drink a great deal and whose daughters attend church wearing T-shirts and miniskirts.

"Are there Old Believers who shave their beards these days?" asks Adam.

This question is answered by Pani E.'s father, a frail man in his mid-seventies with a long, white beard. "How would a rooster look if you cut off its comb?" He blinks against the sun. His daughter says that of course there is the occasional individual who has turned his back on religion. It isn't easy, she says, in today's Poland. Her husband is often made fun of in Augustów. People make derisive, scissor-cutting gestures when he goes by.

"It wasn't easy in the past either," her father points out. The Nazis often mistook the bearded men for Jewish rabbis; under the Communists, they had to worship in secret. The irony of the latter is noted by Alicja who says that under czarist rule, any Pole with serious ambitions was obliged to convert to Orthodoxy, as well as to learn Russian.

I wonder how Old Believers feel about intermarriage, and Pani E. says it leads to instant excommunication unless the outsider agrees to convert. We are going through her parents' gate as she says this and, the old man having disappeared in the direction of the outhouse, Pani E. lowers her voice and says that, in truth, the community could use some fresh blood. There has been too much inbreeding, and many of their children are being born with genetic defects.

"But don't say I said so." She smiles and ushers us into her parents' kitchen. It is a large, sunny one with a wood-burning stove as well as a gas range. There is a plate rack on the wall, and baskets, and jars of preserves above the pine table. At the table sits an old, rather fat woman, pitting cherries with the help of a safety pin. She pauses for a moment and gives us a toothless smile, then goes on with her task, explaining, "Cherry jam!"

She invites us to sit down and tells her daughter to pour us some *kisiel.* The thick, jellied, red-currant juice is something else I remember from my childhood, and this one is delicious. There was a time, says the mother, when she would go currant picking herself, but these days she can't even get to church, her legs are so arthritic. We commiserate, and praise the *kisiel,* and I make a mental note to send a cherry pitter when I get home.

And then Pani E.'s father comes in and brings out his old hymn book from the adjacent bedroom. Each hymn has eight melodies, to be used on different occasions. He sings a few bars for our benefit, telling us all Orthodox liturgy is sung—that of the Old Believers in Old Church Slavonic, as opposed to the more prevalent Byzantine. Peter the Great, who introduced Orthodox Church reforms, is to this day regarded by Old Believers as the Antichrist.

At this point, Pani E.'s mother looks up from her huge enamel bowl and asks whether we've visited the Wojnowo convent. We haven't, and the old woman gives a deep sigh before lapsing into silence. She is right to sigh, for the famous Old Believer nunnery, a spiritual center since its establishment in the nineteenth century, is all but deserted now. Two old nuns, both in their eighties, still live there. "But they're too old, those two, even to show tourists the lovely icons," says Pani E. She hastens to tell us, however, that there is a caretaker, should we wish to visit the place on our westward route. "Don't worry, you're going to be well received," she adds, recalling our arrival.

It is only then that she explains the old parishioner's anger back at the church. It seems that icons and holy books have disappeared following outsiders' visits. Also, in recent years, there have been articles in the Polish press depicting Gabowe Grądy in what some villagers thought was an unflattering light.

"We're not inhospitable people," says Pani E., "but we've learned to be cautious." Eventually, having looked at photographs of baptisms, confirmations, weddings, we get up and say goodbye, and I ask permission to use the outhouse before we head back to Augustów. Pani E. says not to expect the Marriott and I don't; I've used my share of outhouses in various parts of the world. And yet, I find myself utterly unprepared for this one, for the black mountain of human excrement that apparently no one has attempted to clean up for weeks. This seems all the more shocking because the house is not a primitive one, the owners clearly not among the village poor. I remind myself that the grocer and his wife are elderly, that the daughter must have her hands full when she comes on Sunday. But isn't there anyone they could have paid to maintain the outhouse? And who would possibly want to deal with the problem now?

I remember Adam and Alicja saying on the way to Gabowe Grądy that western Poles have a somewhat condescending attitude toward their eastern compatriots. The farther east you go, they told me, the more primitive and dirty are the conditions. This is usually attributed to the fact that Polish areas previously occupied by the Russians have generally been more impoverished than those under Austrian or German rule.

I don't use the outhouse, nor tell the Gutowskis about its condition. But I find myself preoccupied by the question of whether decency permits even writing about it. It is not, of course, that the outhouse is indispensable to the Old Believer chapter, but it strikes me as a good metaphor for a problem all writers sooner or later face: to keep the dirt to oneself, or tell it like it is, and to hell with wounded feelings. I think of Pani E.'s hospitality, her critical reference to previous journalists, and I am frankly torn. Would I be betraying her hospitality; would the angry parishioner back at the church not be vindicated? On the other hand, I remind myself, no one in this village is likely ever to read my work. As this argument fails to alleviate my doubt, I tell myself I will change not only the names but all the telling details. I decide to go ahead and do so because the ethical problem, if not the condition of the outhouse, seems worth sharing with my readers. I know no one will be able to identify the Gabowe Grądy family who so kindly and trustingly invited us into their home. I know all that, but all the same can't help thinking of Hemingway's words to one of his wives: "Never trust a writer, they're all jerks."

CHAPTER 11

MAGDA STEIN was a postwar friend of my mother's, a woman everyone seemed to like, except her own husband. Artur Stein's parents had owned a knitting factory in Łódź, where the young Magda worked as a shipping clerk. She was a Polish country girl, both bright and beautiful, living with her married sister in the city. Magda's brother-in-law worked at the factory too; he was the Steins' foreman and, when the war broke out, persuaded his own family to take in Artur's parents, while his wife's family agreed to shelter Artur in another village. Artur's parents were found out and shipped to Auschwitz along with their keepers, but Artur survived the war and went on to marry Magda, then start his own factory.

The marriage did not work out. It may have had something to do with the war, perhaps even the odd human tendency to balk at indebtedness. Whatever the problem, it seemed only exacerbated by Magda's high-minded and determined patience, which, everyone agreed, brought out the worst in Artur's nature. He was by all accounts a decent enough man, and Magda herself fully agreed. She thought a Jew who had spent the war in hiding, who had lost his entire family, was understandably short on inner tranquillity. She forgave him a good deal on those grounds alone.

And then the Steins moved to Paris, and my mother—by then living in Israel—began to receive tearful letters from Magda, reporting mounting marital abuse. Artur had opened a knitting factory in France and was quickly becoming rich, but his temper had only worsened with the years. Magda was beginning to have serious doubts that he would ever recover from his wartime trauma.

My mother learned the details on Magda's eventual visit to Israel. I was ten years old by then and still remember Magda as she was that summer: a slender, elegant woman accompanied by two well-behaved, impeccably dressed daughters, one of them fair, one dark. Magda herself had had her hair lightened and wore a turban whenever she sat in the sun. She was fond of sitting in a reclining chair on our roof, her sculpted face offered to the sun. No one had ever considered using the apartment block's roof for anything but laundry, but Magda thought nothing of resting alone among the flapping sheets, dressed in a bathing suit, her long limbs glistening with cocoa oil. One of her daughters was a year older than I, the other a year younger, but all three of us vividly remember that summer, perhaps because it was the last Magda was to spend as Mrs. Artur Stein.

The following Easter, Magda took the girls to Poland. She went to attend her youngest sister's wedding in Kłodzko. The day after the wedding, Anita, Magda's younger daughter, came down with acute appendicitis and ended up in the local hospital. The surgeon was a handsome, childless widower, gallant with women in the Polish manner, and droll with his young patients.

Magda never went back to Paris. There had been increasingly frequent incidents of physical abuse, and as she wrote my mother, no money in the world was worth living that kind of life. She did suffer some qualms on account of the girls, but their stepfather, she claimed, was far more devoted to them than Artur had ever been. They were all living in Kłodzko now, not far from the Czech border. The girls had begun going to a Polish school; Magda was working in the hospital's admissions office. It was, to be sure, not an easy life, but she had no regrets, none at all, she wrote again as she lay dying of cancer two years ago. My mother by then could not remember who Magda was, but I still recall her fierce admiration for her friend who had given up a life of privilege—Artur was on his way to becoming a millionaire—to be a provincial doctor's wife, queuing up daily for meager staples, living in two rooms, sewing her own dresses.

I am not sure why it is that as we reach middle age, our childhood connections suddenly seem so precious, but they evidently do. When I knew I was going to Poland, I wrote to Magda's husband in Kłodzko, wondering if I could have his stepdaughters' addresses. I got a letter from Roma, the elder one, informing me that her stepfather had died the year before, and inviting me to come visit her in Kłodzko. She enclosed Anita's address and phone number in Gdańsk: they would both be thrilled to see me, she wrote. I called Roma when I got to Warsaw, and then her sister in Gdańsk. Anita and her husband were planning a visit to her in-laws in Suwałki and, learning that I too would be in the region, suggested we meet and drive together to Gdańsk, across the Mazurys.

My introduction to the Mazurian lakes took place years ago with *Knife in the Water*, the Polish film that catapulted Roman Polanski into the pantheon of world-class directors. The film being black and white, and Polanski being Polanski, the featured lake looked gray and desolate, its bleakness mirroring the unfolding inner complexities. It was summer in the film, but with the exception of the three protagonists, there was no one to be seen anywhere near the lake. I *know* the film was set in the Mazurys but have trouble believing it when I finally find myself going through the region. What I see, driving west with Anita and her husband, is a seemingly endless number of sparkling blue lakes surrounded by green, undulating hills; a sunny, vivid landscape crowded with swimmers, canoes, waterskiers. The Mazurys are known in Poland as the Land of a Thousand Lakes. Actually, there are three thousand of them, stretching right across the north much as the mountains do across the south. (Altogether, Poland has nine thousand lakes, more than any other European country, except Finland.) The Mazurys are far more developed than the Suwalszczyzna and, offering as they do better facilities, have for decades been Polish families' favorite summer playground.

But this picturesque holiday landscape—formerly part of East Prussia—is equally famous for its wealth of ancient churches, castles, monasteries, and other historic sites. Indeed, it seems virtually impossible to go anywhere in Poland without stumbling on some reminder of the country's turbulent history. In the Mazurys, one comes upon ruins of medieval castles beside graves of anticzarist rebels, trenches from the two world wars, and even old Swedish trenches dating back to the seventeenth-century Swedish invasion. I have heard of determined collectors digging up coins stamped with the czars' two-headed eagle; a few have managed to unearth fragments of old Swedish and Teutonic armor. The Mazurys may not be familiar in the West, yet this is the region that once sheltered Hitler's infamous Wolf's Lair, the twenty-seven-acre complex of Nazi bunkers from which the eastern campaign was conducted between 1941 and 1944. Surrounded by dense forest and carefully camouflaged, Hitler's bunker had walls and ceilings up to sixteen feet thick, the compound sheltering not only the *führer* but much of the top Nazi brass. It was, Hitler said, one of the few places in Europe where he felt safe. Ironically, it was in the Wolf's Lair that he came within a hair's breadth of losing his life.

The July 1944 assassination attempt was carried out by one of Hitler's most trusted officers. Count Klaus von Stauffenberg was the one carrying the briefcase with its ticking bomb, but the plot involved several high-ranking officers desperate to rid Germany of Hitler. The fact that they failed—the way they failed—is one of those historic tales through which the Devil's gleeful laugh will forever echo.

Having arrived at the Wolf's Lair to attend a meeting, von Stauffenberg placed the briefcase under the conference table, close to Hitler's feet. He then left the room on a pretext, unaware that a colleague had promptly taken his place and, finding the briefcase in his way, moved it aside, away from the *führer*. The ensuing explosion killed four of the officers, but Hitler himself was only badly shaken. Quickly recovering, he went on to meet Mussolini that very afternoon, having issued orders for the immediate arrest of all connected with the plot. When it was over, five thousand Germans had been arrested, and two hundred executed, most of them the conspirators' innocent friends and relatives. Six months later, Germany lay in ruins.

Dubbed the Mazurian Venice, Mikołajki is probably the most attractive of the area's resorts. A fifteenth-century fishing village, it straddles a channel connecting two small lakes surrounded by deep forests. Named after a legendary villager who managed to ensnare an aquatic monster terrorizing the fishermen, Mikołajki has winding cobblestone streets, quaint houses and shops, and a picturesque port with yachts and fishing boats. An old center for the region's Protestant community, it has an early-nineteenth-century Protestant church and a museum devoted to the Polish Reformation, which flourished here around the middle of the sixteenth century.

These days, however, Mikołajki's citizens are more preoccupied with tourism than either the state of their souls or the fishing industry. The tourists are mostly young, and there are hundreds of them all over the village. Germans in particular are fond of visiting places once occupied by their ancestors. At least this is what Anita tells me as we sit at a crowded waterfront restaurant, waiting for our midafternoon dinner. Anita doesn't look much like her mother but is an attractive woman in her own right. She has a wide face with prominent cheekbones and dark eyebrows contrasting with her cloud of honey-blond hair. What she has inherited from her mother is her facial expression, a smile so radiantly familiar it led me straight to her at the Suwałki railway station.

It has been some forty years since Anita and I last saw each other, but our meeting has been marked by an odd, almost instantaneous, sense of camaraderie. Did I remember the summer village where we stayed as children? The time I bit the dentist's thumb? The bear in the Łódź park? My frequent preference for solitude? No, not the latter, I said, but Anita assured me it was a fact. Roma, being older, will confirm it: I would play with the children for a while but, sooner or later, would abandon them to go and sit brooding on a stone, at the edge of the village forest.

By the time we stop for dinner in Mikołajki, we have said most of what there was to say about our respective families and, eating our creamed herring, are beginning to branch off in more general directions. The herring here is excellent but, Anita's husband says, is probably not Polish. Much of the Baltic being polluted, Poles have started importing one of the traditional mainstays of their diet from Finland. The diet, however, is a good deal more varied than it used to be.

"You can get just about anything in Poland these days," says Anita, "provided you have the money." It was very different before 1989, when Poles were perennially short of everything except ingenuity. Imagine having to bake a birthday cake without something basic, like flour. "I still remember my mother telling me she had a new recipe for almond cake, using ground beans and artificial syrup. Beans! Can you imagine?"

We talk for a while about Magda who, Anita confirms, never regretted her choice to stay in Poland. Her second husband was a remarkable man, but he lost the will to live after Magda died. Anita doesn't know whether her biological father is still alive. Having failed to obtain custody of his daughters, Artur Stein simply shut the door on his Polish past; they never heard from him again. Occasionally, Anita and Roma have talked of going to France and trying to reestablish contact, but they knew he had a new family and were held back by the fear of having their motives misconstrued.

Anita has no need of her father's money, at least not these days. She herself earns a modest salary, but Ryszard, who spent many summers picking fruit in Germany, studied design and has in recent years become an immensely successful furniture manufacturer. I have already heard that Poles are exceptionally skillful at producing copies of fine antiques, as well as contemporary Scandinavian furniture. In Warsaw, Stefan Kryński told me it would be cheaper to have a solid piece of furniture made to order than to buy a similar, mass-produced one at IKEA. Ryszard specializes in corporate furniture: for conference rooms, reception areas, executive offices. The furniture is mostly for the French market; few Polish companies can afford to furnish their offices so lavishly. Ryszard assures me that it is only a matter of time before they do. He too is proud of Poland's burgeoning economy. The 1995 growth rate was 7 percent, he tells me; inflation was down by 8 percent, and the reserve—

"Now don't go boring Irena with statistics," interjects Anita. "She can't write it down while eating anyway."

Anita, who studied languages, works as a commercial German and French interpreter. With the rush of foreign capital into Poland, there is great demand for someone with her language skills, and she too speaks with approval of the new Poland. Her only disappointment stems from the fact that their daughter married a Swiss and lives in Geneva. There is also a son—an energetic, successful one who studied management and is now in Gdańsk, involved in executive training.

In recent years, an increasing number of Poles have found themselves working with foreign colleagues and sometimes foreign bosses. Since most Poles have been trained in radically different circumstances, many large corporations have been investing in intensive retraining sessions, hoping to change Poles' unprofessional mindset and low production standards. The Communist system having failed to provide incentives, Poles were so blithely unconcerned with productivity that it came as an utter shock to suddenly find themselves fired for inefficiency.

"The older ones have found it especially difficult to adapt," says Anita, "but our son's generation works much harder than they do abroad and are proving themselves as resourceful as anybody."

But the plight of the older generation has been painful to watch, they concede. Some who failed to adapt ended up taking early retirement, occasionally surprised to find themselves actually enjoying it. Ryszard tells me about his brother's father-in-law who, after some three decades with an electronics firm, became a beekeeper, like his father and grandfather before him.

"You'll probably meet him at Borek and Mariola's, and if you do, watch out. He'll talk about nothing but his beloved bees," Ryszard says with a smile. In his early fifties, Anita's husband is a mischievous-looking man with graying, surprisingly bushy, hair. Borek is his younger brother, his partner in the furniture business and the proud owner of a new, not-quite-finished home. The Górniaks live outside Gdańsk, in the country, and I have been talked into spending the night at their place. In fact, it had all been arranged beforehand, and since Mariola and Borek are still without a phone, there seemed to be little choice in the matter.

Mariola, the beekeeper's daughter, is Borek's second wife and represents, says Anita, a new Polish phenomenon: the stay-at-home housewife. The breed is still rather rare in Poland, and we both chuckle over the fact that Mariola, a trained economist, is delighted to be able to stay home with her four-year-old son, and perhaps even proud that she can afford to. Both she and Borek are happy to be living in the country, a possibility no one contemplated until Mariola's father resolved to get out of electronics. One day he chanced to come across a good land deal near a Kashubian village. He bought it together with his son-in-law, setting up his apiary business while Mariola and Borek began to plan their house.

I have expressed only the mildest interest in the Kashubes, but it is enough to prompt Ryszard to stop at the Regional Kashubian Museum in Kartuzy, all three of us forgetting that it is Monday. Finding the museum closed, Anita and Ryszard take me instead to a nearby Gothic church, built in 1380 by Carthusian monks. An exceptionally austere order, the Carthusians originated in Grenoble, France, and were known above all for their determined contemplation of death. With Memento Mori as their motto, they routinely slept in coffins and in Kartuzy went so far as to construct a church whose roof resembles a giant coffin. We don't spend much time here, but long enough to see the Angel of Death on the church clock's pendulum, and to read the irrefutable inscription: "Every passing second brings you closer to death."

This is hardly what I expected from the Kashubian region, but far from casting us into a somber mood, the visit to the church perversely throws us into a fit of irrepressible hilarity. We laugh like schoolchildren on the way to the jeep, and spend the rest of the ride swapping jokes. Ryszard tells one lampooning Poles' national self-centeredness.

A German, an Englishman, a Frenchman, and a Pole are asked to write a treatise on the elephant. The German writes on the elephant's anatomy, the Englishman on a typical elephant hunt, the Frenchman on the elephant's love life, and the Pole on the Elephant and the Polish Question.

It is dark by the time we get to the country, greeted by a clear, tranquil evening, surprisingly cool for August. The Górniaks' house stands alone in a forest clearing, and getting out of the jeep, we linger for a moment under the starry sky, breathing in the scent of the surrounding woods, listening to a night bird's call. It is an eerie, repetitive, burring sound made by a bird whose English name turns out to be goatsucker. The name stems from the ancient belief that the bird is fond of feeding on goat's milk. Though goatsuckers are indeed plentiful around goats, this is most likely due to the presence of insects specifically attracted to goats.

We have arrived later than expected, and Mariola, meeting us at the door, says she was beginning to think we had been in an accident. Road accidents are a matter of particular concern here, for many more drivers die in Poland than in the West (14.6 percent of all accidents, compared with 3.5 percent in Western Europe). Ryszard assures Mariola there has been no accident but reports that he had his car radio stolen in Suwałki. This too is an increasingly common problem in Poland, one that has Poles forever fretting everywhere they go. I have been told that it is not at all uncommon to see concert- and theater-going Poles in evening dress clutching car accessories during intermission. Mariola says she went to Gdańsk with her son last week and saw schoolboys breaking into a foreign BMW.

She leads us into the living room, where a cozy fire awaits us. Tomek is asleep, she says, answering Anita's inquiry. He has come down with fever, and Mariola feels it is all her fault: she let him go for a swim late the other day, when it was already growing chilly. "But it's barely over thirty-eight," she says, "nothing to worry about, I guess."

"I can't believe my own ears!" exclaims Mariola's husband. "All afternoon she's been wringing her hands as if he were on his deathbed. Now, suddenly, it's nothing to worry about!" Borek puts his arm around Mariola, smiling indulgently. He is a fair-haired, compactly built man in his late forties; rather boyish-looking. Mariola is small and dark and slender as a schoolgirl.

"I was not wringing my hands!" she protests, sitting down. "All I said was we should call the doctor if the fever gets any higher."

Ryszard turns to me. "All Poles are hypochondriacs, as you've no doubt noticed." He gives me one of his wonderfully crooked smiles and I smile back, remembering all the public discussions of physical symptoms; also, the apparent obsession with changes in atmospheric pressure, to which Poles feel singularly susceptible. The thought of national hypochondria will strike me again in Malbork, on seeing a long queue in front of a free blood pressure clinic. What will give me pause is the information that the clinic, set up in a tent on a busy side-walk, is a promotional ploy used by a local radio station!

Borek and Mariola have meanwhile invited us to sit at the dining table, which Mariola's mother has set with the usual Polish delicacies: cold cuts and smoked trout, cheese, good country bread, and honey. The honey comes from Mariola's father's beehives and is wonderfully scented with linden. Pan Moroz, the beekeeper, has been out chopping firewood and, coming in, smiles on being told that I like his honey. I also like Pan and Pani Moroz, who are energetic and hospitable and highly animated. Did I know that apiculture was one of the oldest occupations in the world? asks Mariola's father. Having been told that I lived in Greece, he adds that, in fact, the ancient Greeks were probably the world's first beekeepers. But there he is wrong, I eventually discover. Apiculture is actually said to have originated in ancient Egypt. The Egyptians believed that the first bee known to man had flown out of the horns of Apis, the sacred bull; hence the term *apiculture*. Whatever the bee's origin, the Egyptians eventually discovered honey's culinary potential as well as its cosmetic properties. They also discovered that bees provide a gluelike substance (propolis), which was used to embalm corpses.

Pan Moroz, however, talks mostly about Polish apiculture, which is at least several centuries older than the Polish state. In fact, Piast the Wheeler, whose son founded the first Polish dynasty, is said to have been a beekeeper. Poland, with its vast forests and meadows, apparently has ideal conditions for the propagation of bees.

"Unfortunately, bees too are beginning to suffer from progress." Pan Moroz gives the word an ironic emphasis. The use of insecticides, he says, has led to the total destruction of bees in some parts of Poland, seriously undermining the quality of local crops.

"That's true," says his daughter, "but just think of all the positive things progress has given us. Do you think Uncle Jan would be alive today without all our new medical technology?"

"Uncle is alive, but thousands of people are dying from industrial pollution and other such gifts brought by progress. Polish hospitals are full of sick people, even tiny children."

At the mention of sick children, Mariola's mother gives her husband a baleful look. "What I'd like to know," she says, seemingly resolved to change the subject, "is why it so often takes hundreds of years to discover things people have always known." Bee products, she points out, have been used in folk medicine since ancient times, but it is only recently that hospitals have recognized their efficacy. Everybody knows that honey is beneficial to the heart and metabolism. She herself has felt much healthier since she began substituting honey for sugar.

Mariola says something in response to this, but I miss its gist, for Ryszard takes the opportunity to say, sotto voce, "You see, I told you all Polish conversation sooner or later leads to discussions of physical ailments."

I chuckle at this, and then ask whether it's true, as my daughter once told me, that queen bees fight each other for a mate.

"You could put it like that, I suppose," says Pan Moroz. In any colony that has lost its queen bee, he explains, the first new queen to hatch stings all the others as yet in their cells. Only if two queens happen to hatch simultaneously do they fight until one of them is killed. "And then mating does take place, of course."

"Of course!" says Mariola. "And they live happily ever after." She grins at her father over her glass of milk, her pert, suntanned face looking much younger than her thirty-five years. She is twelve years younger than Borek and, Anita and Ryszard told me, had grave doubts about marrying him. There was the age difference but, more important, Borek was divorced and Mariola had a hard time accepting the inevitable excommunication. To this day, she and Borek cannot participate in Church sacraments, though they both continue to attend mass without fail.

When I ask Mariola about this the following day, she surprises me with her unequivocal support of the Church's position vis-à-vis divorce. This may seem like a case of hypocrisy, but Mariola defends her point of view, saying that human beings are obviously fallible; the Church recognizes that, but it can't, and shouldn't, compromise its own moral standards to suit its straying followers. "After all," she argues, "the Church is supposed to be Catholics' moral guide, isn't it? What would happen to the shepherd, I ask you, if he allowed himself to be led by his own bumbling flock?"

"Not German enough for the Germans, nor Polish enough for the Poles." This observation about the Kashubes is made by Günter Grass's Grandma Koljaiczek in *The Tin Drum*. A Slav people related to the Pomeranians, the Kashubes have lived for generations along the Baltic coast, in a hilly, well-forested area dotted with more postglacial lakes. Unlike the various tribes that gradually came to form the Polish nation, the Kashubes have managed to retain much of their ethnic identity—at least until recently, when assimilation into Polish culture became inevitable. Today, only the elderly and middle-aged routinely communicate in Kashubian, a language that Poles are unable to understand. (Though often mistaken for a Polish dialect, Kashubian is in fact an independent language, with its own grammatical constructs.) Unlike other Polish minorities, the Kashubes were particularly fortunate in managing to avoid relocation after the postwar Communist takeover. They maintain their northwestern farms to this day, some of them having become highly successful in strawberry cultivation.

I hear about the local strawberry industry on a morning hike with Ryszard and Anita, who tell me I have missed the annual Kashubian strawberry festival. We have been walking along a strawberry field, heading for a green hill on our way to a Kashubian hamlet. The hill offers a sunny, serene rural vista: a forest and shimmering blue lake on one side, a golden field of wheat on the other. It is a warm morning, alive with singing birds and buzzing bees and, though it is by now late morning, the call of a distant rooster. Having had a good night's sleep and a swim in the lake, I feel calm and invigorated, glad to have been persuaded to spend the night in Kashubia. I have been greatly looking forward to seeing Gdańsk, but it is good to have this brief bucolic interlude, breathing in the fragrance of wild herbs, the heady smell of freshly cut hay and animal fertilizer. A farmer comes down the gravel road, sitting atop a long, horse-drawn cart laden with hay. He salutes us and keeps on going, followed by a beagle. Having visited several rural areas, I am beginning to understand the government's determination to modernize Polish agriculture, for everywhere I go I see primitive harrows, reapers, plows; occasionally, an old tractor or combine. If there is any new wealth here, it is not in evidence, though neither is there the rural squalor I have seen in the east. In the Kashubian hamlet, some of the recent houses are made of stucco, but most are old timber houses, blackened by time. They have shingled roofs and are so low they seem to be slowly subsiding into the earth. We stop to photograph one of them, a picture-book house that makes me think of Hansel and Gretel, perhaps because of the two flaxen-haired children playing under a plum tree. And then we are chased away—I for the second time—by a flock of geese. The geese seem a good deal more aggressive than the barking dog, and we take to our heels, followed by the children's laughter.

Crossing a potato field, Ryszard bends down and points out a small insect on one of the plants. In the 1950s, he tells me, schoolchildren were routinely taught that the CIA was infesting Polish fields with these insidious insects.

"That's true," Anita remembers, laughing. "*Everything* used to be blamed on the Americans. Now we have no one to blame any more, so our political parties constantly blame each other."

This is how a potato bug, like seemingly every other topic, eventually leads to a discussion of Polish politics. Anita and Ryszard confirm that the elderly, and all those opposed to Wałęsa, voted for the neo-Communists, but add that there was another segment of Polish society that chose Kwaśniewski: well-educated, ambitious men and women who apparently see the Kwaśniewskis as the embodiment of their own aspirations.

"Our own Bill and Hillary Clinton," says Anita. Many Poles, she tells me, are relieved that at last they needn't be ashamed when their president goes abroad. In contrast with the gauche, ill-educated Wałęsa, Kwaśniewski and his wife are articulate, presentable, worldly. They reassure ambitious Poles that they too can some day attain such sophistication.

When I muse out loud on the irony of a neo-Communist serving as a role model for Polish yuppies, Ryszard makes a dismissive sound. "Kwaśniewski is no Communist, not even neo. He's just a very shrewd politician who understands the Poles—a true opportunist, that's all."

Having themselves voted for Kwaśniewski, Anita and Ryszard feel that the president's biggest problem lies in his wish to be all things to all Poles. Determined to please everyone, he does no harm but not much good either. They, like most Poles, continue to hope for a truly great leader. Indeed, if opinion polls are to be believed, this is Poles' single most common preoccupation. Asked in December 1995 to make a new year's wish list for their country, the majority of respondents wished above all to see Poland ruled by wise politicians. Three times as many people wished for this as for an end to unemployment.

We are still chuckling over this when a farmer stops to talk to us outside his barn. He was born and raised in the region, and so were his parents and grandparents, but these days, he says, most young Kashubes end up working in the city. Four of his own children went to Gdańsk, though one of them has recently come back, unhappy with urban pressures.

This reminds me of Mariola's father, who gave up electronics for apiculture, and we talk about him and his wife as we head back through a dense, cool, intoxicatingly musty forest. Mariola's parents were opposed to her marrying Borek and, until Tomek's birth, kept a determined distance. They are still unhappy about the excommunication but have learned to live with it.

"There's a spoonful of birch tar in every barrel of honey." Anita offers this old Polish proverb to support her view that despite everything, Borek and Mariola's marriage is remarkably successful. Borek's first wife was a perfectly nice woman, but they were temperamentally incompatible, and once their children were grown, decided to separate. In Poland, divorce is still associated with grievous fault. When Ryszard tried to explain Borek's decision to his own parents, he told them that neither their son nor his wife was guilty of any major transgression; he emphasized this, pointing out the couple's basic differences. His parents heard him out, wagging their heads sadly. "Now tell us what really happened," they said when he was done.

Borek's parents live in Suwałki, but Mariola's have a house nearby and spend much of their time helping their daughter and her husband. The new house, a rustic one with high, beamed ceilings and a stone fireplace, is still without a bathroom. It was supposed to be finished by now, but the workers abandoned it to take up a more lucrative contract in Gdynia.

The Górniaks' outhouse, however, is a clean, solid one on the edge of the forest, and the path to it is lined with translucent red-currant bushes and sunflowers the size of dinner plates. There is also a flourishing vegetable garden and, at the entrance, bushes of blood-red rambler roses. Coming out of the forest, we see a stork sitting on the Górniaks' chimney, as if to underscore the family's rising fortunes. Anita tells me that storks return to the same nest every year, which is why Poles are so fond of them.

"They are very domestic creatures, just like us," she says, smiling. As for the myth of the baby-bearing stork, it may well have its origin in Polish folklore, according to which a stork's return inevitably signals imminent birth.

"I thought it's supposed to signal good luck," I say.

"Children *are* good luck," says Anita.

I concur with the sentiment and also, as we enter the house, with Mariola's decision to summon the doctor after all. We may have little in common, but it takes a worrywart to understand one, and I remember all too well my own anxiety whenever my daughter came down with a high fever. As for Tomek, he seemed much better this morning, says Mariola, but his fever started to rise rapidly in the afternoon, and with Borek away at the office, she decided to send her mother for the doctor.

He turns out to be an elderly rural GP carrying a battered black doctor's bag and a larger one containing an old-fashioned cupping set. But this I gather only a few minutes later, when Mariola returns to the kitchen in search of matches.

"He says it's only an ordinary grippe," she says, looking visibly relieved.

Tomek can be heard crying from the adjacent room, and I don't blame him. I know that, despite Western physicians' disdain, doctors in many parts of the world routinely use cupping to relieve minor chest ailments. I also know, having been subjected to the treatment in my own childhood, that to a four-year-old the procedure taking place next door must seem as terrifying as black magic.

It involves the use of perhaps two dozen tiny transparent cups, which are warmed before application. In my childhood, this was done with a bit of cotton moistened with rubbing alcohol, wound around an instrument, and set aflame. To this day, I remember the hot, airless cups traveling toward my afflicted chest; the pale, helpless flesh sucked into them like rising dough. Soon, my entire chest was covered, resembling the body of some rare marine creature. It was not a painful procedure, but it gave me the obscure feeling of being robbed of something for which I had no name, something vital to my existence. It was a feeling I would remember as an adult, learning about primitive Africans' fear of losing their souls to the camera. Eventually, I would read that cupping originated in the Middle Ages, a practice widely sought for sucking evil spirits out of a bewitched body. It is perhaps this old belief that has led Western physicians to dismiss cupping out of hand. And yet, it seems to me a perfectly apt metaphor for the body's submission to noxious powers beyond its control, which germs certainly are.

Indeed, I have come to feel that all superstition is ultimately an expression of human vulnerability—the awareness that our destiny is at the mercy of unknown, manifestly capricious forces. This may not be within the average peasant's ability to articulate, but he has always known that all he can hope to do is alleviate the intolerable sense of his own impotence. And so he prays, and makes offerings to the powers that be, and hangs amulets on his home, livestock, children. A Polish farmer having his field blessed by a priest, a Greek wearing a blue-bead eye, an ancient Aztec making religious sacrifice—all these seem to me infinitely poignant gestures whose main aim is to convince us that whatever happens, we have at least done our best to keep at bay the chaotic forces ruling our universe.

CHAPTER 12

I T IS IN Gdańsk that I am finally persuaded to extend my Polish stay. This has a good deal to do with Gdańsk itself, but also with the growing awareness that a rest is called for. I have been moving at an increasingly frenzied pace, talking almost incessantly, taking in as much as time has permitted by day, and staying up most nights with my recorder and my journal. I have been at it for five weeks and have five to go, but it's doubtful I'd be able to keep up this hot-footed pace much longer. And so, encouraged by Anita's warm hospitality, I decide to extend my stay by two weeks, with five days for Gdańsk and the seaside. Though Gdańsk's own waters are still polluted, two and a half hours away by boat are the clean, often deserted beaches of the beautiful Hel Peninsula and, west of Gdańsk, those of Wolin Island. The island is barely known to foreigners, despite its dramatic coastline and remarkably varied landscape. There are sand dunes here, and lakes, forests, meadows, moors, and famous thermal springs. The sea at Wolin is reportedly the warmest in Poland and also, it is said, the cleanest.

And then, there is the famous Sopot, where Anita and Ryszard live. It too has fine white-sand beaches but less reliable water. In recent years, dramatic measures have been taken to deal with industrial pollution, and since 1995, the Sopot beaches have been certified safe for swimming. But the water continues to be tested daily for toxic levels, and now and then the beaches are temporarily sealed off. All the same, thousands of people visit Sopot every year and have been doing so for decades. It was one of Napoleon's physicians who, in 1823, established Sopot as a seaside resort, with spas, hotels, and luxury villas sprouting throughout the nineteenth century. In the interwar years, Sopot had a dazzling international clientele, and a nightlife reportedly worthy of Monte Carlo.

Sopot remains immensely popular (above all with Swedes and Germans) and retains much of its prewar charm. It has upscale restaurants and shops, bars, cafés, discos and, once again, a flourishing casino. Also, the longest pier in the Baltic, jutting 1,680 feet into the blue sea. Ryszard and Anita live in upper Sopot, in a quietly affluent part of town. Like me, they love to be near the sea and share a luxurious, two-family villa with their son and new daughter-in-law. Sopot is less than seven miles away from Gdańsk and, along with nearby Gdynia, belongs to a jointly administered urban complex known as the Tri-City.

Originally a small Kashubian village, Gdynia belonged to Cistercian monks for several centuries. It was still a village in the 1920s when the Polish government undertook aggressive measures to transform it into an international port. Within ten years, Gdynia had the most modern port in the Baltic, with cargo vessels, fishing ships, passenger liners, and naval craft setting sail daily.

Today, Gdynia has an increasing number of wealthy Poles' yachts but remains a bustling commercial harbor. Of the three Tri-City towns, it is the least visited by tourists, but prompted by personal curiosity, I visit it on my second day in the area and, standing beside a monument to Joseph Conrad, take mental sail back to September 1950 when my family and I left on an ocean liner heading for Israel.

I have only the vaguest recollection of Gdynia, but a fairly vivid one of several events connected with our departure. The state of Israel having recently been proclaimed, thousands of Jews emigrated from Poland in those first years of Israeli independence. There were no impediments to their departure, except for a strict quota on all valuables taken out of the country. Arriving in Gdynia, we were all ruthlessly searched by grim port officials. My father was led away by a male inspector, while my mother, brother, and I were ushered into a small cubicle and ordered to undress. There was no heat and the woman's hands were cold, searching our bodies. Even my three-year-old brother was not spared her intrusive scrutiny, though he was the only one who felt free to wail in outrage. Done with us, the official opened our luggage, promptly confiscating our flatware. My mother protested weakly. She pointed out that it fell into the permissible category of household items. The official, heedless, went on rummaging through the suitcases, but it was only when she confiscated a large container of powdered milk that my mother looked on the verge of tears. She had the idea that we might find ourselves living in tents in Israel, with inadequate nutrition. And so she resumed her protests, demanding to see the woman's superior. But this request only made the corners of the official's mouth turn up slightly.

"You can go look for him," she said and gave a shrug. "But you'll see this milk the way I see my own ears."

These words, this Gdynia cubicle, have for decades been the last memory I had of Poland.

Ask North Americans what Gdańsk conjures up for them, and most are likely to say shipyards. They imagine, as I once did, a gray, gritty port town populated by plucky but graceless dock workers. They hear Gdańsk and they think Solidarity. And of course Gdańsk *is* where Solidarity was born and the city has not only shipyards, but several other successful industries. All of which explains the astonishment experienced by many first-time visitors: Gdańsk is an urban beauty; a coastal town traversed by two tributaries of the Vistula, with picturesque ports, canals, bridges, Gothic churches, and narrow medieval streets. Gdańsk remains an important industrial center, but also a scientific and cultural one, with five institutions of higher learning and a wealth of historic and architectural treasures. Capital of the Pomeranian region, Gdańsk is one of Poland's great visual treats—a thousand-year-old town, but one strongly reminiscent of sixteenth-century Flanders.

One of the fascinating things about Polish cities is the diversity of their architectural offerings. The southeastern town of Zamość, for example, was built by one of Poland's wealthiest magnates but, having been designed by a Padua architect, bears a striking resemblance to an Italian Renaissance town. Old Warsaw and Kraków are reminiscent of medieval German towns, Gdańsk of Amsterdam. Known for much of its history as Danzig, Gdańsk was largely designed by celebrated Flemish and Dutch architects after the coastal city joined the Hanseatic League.

The League, a trade merchants' alliance, originated in medieval Germany, its main aim being the protection of its members' commercial interests. By the middle of the fourteenth century, having grown quickly and immensely wealthy, it boasted one hundred coastal and inland towns, from Holland to Poland. In time, Gdańsk became one of the League's four chief towns, its prominence largely due to its strategic position at the Vistula-Baltic estuary. Both Napoleon and Frederick the Great understood Gdańsk's strategic importance, the latter saying that whoever controlled Gdańsk "might be considered more master of Poland than the king ruling there."

Naturally, there have been many interested parties. At different times, Gdańsk was held by Pomerania, Prussia, Poland, Brandenburg, and Denmark, with the Teutonic Knights in ruthless control for some 150 years. The key players have been the Prussians and the Poles, with the Swedes, the French, and the Russians contributing their bit to what is, even by Polish standards, an exceptionally tumultuous history. Adding to the complexity have been commercial invasions by Dutch, Scottish, Italian, and Scandinavian traders, eager to join the increasingly successful Polish-German population. By the sixteenth century, Gdańsk was the richest city in Poland and one of the richest in Europe. Its economy was based on trade in amber, wood, and above all grain. It had three hundred granaries and by the fourteenth-century the biggest mill in Europe. The Great Mill—now an upscale shopping center—was to grind wheat for six hundred years, contributing to the wealth of Gdańsk merchants, regardless of their origins. Indeed, it was the tradition of religious tolerance as much as trade prospects that encouraged the sizable Protestant settlement in the area. The town flourished under Polish hegemony but, besieged and fought over, went into decline in the seventeenth century. The Gdańsk Town Hall bears a gilded statue of the last Jagiellonian king, Zygmunt August. Its Latin inscription says, "Oh that our golden Polish times might return!"

Eventually, the town would revert to Poland, but in 1919, after years of war and ruthless partitions, the Treaty of Versailles declared Gdańsk —for the third time in its history—the Free City of Danzig, more or less autonomous but now under the protection of the League of

Nations. Poland having regained its independence, the Treaty gave it a strip of land stretching from Toruń to the Baltic. Known as the Polish Corridor, this strip was provided to give Poland access to the sea. Since it excluded Gdańsk, however, Poles urgently needed a port and it was then that they set about building up Gdynia.

But the Versailles Treaty seemed a blueprint for ongoing conflict. For one thing, though Poland had lost Gdańsk, it was left in charge of the Free City's railroad system, customs, and, most important, its foreign policy. Moreover, the Polish Corridor cut through an area heavily populated in the nineteenth century by Germans, providing Hitler with one of his early propaganda tools. In 1939, he demanded that the Corridor, including Danzig, be reincorporated into the Reich and, meeting with categorical refusal, promptly launched the battle that soon grew into World War II. It was in the Danzig area that the first shots were heard, the Hel Peninsula being the last place in Poland to surrender to the Nazis, and the last to be liberated. Soon, Danzig was annexed by the Germans and remained in the Reich until 1945, when the Allies returned it to Poland, renaming it Gdańsk.

Tragically, there was little to be returned. Flying over Pomerania, Soviet planes had distributed fliers warning the Nazis of the inevitable destruction should they fail to surrender. But the Nazi authorities under Gauleiter Albert Forster refused to submit. Later, it would be learned that while the city with its treasures and thousands of German citizens was in imminent danger, Forster himself was busy transporting his private furniture and valuables west to safety.

When it was all over, 90 percent of Danzig had been reduced to rubble. The German population—384,000 before the war—had either perished or fled west, leaving behind on the town's crumbling walls black inscriptions saying, in German, "REVENGE!" The panic-stricken transports heading west soon gave way to others from the east, bringing in repatriated Poles from areas lost to the Soviet Union. Like the Varsovians, they promptly set about rebuilding the magnificent city, undeterred by the anonymous letters arriving from across the border. "Don't think you own it—we'll be back someday!"

It is the knowledge of all this lamentable history that makes a visit to Gdańsk, as to Warsaw, such a moving experience. In Gdańsk, the tall, narrow row houses line graceful, cobblestone streets, many of them along the canals or river, their terraces and lofts and richly ornamental gables reflected in the water. When I think of Gdańsk, its predominant colors are peachy and brown, with red-tiled roofs and lofty church spires. In the Main Town, some of the newly refurbished houses have been taken over by elegant boutiques displaying jewelry, art, antiques. People who lived here only thirty years ago are barely able to recognize this stylish, bustling town, with its statues and fountains and outdoor cafés, and meticulously restored monuments.

One of the city's predominant landmarks is the medieval Gdańsk Crane. A massive, dark timber edifice, it looms over the Motława River, on a busy promenade where, in the fifteenth century, hundreds of ships loaded and unloaded their cargo, storing it in the nearby granaries. Capable of hoisting loads of forty-five hundred pounds, the Crane was the biggest in medieval Europe and is the only such structure to be seen anywhere in the world today.

A medieval edifice of a different sort is the House of Torture, which is closed the week I visit because, a workman informs me, of an upcoming theatrical production. What are they putting on? He doesn't remember the name—something by Shakespeare, though; he's sure of that. The House of Torture stands next to the Prison Tower, near a square where public executions occasionally took place. The square was reserved for noncitizens; local offenders were usually hanged at the more public Long Market. For those whose taste runs to such things, Poland offers many reminders of the more gruesome aspects of the Middle Ages. In the southeastern town of Biecz, for example, there used to be a famous school for public executioners. A school? I asked, wondering how much instruction pulling the noose required. I was told that medieval executioners were also called on to serve in the torture chambers, and this apparently required training as well as aptitude.

And then there is Gdańsk's celebrated St. Mary's, reputedly the biggest brick church in the world. Begun in 1343 and built over a period of 150 years, St. Mary's became a Protestant church during the Reformation. After World War II, it reverted to the Catholic Church and, under the 1981 martial law, reportedly accommodated crowds exceeding twenty thousand. Today, St. Mary's cavernous interior holds many treasures spirited away during the war, including the famous astronomical clock constructed in 1460 by Hans Düringer. Forty-six feet high, the clock was at the time the largest in the world, showing not only the hour, day, month, and year, but also the phases of the moon. There was also a calendar of saints' days, with saints and apostles making regular appearances, and Adam and Eve chiming an hourly bell. So prized was this magnificent clock that its builder, like the one hired by Ivan the Terrible for St. Basil's Cathedral, was blinded to prevent possible duplication. I go around the church; then, glancing at my watch, see it is almost one o'clock. I have been given the phone number of a well-known Polish feminist, a local university professor with an interest in the role of women in public life. Having been told to call between twelve and three, I decide against climbing the 405 steps to St. Mary's lookout and, stepping out into the sunny street, hurry toward the Main Town's thousand-foot Long Street.

It is in Gdańsk that my relationship with Polish phones reaches the breaking point; this despite the city's glossy exterior and a chance encounter on a Warsaw train with a Dutchman working for AT&T, in Poland to improve the communications system. The Dutchman assured me things are quickly improving, as have my Polish hosts. They still remember the days when making a phone connection seemed at times like a small miracle; one that often took hours to perform. This no doubt explains Poles' remarkable patience in the face of what seem to me obstacles of farcical proportions. I know by now that my best chance of finding a public phone is at the post office and, fortunately, there is one within easy walking distance. Being very central, it is also exceptionally busy, and in all fairness, it must be stated that the following experience takes place at the height of the tourist season. There are long lineups for cards and tokens, and equally long ones for the telephones. It is at such times, waiting my turn, that I have occasionally wondered how I would have possibly survived the Communist era.

Eventually, thirty-five minutes later, I find myself dialing the scribbled number, only to get a busy signal. I try three times, then give up and gloomily step aside. I am not sure what the rules of public phone etiquette are here but suspect it would not do to keep dialing indefinitely with a long line of perspiring Poles and flushed tourists breathing down my neck.

And so I go out and have a quick lunch and return half an hour later to find the telephone line still busy. Experience tells me that busy can also mean the number has been changed, or the phone is out of order, or the circuits are temporarily jumbled.

I decide to call Information, and, miracle of miracles, I manage to get a line. It is not busy; I can hear it ring. And ring and ring and ring. Finally—no doubt through AT&T's intervention—I get a recording. I am placed on hold but wait patiently until, at long last, an operator says, "I'm listening." Breathing a sigh of relief, I blurt out my question and am about to obtain an answer when my token expires and I find myself abruptly cut off.

I use another token. I try the original number, which is still busy, and then Information for the second time. Eventually, I get an answer. Eventually, I am told the number has indeed been changed. I am given a new number, which I try to call, experiencing an altogether new problem: I have been sold an outdated token! I rummage for another and insert it successfully, only to get a wrong connection. I know from past experience that I am likely to get the same connection for the next few hours, at least from this particular phone.

And so I line up before another phone and wait for another fifteen minutes, thinking, When I tell people back home about this, they will suspect me of exaggerating. I congratulate myself on having learned to obtain tokens as well as a calling card. But I know that on a day like this, one of several things is likely to happen: I may get a wrong connection again, or a busy circuit, or have the call box reject my card, or worse still, gobble it up! All of these things have happened to me at one time or another, usually in a lightless telephone booth where just reading the number and dialing it correctly is something of a challenge. But the Gdańsk post office is clean and spacious and brightly lit and none of the feared possibilities materialize. I do get a line, the right line, and hear a pleasant female voice answer when, just outside the large windows overlooking the busy mall, an accordionist begins to play. The music is loud and exuberant, but plugging my left ear, I do manage to make out the answer to my question:

"Sorry, madam, she has just left for Toruń."

This is how a grown woman—a decorous foreign *pani*—comes as close as she ever has to having a public tantrum.

The next day, however, it occurs to me that had I in fact been forced to live under the Communists, I might have eventually come to possess a healthier sense of perspective. It would have been ludicrous, not to say futile, to lose one's equanimity over something like telephones at a time when arrests, imprisonment, and death were commonplace; when survival itself was for years a challenge. All this comes to me as I stand outside the Gdańsk shipyard gates, gazing up at a steel memorial to local shipyard workers: three 140-foot crosses, each supporting a huge black anchor, a symbol not only of the sea but, for Poles, of struggle and redemption.

The shipyard memorial was put up in Gdańsk in honor of workers killed in a 1970 protest against government price hikes. Thousands of shipyard workers took part in what was soon a riot; one ending in violence when fire was set to Communist Party headquarters. When it was over, forty-four striking workers lay dead, but the Lenin Shipyards, like the Nowa Huta steelworks, remained a center of trade labor agitation. Eventually, it led to the formation of Solidarity, the first industrial trade union in the Soviet bloc. Now that Poland is a democracy and Wałęsa has in the eyes of many discredited himself as national leader, it is easy to forget the headline-making days when workers led by a forklift electrician took on the Communist Goliath and, undeterred by the tragic precedents in Prague and Budapest, won the battle. They had, at the start, hoped for no more than better working conditions, but were soon demanding basic human rights, the release of political prisoners, freedom of the press, and so on. What made Solidarity so seemingly indomitable was the righteous, united facade it presented to the watchful world. By 1980, its membership numbered ten million Poles, including workers, intellectuals, prominent members of the Church, and assorted political activists. What had begun as a trade union was by then a powerful social movement, and though its members were hounded, imprisoned, tortured, and sometimes killed, and despite the 1981 martial law aimed at suppressing it, Solidarity continued to agitate for change, in time bringing about the first democratic elections in over fifty years.

And now the shipyards are bankrupt, a fact as lamentable as the eventual disintegration of that celebrated worker-intellectual alliance. There are Poles today who are reportedly nostalgic for the purposeful, idealistic era that has given way to one of rapid, heedless consumerism. As for the unemployed shipyard workers, they remain uncertain about the future, hoping for Polish or foreign investors to make the yards viable again. It is said here that the shipyards got caught between "rotting Communism and raw capitalism." Like much of Polish industry, they were run down and poorly managed and, once Russian subsidies had stopped, found themselves ill-equipped to match world production standards. In the past three years, the shipyards had suffered losses of some U.S. $13.5 million and the Polish banks, which hold the majority of shares, saw no choice but to close them down.

Despite the shipyards' demise, Gdańsk appears to be flourishing, its merchants doing brisk business, its Main Town teeming with shoppers, tourists, performers. There is a costumed Kashubian group singing beside Neptune's fountain and, a little farther on, a Gypsy tenor bellowing "Celeste Äida." Gdańsk has an annual August fair named after the Dominicans and, for better or for worse, it coincides with my visit. All along the broad promenade overlooking the river, hundreds of vendors and craftsmen have set up their makeshift stalls, selling everything from jewelry to antique chamber pots. Most of all, they sell Baltic amber. Amber is everywhere in Gdańsk: at the glittering jewelry shops where the salesclerks speak two or three languages, as well as on creaking wagons pushed through the cobblestone streets by wizened old men. I had no idea amber could come in so many shades, from bone white to dark brown, and in so many grades. There are necklaces and brooches and earrings and cufflinks; such dazzling quantities of them that, after a while, having bought several pieces, I can't bear to look at any more amber.

But the fair is as much carnival as bazaar, with knights' tournaments and street theater, and traditional dance troupes performing for two solid weeks. There is also a small flea market, and hesitating over an antique Tatar bracelet, I see that the adjacent stall is selling Nazi medals and photographs of the German Occupation. I watch a young German couple buy one such medal, laughing in the sun, then running to catch a river cruise boat. There are several such boats at the quay, white and festive, moored beside small private yachts. The tourists line up for the cruises, eating hot dogs and ice cream and pink cotton candy. It is by now almost two-thirty and I too decide to stop for something to eat. There are, among the leather and amber and souvenir stalls, fast-food concessions selling charcoal-grilled shish kebab, sizzling Polish sausage, and deep-fried fish and chips. I know the sausage is laced with fat and the shish kebab likely to be tough, but where does the fish come from?

From the North Sea, I am told by the vendor. But I have my doubts and decide to play it safe by walking a little farther until I come to a pizza stall. It is the most prosaic of decisions but, as it turns out, an extraordinarily lucky one.

This perhaps is the time to confess: like most writers engaged in an absorbing project, I have had moments of doubt about this book—its merit, its marketability. Traveling around the country, however, I have had several fortuitous encounters whose very improbability has helped convince me that this is a book I am apparently meant to write. Stopping for a slice of pizza at the Dominican Fair turns out to be one such affirmative occasion.

There are a few picnic tables in front of the food outlets but not many, and so perfect strangers end up sharing a table for the duration of a snack or meal. This is how I find myself sitting with two middle-aged men and a woman, eating pizza with plastic cutlery and watching the passing cruise boats, the flow of pedestrian traffic. Eventually, the woman notices my English guidebook and engages me in conversation. We talk about this and that—the origins of the fair (celebrated by the Dominicans as far back as 1260), the recent Quebec referendum. The three seem surprisingly well informed, as well as curious. They wonder where I have been in Poland, what I have seen in Gdańsk. I tell them about my visit to the shipyards and, a little earlier, the famous St. Bridget's, Lech Wałęsa's church. Having been destroyed in the war and rebuilt, the Gothic church contains many reminders of its long-standing association with Solidarity: a collection of crosses from past protests, a painting of the Black Madonna wearing a Solidarity T-shirt, a tomb-stone for Jerzy Popiełuszko.

We talk about the still-mourned assassinated Polish martyr—a charismatic and influential priest who became a dedicated Solidarity activist, so outspoken and fearless in his activities that, in 1984, he was finally murdered by the security police. The uproar that followed was such that the authorities thought it prudent to jail the perpetrators. But Popiełuszko's death only contributed to Solidarity's momentum. His funeral was attended by nearly half a million Poles; his Warsaw church has become a shrine.

Equally outspoken but far more controversial is St. Bridget's Father Henryk Jankowski, the priest whom the drunken Ignacy Kielak quoted back in Augustów. The priest's latest headline-making sermon expressed the view that the Polish prime minister's apology to Jews for the Kielce pogrom was "an insult to the Polish nation." It also accused Jews of having murdered Poles between 1944 and 1956, after the Soviet takeover. I have read that Jankowski's sermons have caused Church authorities profound embarrassment—there have been threats from the local bishop to defrock Jankowski—but also that they have done nothing to diminish his local popularity.* Eating my Polish pizza, I wonder what three seemingly intelligent, well-informed Poles might think of Father Jankowski, but my question meets with abrupt silence. I see the woman's odd little smile, see her exchange looks with one of the men, and think to myself, You're in for it now.

"You happen to be speaking to a priest," the woman says at length. A *priest*! I have been hoping to speak to one but have not gotten around to arranging it. And here, without any effort on my part, is a rather genial one in street clothes and, it would seem, with time on his hands. He turns out to be an out-of-town priest visiting his married sister. He works with orphans, I eventually find out, though I never learn his name or that of his town. Indeed, for a moment or two, I think I will learn nothing at all, for just then, the priest's brother-in-law looks at his watch and says they'd better go: he has to call Warsaw. Would I like to have coffee with them while they wait, the priest's sister asks.

And so we make our way through the crowded streets to an outdoor café, and just as I find myself thinking they have managed to deflect my question, the priest, whom I will call Father X, looks at me earnestly through his spectacles.

"To get back to Jankowski," he says, with a smile suggesting he has read my mind. He will try to explain to me the priest's phenomenal

---

*Since this was written, Jankowski has been charged with propagating racial hatred. If convicted, he faces up to three years in jail. "In my own country, I feel persecuted by the Jewish minority" was Jankowski's response.

popularity. "What you have to understand," he says, "is that many people disagree with Jankowski's views—I would say most of them do—but they stand by him because he stood up for them, fighting all those long years for a free Poland."

Under the Soviets, the Church was not only the voice of public opinion, but it also helped Poles preserve a sense of their own identity. Above all, it was the staunchest defender of human rights in Poland, providing a sanctuary for political opponents of many stripes. In those days, even an avowed atheist could count on the Church for shelter.

"And Jankowski, you know, was one of the most active among us. He risked imprisonment and even death, supporting the shipyard workers. His supporters cannot forget that, you see."

It occurs to me that Father Jankowski too has lost the enemy that gave his life much of its former meaning, and is now trying to fill the resulting vacuum with an imaginary one: the Jews. The fact remains that Jankowski's sermons attract thousands of worshipers and that, if the Polish press is to be believed, interviewed parishioners have echoed Jankowski's drivel.

"That's what's so puzzling to an outsider," I tell Father X. "There are after all hardly any Jews in Poland. How can Poles possibly be ruled by them, as Jankowski claims?"

"You're asking me to be the devil's advocate," Father X says, smiling. "I can't do that. I can only say that the Jews seem to have become a kind of metaphor in Poland. Jankowski's parishioners don't think of actual people; they think of what, in their minds, a Jew happens to stand for."

This is another part of the puzzle I have been trying to work out ever since I arrived in Poland. Knowing of the poverty of my father's family, and of the vast majority of Polish Jews, how to explain the tenacious stereotype of the wealthy, exploitative Jew? I am not sure Father X is likely to illuminate the issue, so I point instead to the irony of a man like Jankowski, with his Mercedes and his lavish ways, his treasure-filled rectory, representing the struggle of Gdańsk's downtrodden workers.

At this, Father X smiles. "People expect priests to be not only poor but saintly," he says. "But a priest is not a saint; he's as flawed, as contradictory, as the rest of humanity."

The statement—and perhaps Father X's work with Polish orphans—reminds me of the recent Canadian scandals involving sexual abuse of boys at priest-run orphanages. Also, of Mariola Górniak's recent statement that the Church is there to serve as Catholics' moral guide. I ask Father X what he thinks of the Western influences taking hold in Poland.

The question elicits a tightening of the lips, a deep sigh. He is having trouble, the priest admits, witnessing some of the recent changes in Polish society. They all struggled, hoped, for democracy and freedom. "And, well, you know the old saying: Be careful of what you wish for; you may end up getting it."

Is he wishing for the return of Communism, I wonder. No, not that, but some measure of restraint, yes. Democracy has come too abruptly to Poland; it has caught people ill prepared to deal with its complexities.

"It's like suddenly giving a small child unrestricted freedom," his sister interjects. "How can you expect an inexperienced child to handle such freedom wisely? He's bound to get lost, don't you think? Well, that's what we're up against in Poland today. That's why the Church tries so hard to curb what is happening."

We talk for a while then about the current campaign to prevent the liberalization of abortion laws, and I am reminded of an article I have read in which a priest, listening to arguments in favor of abortion, suggested that the proponents of such views should consider legislation permitting children to have their parents killed off once they are infirm and unproductive. "Parents are killing their unborn children for material reasons; children should have the right to do the same," he argued to a Polish journalist.

This eventually leads to a discussion of Polish "orphans," most of whom are given up by their parents for economic reasons; some are taken over by the state on grounds of physical or sexual abuse. What has inflated the Polish clergy's workload is the increasing abandonment of foreign children: Romanian, Belarussian, Ukrainian. "Only 0.2 percent are natural orphans these days," says Father X.

Knowing how long childless couples often wait for an adoptable child in the West, I ask whether any efforts are being made to place unwanted children outside Poland. Father X tells me that out of some twenty-five hundred adoptions in 1995, fewer than 10 percent went to couples abroad, and even then only to families with at least one of the partners having Polish roots. The real problem is finding homes for handicapped children. They are not wanted by Polish families and seldom by foreign ones. In rural Poland especially, an irrational sense of shame accompanies the birth of a handicapped baby. There is a new program, however, to educate Polish families and help them cope with a child who would otherwise end up in an orphanage; also, a highly successful practice of letting friendly families "adopt" an orphan for weekends or holidays.

When he speaks of his charges, Father X's tone is notably different from that used in our earlier discussion. He sounded a little weary before, perhaps even wary, but his face has visibly relaxed in the past few minutes, and after we say goodbye, I reflect that his wistful, indulgent look was that of a parent temporarily separated from his own children. This is when I remember another, more famous, man devoted to orphanage work: Janusz Korczak, the eponymous hero of Andrzej Wajda's documentary film. An assimilated Jew, Korczak claimed never to have thought about his religious identity until the Nazis forced him to do so. A trained physician, he was famous for writing popular children's books, an occupation abandoned in wartime so he could care for Warsaw's Jewish orphans. He went on caring for them in the ghetto and, despite repeated offers to save his life, chose to accompany his charges to Treblinka. In Warsaw, Korczak's orphanage was one of the few buildings to survive the war. It still stands today, fronted by Korczak's statue, a few minutes away from the Jewish cemetery. It is still sheltering orphans.

Gdańsk too has had several celebrated sons, among them Gabriel Daniel Fahrenheit, inventor of the mercury thermometer, and the philosopher Artur Schopenhauer, who throughout his life insisted he was not German but rather a citizen of the Free City of Danzig. There was also Jan Heweliusz (Johannes Hevelius), the first astronomer to chart detailed maps of the moon surface, an occupation that did not prevent him from enjoying the more prosaic pleasures of owning a private brewery, whose beer to this day bears his name. And then there is

Günter Grass, who was born here in 1927 and spent World War II in what is now the Wrzeszcz district. It was Günter Grass who, two decades before Solidarity, brought his Baltic hometown's vicissitudes to the world's attention. As it happens, one of the landmarks he immortalized in *The Tin Drum* is of some personal interest to me. It is the Old Polish Post Office, a prewar institution existing improbably within the Free City of Danzig. Maintaining their own local post office was one of the concessions made by the Versailles Treaty in favor of the Poles, and its employees' heroic resistance against the Nazi onslaught has acquired mythic proportions in the Polish imagination.

The attack took place on September 1, 1939—the first day of World War II—simultaneously with one on the Polish Army Depot at nearby Westerplatte. The Westerplatte garrison consisted of poorly armed men—fewer than two hundred of them—attacked by the Germans from land, air, and sea. The Nazi troops numbered some three thousand soldiers, against whom the small Polish contingent battled for a week before capitulating. By then, enemy tanks were rolling toward Warsaw, and the Polish Post Office had been burnt down. Indeed, it was only after the Nazis had torched the building that the postal employees surrendered, most of them to be summarily executed.

The restored Old Post Office still offers postal services, but one of its wings is devoted to a display of wartime documents, and black-and-white photographs of the famous battle. If I study the photographs more closely than the average tourist, it is because, over a quarter of a century ago, I had the misfortune of falling in love with a young German Canadian; a fair-haired, gray-eyed architect whose father had been wounded in the Post Office attack, when Werner was a newborn infant living in Hamburg. I never learned more than that; did not *want* to know anything about his family for fear of what I might learn. Werner was the first man I had truly loved and quite possibly the man I should have married. But I couldn't find a satisfactory way of solving the diabolical dilemma fate had inflicted on me; could not bring myself to tell my father, who had lost his entire family in the war, that I wanted to marry a German officer's son. Several times I came close to doing so, only to hesitate before the imagined, inevitable, response. "Is there a shortage of eligible men in Canada that you had to pick yourself a Nazi?"

Werner was no Nazi, but could I expect my haunted father to be rational about it; to suspend his lingering horror for the sake of what was bound to seem like a spiteful passion? I considered trying to pass Werner off as a Swiss but knew he was a poor dissembler and that one way or another my inquisitive father would arrive at the truth.

But so what, another part of me argued. Could I reasonably be expected to give up a man I loved to spare my father's feelings? Above all, I asked myself over and over, was it fair to turn my back on a blameless man for the imagined sins of his father?

Many years have gone by since I asked those questions, but studying the black-and-white photographs on the Post Office walls, I ask them all over again.

"The answer to all three is obviously no," says Anita on hearing about Werner. She looks at me in the moonlight, shaking her head sadly. How did I resolve this impossible dilemma? she wants to know.

I didn't—at least not consciously. Unable to find my way out of the conundrum, I ended up slowly but surely destroying the relationship. It took a long time to die but die it did, victim to my own exaggerated filial sympathy—or was it cowardice?

"You should have listened to your heart," Anita says after a thoughtful silence. God knows it isn't easy to find anything approximating true affinity. Her sister is middle-aged and is still looking for it. "What do you think you'd do now, given a chance to relive your life?" she asks.

"I think I'd go for it," I say finally. "I think my father would have come around to accepting it, just like Mariola's parents."

We talk about our respective parents—their troubled marriages and whether our fathers would have made better spouses married to Jewish women. Anita herself was raised as a Pole but was old enough when they all left Paris to maintain a lifelong interest in her Jewish background. Not that she and Roma were ever encouraged in that direction. In fact, though Anita cannot remember how it came about, they were somehow made to understand it was prudent to keep certain things to themselves.

"My mother—and my stepfather, for that matter—did not have an antisemitic bone in their bodies. All they wanted was to shelter us," says Anita.

This reminds me of Hania Gwiazda, the special education teacher in

Bielsko-Biała, and when I tell Anita about her, she says the decision not to reveal their identity was common among Polish Jews. Also, that though the number of self-declared Jews is small in Poland, there are probably thousands of Poles today with at least some Jewish blood in their veins. If this is true, it may explain the Polish tendency to suspect anyone and everyone of being a closet Jew.* But why should Poles care about it these days? How did a Jew come to take on such a metaphorically hideous shape in Poles' imagination?

I voice these questions to Anita, sharing with her the thoughts raised by my encounter with Father X. Our talk has started with an evening walk on the Sopot beach but goes on in the living room, long after our return. Ryszard having left for Paris this morning, Anita and I are alone in the Scandinavian-style living room, sipping mead made by Polish monks and chatting late into the night.

After Kazimierz the Great passed a fourteenth-century law protecting Jews against persecution, says Anita, Jews began to settle in Poland in great numbers, going into trade and often functioning as the aristocrats' tax collectors. When moneylending was outlawed by the Catholic Church, it was once more the Jews who rushed in to fill the sudden gap, breeding intense resentment among the perpetually strapped populace.

"On the one hand, there was the tax-collecting Jew forever coming to demand money, and on the other hand, a Jew refusing credit, or charging high interest on miserable loans. So you can see, can't you, how it happened; how the Jews gradually came to be seen as bloodsuckers by the oppressed peasants?"

The reference to peasants reminds me of Ignacy Kielak's diatribe in Augustów, and of my lunch the next day with Alicja and Adam Gutowski. When I told the Poznań couple about Kielak's views, they both sighed and said, "That's just the kind of rough individual that gives Poles a bad name abroad."

And, I say to Anita, it is tempting to believe them. After all, there are countless people like Kielak in any society, including Canada. For that matter, I know Jews who express similarly warped sentiments

---

*The current estimate of "Poles of Jewish descent" is forty thousand, but recent polls indicate that the general population overestimates Jewish presence in their midst. One in ten Poles reportedly believes that 10 to 20 percent of the population is Jewish.

about other minorities. All the same, it cannot be said that Polish peasants have been the only ones guilty of antisemitism. The fact is that it was sometimes rampant in highly educated circles. For example, when in the late 1930s Jewish attendance at Polish universities began to exceed 20 percent, there were increasingly vociferous demands for both a quota and segregated seating. I point this out to Anita, conceding at the same time that Montreal's famed McGill University also had quotas on Jewish admission and that at one time, the university even rejected the offer of an endowment from a prominent local Jew.

"Well, there you are," says Anita. She goes on to explain that while the peasants felt oppressed by the Jews, the educated minority felt increasingly threatened by their incursion into the professions.

"The fact is that Jews who got an education became immensely successful. They dominated prestigious professions like medicine and law, as well as Polish industry and commerce." Prewar Jews represented only 10 percent of the population, yet they paid close to 40 percent of Poland's taxes. "It just goes to show you how much of the country's wealth was in Jewish hands," says Anita.

This surprises me. I am still having trouble reconciling it with the historical and literary evidence of widespread Jewish penury. When I voice this to Anita, she says that the majority of Jews may have in fact been extremely poor, at least after the eighteenth-century Partitions, but there were those who became extraordinarily successful and thus highly visible. Certainly, in the prewar years, there was a minority of wealthy, prominent Jews on whom many downtrodden Poles depended for survival. Thousands of them were in Jewish employ, seething with the usual underdog resentments. Jews' disdain for manual labor only served to reinforce Poles' perception of Jews as incapable of anything but exploitative labor. It fed the notion that Jews thought themselves superior to Poles, who usually took on whatever came their way.

I mull this over for a while, thinking of the experience of countless Jews who, visiting Israel in the early years, were astonished to come upon Jewish janitors, garbagemen, sweepers.

"In *Israel*," says Anita, "but certainly not in Poland. Well, try to see it from Poles' point of view. A middle-class Jewish family needs a handyman or a maid. What do they do? They look for impoverished Poles from the countryside and hire them for a pittance. But—" she says and gives a wan smile, "I don't think a Jew, no matter how poor, ever went to work for a Polish household. Does that tell you anything?"

I think about this for a while: the Jewish families we knew in Łódź, all of them with Polish maids; of the cumulative resentment this social divide apparently generated. What I still don't understand, I tell Anita, is how Poles can persist in thinking of Jews as both bloodsucking capitalists and ruthless Communists. I raise the question because, since World War II, much of the hostility toward Jews has been due to their alleged association with the Soviet regime.

"That's quite true," says Anita. What I must bear in mind, she explains, is that Poles have always felt such deep antipathy toward Russia that, after World War II, Stalin had a lot of trouble coming up with trustworthy Polish Communists. Though there were certainly Poles who believed in the Communist cause, most of them saw the Soviets as the old Eastern wolf in a new disguise, trying to bring down the walls of Polish nationhood.

Postwar Jews, on the other hand, had every reason to embrace Communist ideology, promising as it did an international brotherhood impervious to ethnic origins. This was how some of the most important government positions in postwar Poland came to be occupied by Jews who, though they were sometimes used as Communists' scapegoats, once again became identified with a hated oppressor.

I am still thinking about all this when, suddenly, Anita flashes me a grin and, putting on a mock broadcaster's voice, ad-libs, "This has been a symposium on the roots of Polish antisemitism. For solutions to the problem, please tune in again tomorrow."

CHAPTER 13

F POLES SEEM AT TIMES obsessed with real and imaginary oppressors, their history makes such obsession seem if not reasonable then at least comprehensible. What I find myself repeatedly grappling with is the oppressors' prodigious capacity to rationalize their own aggression. Though the phenomenon is hardly unique to Poland, the more I learn about the country, the more often I find myself thinking of Zofia Russak, the Auschwitz schoolteacher whose injunction "Doubt yourself!" underlined the universal capacity for legitimizing terror. One of the places where Russak's words resonate most strongly is the Malbork Castle, the vast, truly extraordinary stronghold of the Teutonic Knights.

There is a central well in the Malbork Castle courtyard, above which stands the bronze sculpture of a pelican; a bird that, faced with shortage of nourishment, will feed its young with its own blood. It is the ancient symbol of the Teutonic Knights, who—with some early justification—clearly saw their mission in the world in self-sacrificial terms.

The Teutonic Order of the Hospital of St. Mary was founded in 1190 in the Holy Land, one of three medieval orders that sprang up from the Crusades. Originally dedicated to caring for the sick and dying, the Teutonic Order was soon aiming to reconcile monastic and military ideals, its followers vowed to chastity, poverty, and obedience, in hopes of redeeming their sins. Committed to a stark military existence in an alien land, these Augustine soldiers kept a monastic silence in camp, read the breviary on the march, and took care of the needy. Eventually, having lost their Palestinian base to Islam, the Teutonic

Knights took up temporary quarters in Venice, and then in Transylvania, before responding to an urgent call from a beleaguered Polish ruler.

A thirteenth-century Mazovian duke, Konrad appealed to the crusading monks to help him subdue his unruly Prussian neighbors.* Since the Prussians were still pagan, and since the Teutons' putative mission was to spread and defend Christianity, they promptly responded to the call, soon solving the Poles' Prussian problem. They did so by wiping out the Prussian population and taking over not only their land but also their name. The original Prussians had been a Baltic people related to the Lithuanians. Ironically, all subsequent generations would associate the name with the Germanic conqueror that had decimated them.

The Teutonic Order continued to evolve. Having begun as a charitable society and grown into a military fraternity, it was soon to become a theocratic state under papal suzerainty. In 1274, having established their capital in Malbork, they began the construction of an impregnable brick edifice they called Marienburg—the fortress of Mary. Not content with the Virgin's patronage, they went on to secure the backing of several German overlords who welcomed what they saw as an unexpected opportunity for eastward German expansion. A no-longer-humble brotherhood, the Teutonic Order was by then restricted to German noblemen, who seemed for a long time superior to their neighbors in military strategy as well as armaments. On the battlefield, they appeared both indomitable and resplendent, wearing silver armor and white capes emblazoned with a large black cross. The cross, and the pelican, apparently helped persuade them of their own high-mindedness, even as they went about pillaging their neighbors. Since much of the region's wealth was generated by Hanseatic trade, the knights quickly and ruthlessly gained control over strategically situated cities, cutting the Poles off from the sea and encouraging German peasants to take over Poland's most fertile land. The Poles thus found themselves battling a relentless enemy whom they themselves had given a foothold in the region. It must have been intolerable to contemplate their own shortsightedness, and galling to be forced to acknowledge the formida-

---

*Mazovia, the region surrounding Warsaw, was an independent dukedom before being permanently incorporated into Poland in 1526.

ble might of the wily aggressor. Nonetheless, the Poles never gave up the battle. The conflict born of the Mazovian duke's invitation would last for two centuries, generating grievances between Poles and Germans that have yet to be laid to rest.

Poland possesses a remarkable number of castles, most of them dating from the thirteenth to sixteenth centuries. But nothing—no guidebook or photographs or other medieval castles—has quite prepared me for the unforgettable experience of visiting the ultimate Teutonic castle: Malbork. Covering an area of fifty-two acres, it is the largest feudal castle in Europe, a truly awesome red-brick fortress looming above the Nogat River as it has for over half a millennium. Though it is often held up as a typical example of classical medieval fortress architecture, Malbork's grandeur is breathtaking. Surveying it from the footbridge over the river, I find it impossible not to think of treachery and carnage, but equally difficult to deny the evident genius of the crusading knights. It is when I come upon a large black swastika spray-painted on one of the defensive walls that I remember Russak, whose words inspire a possibly inevitable mental connection between the two historically formidable black crosses.

Malbork served as the Teutonic capital from the beginning of the fourteenth century to the middle of the fifteenth, and unlike many medieval castles constructed as temporary shelters, it was built with as much regard for aesthetics as for solidity and self-sufficiency. I am far from being a castle enthusiast, but Malbork's Gothic complexity is mind-boggling; it defies description. There are, of course, the typical medieval ramparts, bastions, and towers; the usual drawbridges, moats, and turrets. But what astonishes is the architectural intricacy within the brick vastness; the outer and inner splendor of what seems more like a fortified town than a castle. There are ornamental facades and stained-glass windows, gorgeously sculpted portals, statues, frescoes, friezes, countless bas-reliefs, and some truly magnificent interiors. It is intolerable to think that a later generation of so-called Prussians could bring themselves, after Poland's First Partition, to contemplate demolishing this fortress, damaged in the seventeenth century by invading Swedes. The Prussians planned to use the castle's bricks to build vast store-houses at Malbork. Checked only by the enormous cost of such an undertaking, they satisfied their pragmatic impulse by turning the fortress into military barracks, dismantling in the process much that seemed superfluous to sheer military purpose. It was only toward the end of the nineteenth century, with the growing interest in historic German monuments, that restoration was finally undertaken. But then came World War II and Malbork became a prisoner-of-war camp, its eastern section damaged by Allied bombs. It is remarkable that over 50 percent remained unscathed, and more remarkable still that the Poles elected to restore this grand monument to their archenemy, and have done so with the same dedication and meticulousness brought to the restoration of their own royal castles. Though some of the interiors are still undergoing restoration, today's Malbork Castle looks much as it did in the Middle Ages.

The fortress is divided into three castles—Upper, Middle, and Lower—each representing a different stage of construction and purpose. In the Middle Castle courtyard stand bronze statues of the Teutonic Order's Grand Masters—three draped, strong-featured men whom I find myself trying to imagine inhabiting the chambers I visit. The Grand Masters' residence was the magnificent Malbork Palace; a crenellated, turreted edifice whose spacious interiors display the knights' determination to match the splendor of any European residence. Its Great Refectory, used for special banquets, measures 538 square yards and has a spectacular palm-vaulted ceiling supported on incredibly slender octagonal pillars. The only place in Poland where I have seen a more remarkable ceiling was at Kraków's Wawel Castle, where the Envoys' Hall boasts a coffered timber ceiling, each square containing a splendidly carved human head.

Exploring other parts of Malbork, I come upon churches, cloisters, dormitories, kitchens. Having long since forgotten the vow of poverty, the knights had vast granaries and storehouses for their loot, as well as barns, stables, arsenals—and a small hospital. In fact, the knights continued to maintain several great hospitals along the Baltic. In the Upper Castle, where the toilets are to be found, there is a trap through which unwanted guests found themselves hurtling toward the sewage moat— a fate preferable to the torture chambers which were certainly in existence but are currently closed to the public. For that matter, so are the dungeons, where prisoners reportedly languished until such time as their families managed to come up with adequate ransom. They are sealed off these days because of their dampness, darkness (there is no electricity), and the presence of "rats as big as cats."

I learn all this from an off-duty tour guide enjoying a Coke against the central well. There are many guided tours in progress, but I make my way alone with the help of a guidebook and sturdy walking shoes. Leaving the Polish guide, I move on to climb a maze of winding passages until I find myself high up in one of the turrets, looking out through the slit windows at the flat countryside below. It is, as Poles often ruefully point out, an ideal terrain for a battlefield and, along with their geographical position, explains much about Polish history. The biggest and bloodiest battle in medieval Poland—indeed in all of Europe—actually took place southeast of Malbork, at a place called Grunwald, but I think of it as I scan the approach to Malbork because this was the event that marked the beginning of the Teutonic Order's decline.

The battle of Grunwald was fought in 1410 by combined Polish and Lithuanian forces, following the marriage of Lithuania's grand duke to the reluctant Jadwiga. While the princess sat in her Wawel chamber, shedding tears for her lost Austrian lover, her Lithuanian husband and Poland's new king was fighting the battle that would change the course of Polish history. He had thirty thousand soldiers with him, as did the formidable knights. The carnage lasted for ten hours, ending with the Teutons' defeat. Against all odds, Władisław Jagiełło found himself the head of a kingdom that was to stretch from the Baltic in the north to the Black Sea in the south; in the east almost as far as Moscow. Ironically, though the Polish-Lithuanian union had been sought above all in hopes of vanquishing a common enemy, Jagiełło's prenuptial baptism soon brought about the Lithuanian conversion that the knights had in vain tried to accomplish for two centuries.

Although the battle had been won and a treaty signed, the war was not yet over. Having retreated to their impregnable Malbork fortress, the knights remained a thorn in the side of the Polish monarchy. They had lost some of their conquered land and their ostensible mission in the region, but their persistent disregard for the terms of the Toruń Treaty eventually led to the Thirteen Years' War (1454-66), fought by Jagiełło's son. They lost this battle too, but the coup de grâce was dealt by the

Teutonic Grand Master himself. Having converted to Lutheranism, he dissolved the order and declared what was left of Prussia a secular duchy with himself as ruler under the Polish crown. In 1525, he paid public homage to the Polish king in Kraków's market square. As far as Poland was concerned, the Teutonic Order was no more.

By the time this momentous event took place, the knights had left their mark in every sphere of Pomeranian life, matching their skills on the battlefield with those in finance, architecture, and trade. One of the irresistible economic attractions of the Baltic coast had always been amber, and it was not long before the Teutonic Knights had virtual monopoly on its trade. This presumably is the rationale for placing Poland's—perhaps the world's—greatest amber collection in the Malbork Castle.

It is a dazzling display, including everything from ancient amulets to a five-pound raw amber rock as large as a human head. There are pieces with prehistoric plants and feathers trapped in the fluid amber; spiders and worms and flies and frogs. Predictably, there is a great variety of opulent jewelry, but also more surprising items: chess games and candlesticks and sculptures and caskets; even elaborate cabinets and altarpieces. It turns out that, though rare, amber can also be gray or green or blue, or a rich, fluorescent hyacinth red. Mined from claylike soil called "blue earth," it is just as often found in shallow Baltic water, sometimes cast up onto the beach by waves. For centuries, it was collected by amber fishermen wading into the sea with their special nets. Attached to poles, the nets were used to haul out seaweed, in which chunks of amber torn from the seafloor were frequently entangled. Since amber is invariably warmer than the bed in which it rests, there was also a widespread practice—common as recently as the late nineteenth century—of hunting for amber with one's bare feet. Shortly before dawn, coastal villagers would be seen walking along the beach, their soles searching out the warm amber concealed by the night-chilled sand.

Amber, as is widely known, is a fossilized coniferous resin, but I had no idea that it comes from now-extinct trees dating back forty-five to fifty million years! That amber was valued in prehistoric times has become apparent through various archaeological excavations yielding Neolithic and Bronze Age artifacts. The ancient Greeks called amber *electron*. It was observed that under friction, amber became electrically charged, and this in time gave etymological birth to the word "electricity."

By the time of the Roman Empire, there was a well-established amber route, stretching from the North Adriatic through the Balkans, all the way to Poland's amber coast. The prevalence of Roman trade in these parts has been confirmed by the great number of first- and second-century Roman coins found along the amber route. It is known that Roman women prized amber ornaments, and that an amber figurine could, for a time, fetch a slave on the Roman market. Eventually, the craze for it waned in Rome and the route was extended eastward, all the way to the Black Sea. In the Middle East, amber remained a prized item up to the modern era. The Turks in particular sought it for the manufacture of worry beads, as well as cigar holders and pipe stems. Amber, they believed, could prevent the transmission of various infections, an ever-present risk in the East, where smoking was traditionally communal.

The belief in amber's healing properties has been surprisingly, tenaciously, widespread. In some cultures, the sick have traditionally been exposed to the smoke of burnt amber, or made to drink an amber-based infusion. Perhaps because of its static charge, it has also been widely linked to superstitious practices, as evidenced by amulets going back to Neolithic times. It was thought to ward off the evil eye, and to offer a sure cure for infertility. Following a successful birth, it was hung around the infant's neck as a charm—and a teething ring.

All this ensured an ongoing demand for Baltic amber, which the Poles, like other Baltic people, have traditionally regarded as their most reliable currency. Like gold, it was prized and saved for a rainy day by villagers as well as aristocrats. For centuries, when the latter sought to gain favor with some great European personage, it was amber they sent or took along on their journey. It used to be said of people living in the Baltic region "They are sitting on amber." The Teutonic Knights sat on it for some 150 years.

Today's Malbork is a small, undistinguished town whose economy rests on sugar refineries, as well as rubber and pharmaceutical industries. It has some thirty-four thousand inhabitants settled on the right bank of the Nogat but, having been virtually razed during the war, has little to offer tourists. Nonetheless, I decide to cross the bridge, hoping to find an open shoe-repair shop. I am carrying a leather shoulderbag whose strap, I suddenly noticed at the castle, is on the verge of snapping. I have been overloading it with books and camera and recorder and suspect it won't last the day. Having stopped several passersby, I am directed to a small, rather dark shop where an elderly, bespectacled cobbler sits hunched up over a high-heeled sandal. I remove my bag and he blinks down at the frayed strap, his hands a little shaky. He can certainly fix it, he tells me, but will have to do it on another machine, in the adjacent living quarters. It will cost 2.5 złoty, he says: a little more than a dollar.

"That's fine." I move to empty the laden bag, only to be told there is no need to worry: he is a Jehovah's Witness, and Witnesses, as everybody knows, are scrupulously honest.

Somewhat embarrassed, I empty it anyway, watched by the owlish-faced cobbler. He looks faintly impatient but doesn't seem to hold my lack of faith against me. When he learns I am Canadian, he grows positively expansive. It turns out he has a cousin in Canada; some place in Ontario whose name he can't remember. He fixes my strap while I sit reading, then comes out, seemingly eager for a chat. There are, he eventually tells me, five million Jehovah's Witnesses in the world, 124,000 of them Polish. Asked how Catholics feel about them, he states that whatever people say, religious freedom is not yet a fact of life in Poland. By way of example, he tells me of a Jehovah's Witness boy who recently fell from an eleventh-floor apartment and was given a blood transfusion against his parents' will. Polish law permits doctors to overrule parental wishes in life-threatening situations. But this, insists the cobbler, is clearly a violation of the right to religious freedom.

"God's law is higher than man's law, after all," he says.

Asked how he came to be a Jehovah's Witness, he tells me that it happened in England, where he found himself at war's end, having been forcibly conscripted into the German navy. World War II was not the first time that Poles were forced to fight against their own, but this is my first encounter with anyone who has lived through the unimaginable agony. The cobbler seems reluctant to discuss this particular experience. He tells me it was a great relief to be captured by the Allies, though he spent the rest of the war in a British prisoner-of-war camp.

Eventually, he married an English girl but had to abandon her after a few years, along with a child who might or might not have been his. This he is not at all reticent about: he had caught his wife in flagrante delicto with an Anglican priest. "A priest!" he says, blinking across the counter, "right in my own bedroom!"

And so he came back home and married a Polish woman and has been in Malbork ever since. He has a son and daughter and four grand-children but from time to time can't help wondering: was it his own flesh and blood he abandoned in Britain?

At this point, an elderly man enters the shop, sitting in the vacant chair. I take him to be a customer, but the cobbler introduces him as his brother-in-law, a recently widowed fisherman from the Hel Peninsula. Hearing that I am Canadian, he looks as astonished as if I had just landed from Mars. *I* am astonished to learn he is almost eighty and still fishing. He is a thickset, garrulous man, with the ruddy face of a healthy sixty-year-old. He looks pleased by my own surprise and eager to impress me with the hardships of his profession. For one thing, the peninsula is very low and, made up of pure sand, is extremely vulnerable to the elements. The whole shape of Hel can change from one day to the next, given a major storm! There was a time when some fisher-men became pirates simply to survive, Pan Bajek informs me. Not so long ago—in his grandfather's time. They don't do that any more, but it's still often dangerous work. He personally used to know men who lost their lives in winter storms, yes! And then there are the times when the Baltic freezes over, and small boats can't go out at all.

"But summer or winter, we all have to eat, no?" He grins at me, revealing a set of poorly fitted dentures. What do they fish for? Cod and sprat mostly, and also eel and flounder. They used to catch sturgeon too, but it has been lost to pollution.

"Tell her about the gobies," the cobbler urges.

It seems there has been a marine invasion of alarming proportions. The Baltic never had gobies, but in 1990 they began to surface in fish-ermen's nets—a great nuisance, since Poles are reluctant to buy them. Where have the gobies come from, I ask. From the Caspian and Black Seas, most likely. It is believed they were inadvertently transported in the ballast of cargo ships. One thing is certain: having multiplied with unprecedented speed, the gobies threaten to eliminate local species.

"It's like the Germans," says the cobbler, looking at me intently. "One day they arrived where they had no business being, and before you could snap your fingers, they had taken over everything."

This reminds him of something he would like to show me. He disappears through the door to his living quarters and comes back clutching a German belt buckle that his son-in-law found on a recent excursion. Can I read German, he asks, adjusting his glasses.

"Not much," I say, but as it turns out, not much is called for. The inscription on the metal buckle consists of three short words—perhaps hopeful, perhaps presumptuous— "GOTT MIT UNS."

CHAPTER 14

GOD WAS DECIDEDLY not with the Swedish invader who, in 1655, arrived in the Polish town of Częstochowa, determined to lay claim to the riches of its famous shrine. Having recently triumphed in the Thirty Years' War (1618-48), Sweden was Europe's leading military power, a country with a vast, suddenly redundant, army and unflagging territorial ambitions. Taking advantage of internal disputes in Poland, the Swedes swept through the country, leaving Polish cities burnt and plundered,* the countryside ravaged, the economy devastated. By the time they arrived at the Jasna Góra shrine, the Poles were so utterly demoralized, it was felt that only a miracle could stop the Swedish Deluge. And a miracle apparently did.

The Jasna Góra (Bright Mountain) monastery at Częstochowa is one of the world's greatest pilgrimage destinations, its drawing power surpassed only by Benares, Mecca, Lourdes, and Rome. For over six centuries, hundreds of thousands of pilgrims have been coming here annually, their personal and national prayers addressed to a reputedly miraculous icon known as the Black Madonna.

The icon's origins are a matter of ongoing controversy. Some believe it was painted by St. Luke on a panel from the Holy Family's table; others insist it is Byzantine in origin, executed somewhere between the sixth and ninth centuries. Donated by a fourteenth-century Polish prince to the newly founded Pauline monastery, it soon acquired a reputation for miraculous interventions. The number of pilgrims kept

---

*Many Polish treasures ended up in Sweden, where they are to this day. For example, two stone lions from Warsaw still grace Stockholm's Royal Palace.

growing, turning the modest monastery into a repository of votive treasures, a fact that did not go unnoticed by various foreign villains. In 1430, a band of Bohemian brigands (believed to have been followers of the religious reformer Jan Hus) made off with many of the shrine's treasures but failed to steal the priceless Black Madonna. Legend has it that the icon's weight had so grown on being lifted that the robbers had no choice but to leave it behind. Frustrated by their failure, they stomped on the icon and slashed it with their swords, bolting at the sight of the Virgin's gushing blood. Though the icon was eventually restored in Kraków, several dark slashes were left by the restorers to commemorate this historic profanation. A second attack in 1466 brought about a new resolution to turn the sanctuary into a fortress, an undertaking that, cynics say, certainly made the Virgin's task easier during the eventual Swedish onslaught.

It lasted for forty days, at the end of which the three-thousand-strong Swedish army and its cannons found themselves ignominiously defeated by a contingent of 260 Poles, only 70 of them professional soldiers. So spectacular was this improbable victory that the Poles instantly proclaimed it a divine miracle, presumably due to the Holy Virgin's benevolence. Her alleged intervention so galvanized the divided Poles that, at the eleventh hour, they finally rallied and rose against the Swedes, eventually recovering most of their lost territories.

After this pivotal event, Jasna Góra became a symbol of religious and political liberty in Poland; a future sanctuary for victims of various persecutions, including Polish Jews. In 1656, the king crowned the Virgin Queen of Poland, consecrating the country to her protection. She came to the Poles' aid again in 1920, after thousands of Poles flocked to Jasna Góra to pray for victory against the approaching Bolsheviks. Not only did the Virgin answer their prayers, but she did so dramatically on August 15, the Feast of the Assumption. The triumph, accomplished through the heroic Marshal Józef Piłsudski, became known in Poland as "the miracle on the Vistula." Ironically, it was the Red Army that would eventually save Jasna Góra, defusing the explosives left behind by the fleeing Nazis.

Though no miracle spared the country the horrors of World War II and its aftermath, Poles' religious faith seems to have been notably strengthened by their travails, blossoming with the unprecedented election of a Polish Pope. When John Paul II visited Częstochowa for the first time in 1979, he encountered an extraordinary crowd of three and a half million worshipers who regarded the Pope's election as a national honor, if not indeed a sign of divine favor. Certainly, the Pope's international stature gave new impetus to the struggle against the Communist regime and, it is commonly believed, was largely responsible for its eventual demise.

Ironically, having achieved its aim, today's Polish Church finds itself in a position of diminishing power. Though Poles are still exceptionally devout, their current allegiance is sometimes divided between God and mammon. Ecclesiastical leaders fear that the Church is on its way to becoming politically marginalized, but their greatest anxieties are focused on what Church fathers often refer to as an encroaching "neopaganism." In the eighteenth century, thousands of Varsovian pilgrims marched on Jasna Góra to plead for an end to the ravaging plague; these days, what Częstochowa's archbishop publicly prays for is to be spared "the plague of atheism."

The threat is no doubt real, but to the casual observer somewhat difficult to credit. Despite reports that attendance is down from the 1980s, Poland's houses of worship are often filled to overflowing, with some city churches offering several masses a day, any day of the week. The Church may have lost some of its political clout, but a visit to Częstochowa leaves little doubt about the unflagging intensity of most Poles' religious faith.

I arrive in Częstochowa in early August, determined to avoid the peak attendance on the fifteenth. All the same, the town is clearly in holiday gear, and I congratulate myself on having for once secured a hotel reservation. Catering to the pilgrim trade has been Częstochowa's raison d'être for several centuries, but its current citizens are given to frequent griping about the dirt and damage inflicted by the pilgrims. The complaints vie for newspaper space with the usual concerns about environmental pollution, a grim consequence of the Communist regime's efforts to undermine Częstochowa's religious base through aggressive industrial development. The regime is gone, but Częstochowa still has iron and steel plants, sawmills and textile mills, and numerous chemical factories whose smoking chimneys share the skyline with Jasna Góra's prominent bell tower. Burnt and rebuilt several times, the slender 350-foot tower rises above a fortified twelve-and-a-half-acre complex comprising several buildings, a park, and a vast square with countless milling pilgrims. Some of these pilgrims are visibly exhausted, having come on foot from great distances, sleeping in parks, haylofts.

The crowds are enormous, though nothing like the ones in the photographs I have seen of religious holidays, when a sea of worshipers fills the immense grounds, carrying banners, flags, crucifixes; on rainy days, hundreds of thousands of umbrellas. Many Poles come to Jasna Góra with their families, but it is common to see them on organized excursions: office and factory workers, schoolchildren, policemen, soldiers, farmers in folk costumes. There are newlyweds coming to have their union blessed, numerous nuns and priests, and many disabled children and adults. There are several gates to go through, and cement steps to climb, but some of the pilgrims fall to their knees at the outer gate, making their way up to the chapel in this manner, praying intently, oblivious to the crowds.

It is Sunday, but on the lower grounds the merchants are doing brisk business in religious memorabilia, the more aggressive of them darting forth to pin a religious brooch to a worshiper's lapel or to offer some cheap trinket. On the sidelines, Gypsy beggars are camped with half-naked children, whining in Polish at the passersby. The crowds, it would seem, are more charitably disposed at Jasna Góra, all the more perhaps as at every turn there is a confessional with a long lineup before it. Everywhere I go, people of all ages are queued up for entry, feeding children, dozing off, taking photographs.

The Jasna Góra buildings are outwardly austere but inwardly opulent, their various rooms dazzling with artifacts and accumulated treasures. There are the historic cannonballs fired by the Swedes; sculptures and paintings and precious gems, and countless religious objects, some dating back to the Middle Ages. There is a tradition at Jasna Góra of dressing up the Virgin in variously gorgeous robes, changing them in accordance with the occasion. Currently, the collection includes seven

robes, two of them on public display. They are encrusted with dia-
monds, rubies, pearls; one of them, "the robe of fidelity" is made of
wedding rings.

Most of the displays consist of accumulated votive gifts offered by
grateful kings and princes, concentration camp survivors, Polish soldiers. Much of Poland's history is lavishly laid out for the visiting
public, one of the most recent offerings being Lech Wałęsa's Nobel
Prize medal.

All of these, and much more, are on display in the much-visited
Museum, Arsenal, and Room of Treasures, but the pilgrims' ultimate
destination at Jasna Góra is of course the Chapel of the Virgin. This is
the only part of the complex to have retained much of its original
Gothic architecture, though a first-time visitor is more likely to be
struck by the collection of crutches and leg braces mounted on the
chapel walls along with countless plaques for fallen Polish soldiers.

I scrutinize all these from a distance, a curious tourist swept along
by a slow river of impassioned pilgrims, all of them intently focused on
the distant presbytery. Here and there, the dense crowd makes way for
a few prostrate pilgrims or supplicants inching their way on their knees
toward the high altar. I remind myself that some of these pilgrims are
peasants who have waited a lifetime to visit Jasna Góra; that this is for
many a glorious event in an otherwise wretched existence. All around
me, small groups of country folk huddle together and break into song.
Every village, I am told, has its own sacred hymn, sung at Jasna Góra
with unsurpassed fervor. The most touching of all, however, are the
mothers with their deformed children—pushing them in wheelchairs
toward the main altar, waiting for the icon to be unveiled.

For the first time in my life, I experience something like shame for
my lack of faith; once more, I feel like a trespasser on sacred ground,
though one deeply moved by this mass of avid, hopeful humanity.
Freud dismissed all religious mysticism as "infantile helplessness," and
perhaps he was right, but what *is* one to feel before the malevolent
forces devastating millions of lives; what did Freud feel when the Nazis
invaded his Vienna?

I have never been taught to pray. And yet, when my daughter was
an infant and had an accident that might have left her brain-damaged,

I found myself praying inwardly, fervently, though I couldn't have said to whom, and still can't. Perhaps Harvard University's Herbert Benson is right, stating in his *Timeless Healing* that human beings may well be programmed for religious faith; "genetically wired for God" to countervail our unique human capacity to contemplate our own mortality.

Dr. Benson is not alone, of course, in drawing public attention to the apparent interdependence of body and spirit, but his eminence underlines the medical establishment's growing receptiveness to this line of thinking. And yet, though serious studies all over the world clearly point to the extraordinary power of religious faith, many of us remain stubbornly skeptical of reported miracles in places like Częstochowa or Lourdes. As Émile Zola said on his way to the latter, "Even if I saw a miracle, I wouldn't believe it."

It is of course easy, even appropriate, to be skeptical of miraculous claims, and the Lourdes authorities are most skeptical of all. Anybody can claim to have been miraculously cured, but official pronouncement demands an exceedingly rigorous process involving two highly respected medical bodies (one of them international) and an equally stringent canonical commission. Despite occasional efforts to discredit the Lourdes process, there have been almost a hundred official, irrefutable, cures of pilgrims with certifiably hopeless conditions; at least ten thousand pilgrims have declared themselves cured.

These facts may be fascinating, but they can't be very encouraging to the handicapped and afflicted: at best, only one in about ten thousand stands a chance of finding a miraculous cure in places like Lourdes or Częstochowa. This fact, however, does not seem to deter the world's religious pilgrims, most of whom are healthy in mind and body and flock to such shrines simply to affirm their faith; to share in what even I can see must be a remarkably uplifting experience for any believer. And yet, when the miraculous icon is finally unveiled (an event that takes place several times a day), I can't help wondering how people can find it in them to believe in *this* particular Virgin's benevolence. Truth to tell, the Black Madonna is so singularly grim as to seem downright rancorous. But perhaps her baleful gaze is aimed only at the likes of me; perhaps it is all in the eyes of the beholder?

What I behold, when I finally get up close to the ebony-and-silver altar, is an icon of approximately four by three feet, darkly painted in the Byzantine style, and further darkened by time and whiffs of incense. The Madonna holds her child, her right cheek cruelly slashed, her slightly asymmetrical eyes heavy-lidded. She looks, it finally comes to me, like any wretched mother after several sleepless nights with a teething child.

But maybe I've still got it wrong. Maybe the painter, whoever he was, meant to suggest that this Madonna knows, has sensed with her exquisite maternal intuition, what awaits her son, and now has to spend all those sleepless nights contemplating the tragic knowledge. It would certainly explain those woebegone eyes.

This line of thought finally comes to an end when I go outdoors, swept by the crowd toward the Stations of the Cross. The Stations are located on what was once the moat—fourteen bronze sculptures at whose pedestals the pilgrims pause, close their eyes, pray intently. At the twelfth Station—Death on the Cross—a group of nuns kneel down to read from the scriptures, joined by a young woman with an elderly mother and a pale, carefully dressed, daughter. The child is about four and wears white kneesocks and beribboned braids much like my own at that age. I take a closer look and see that, fair-haired and blue-eyed, she altogether looks remarkably like my own photographed preschool self—equally restless too. When is she going to climb the bell tower, she insistently demands, and pouts on being told she will have to wait. "Listen to the lovely bells." The young mother resumes praying, a rosary in her hands.

I move on while the bells—thirty-six of them—go on ringing out their hymn, filling me with abrupt, helpless sadness. It is a sharp, not unfamiliar, sort of melancholy, born of feeling myself alone in an alien crowd, acutely aware of the passage of time, of others' hopes and griefs, of their all-sustaining faith. I think of Miguel de Unamuno's Father Manuel Bueno, a village priest who one day loses his faith; who yearns above all to believe again and, failing, begins to long for death. Over and over, the priest contemplates suicide, deterred only by the helpless knowledge that *he* represents his wretched parishioners' life-line; that faithless though he is, it is apparently his destiny to help uphold the faith of those who, without it, would all succumb to the ultimate despair. Father Manuel has lost his faith, but not his faith *in* faith. I understand this perfectly now, but it doesn't make me feel any better. And so I go off to look for a vacant park bench, where I can sit and record all these random thoughts. None of them, I know, will alter existential realities, but it is apparently *my* destiny to go through life clutching a notebook and fountain pen, with nothing whatever to fall back on at times like this, except the miracle of words.

CHAPTER 15

THE FOLLOWING DAY—A gray, rainy morning—I travel
to Kielce. Set in the Silnica River valley, surrounded by green hills,
Kielce is a seemingly ordinary town whose historic name has been
blemished by one of the most gruesome events in Poland's postwar era.
It happened on July 4, 1946, though precisely what happened remains
a matter of controversy, even among Polish historians. What everyone
agrees on are the bare, tragic facts: an unruly mob, fired by rumors of
a Christian child's ritual murder, stormed a small apartment block
inhabited by Jews and killed forty-two of them, wounding sixty others.
Oddly, neither the army nor the police tried to intervene and indeed,
according to numerous reports, actually took part in the massacre. The
failure of the authorities to stop the mob led to the widely circulated
view that the pogrom was masterminded by Soviet authorities. The
regime, it is argued, wished to divert the world's attention from the
recent, allegedly rigged national referendum, as well as the 1943 murder of some fifteen thousand Polish officers whose bodies had recently
been discovered in a Russian forest. Above all, say the proponents of
this theory, the Soviets hoped to discredit the highly nationalistic
Polish Underground, some of whose members were reputed to be antisemites. The truth about the event may never be known now, for at least
four witnesses willing to testify disappeared mysteriously in the
pogrom's aftermath, and the Kielce Security Service archives from
1945 to 1954 were destroyed in a suspicious fire. Arthur Bliss Lane,
erstwhile U.S. ambassador to Poland, is on record stating that "both
government and antigovernment sources admit that [the pogrom] was
not spontaneous but a carefully organized plot." As the Polish histori-

an Krystyna Kersten has repeatedly pointed out, however, regardless of who actually threw the burning match, the conditions for a conflagration were clearly there in Kielce.

No one denies that there was considerable hostility toward Jews in postwar Poland. They were, as Anita Górniak pointed out in Gdańsk, widely perceived as the Communist enemy's collaborators. They were also, in many cases, without homes or occupations, both shops and flats having been appropriated by Poles. Most of the Holocaust survivors in Kielce had recently returned from the U.S.S.R. and were waiting to reclaim their property—an unenviable position and not one confined to Kielce. When a Łódź acquaintance of my parents' returned from Russia to knock on the door to her prewar flat, the Polish occupant opened it a crack, only to exclaim, "Madam is still alive!"

The Kielce events started with the disappearance of a nine-year-old Polish boy who returned home after two days in the country with a cock-and-bull story hinting at forcible confinement. The statement, it is said, was then manipulated by some interested party or parties, deliberately implicating local Jews. The boy, somewhat simple-minded, had allegedly been held captive in some Jews' cellar, where he had come across the bodies of some Polish children killed in Jewish rituals. Several Polish children had, it is said, disappeared in the Kielce region, but the Jewish block identified by the boy had no cellar and of course no Polish children, dead or alive. Mobs are not known for their rationality, and the lack of any incriminating evidence did not stop the frenzied louts. There were, in 1946, some 250,000 Jewish survivors living in Poland, and the Kielce pogrom prompted most of them to emigrate as soon as they were able. Before the pogrom, Jews were emigrating at the rate of about 70 a week; after Kielce, the figure jumped to 700 a day, creating administrative chaos in the American zone of Austria where, in August 1946, some 22,000 Jews arrived from Poland, all seeking shelter.

I have come to Kielce on the invitation of a young English teacher I met on the train from Krynica. An M.A. student in contemporary British literature, she saw me reading Ian McEwan's *The Comfort of Strangers* and started a conversation. She had been trying to decide whom to do her thesis on and we talked about writers we liked, and then about other things. Her name was Anna Bąblewska and she was twenty-three; a beautiful, totally artless young woman seemingly unaware of her own loveliness. She had been visiting her grandmother in Krynica, she told me, speaking excellent English. It was her mother's hometown, though Teresa Bąblewska was born in Germany, after her own parents, along with thousands of other Poles, had been deported to the Reich as slave labor. We talked about that for a while, and then about life in Kielce. Anna was engaged to a music student but living with her widowed mother and two younger brothers. What was it like, growing up in such a notorious town, I wondered, but did not voice the question. As it turned out, I would have an opportunity to see Kielce for myself, for Anna was soon urging me to visit. Her brothers were both at summer camp and there was plenty of space just now, she assured me. She and her fiancé were both free all summer and would be glad to show me around. I liked Anna and said I might stop for a day or two, on my way from Częstochowa.

Kielce is roughly halfway between Kraków and Warsaw, the principal town in the central region known as Małopolska (Little Poland). It is a largely agricultural region made up of green valleys, rolling hills, and a predominantly rural population—quintessential Poland. Though many of Kielce's current inhabitants are educated Poles from other parts of the country, the area still has a certain reputation for pugnacity. While Krakovians are said to be tightfisted and Varsovians conceited, Kielce men, says Anna, are widely referred to as *scyzoryki* because of an apparent propensity to use pocket knives in brawls following soccer games.

This is new to me, but I know by now that the Kielce region is generally considered one of the most backward and superstitious in Poland. It is even said that the site of the famed Święty Krzyż (Holy Cross) abbey was for a long time an important witches' enclave. What has been archaeologically confirmed is the fact that the abbey's mountaintop location was once the site of pagan worship. Legend has it that there was a struggle between heathen and Christian forces, and that the latter eventually won, soon replacing the pagan temple with a monastery.

The Benedictine abbey is in the Świętokrzyski National Park, and I visit it on my first afternoon in Kielce, going with Anna and Michał, her fiancé, in their newly acquired car. It is a small Fiat painted a bright shade of orange. It sounds like a lawn mower and runs, it would seem, as much on faith as on gasoline. Every now and then, the windshield wipers stop working, and Michał must park and fiddle with them to get them going again. My hosts, however, are visibly thrilled to have wheels and treat the Fiat's capriciousness with amused indulgence. They have christened their car Clockwork Orange.

Miraculously, it gets us to the foot of Święty Krzyż, where we leave the car to make our way through the park to the summit. The road winds through a dense forest that, like every forest I have visited in Poland, instantly sweeps me back to my childhood. The forest is shady with ancient trees, lush with ferns and herbs, and full of huge, wild mushrooms. It has stopped raining, and the fragrance of wet foliage and soaked earth hangs in the limpid air. This is a protected wildlife zone with a colony of the nearly extinct white eagle—Poland's national symbol—and also a rare species of poisonous black adder. Thankfully, we see none of the latter but do catch a glimpse of a roe deer darting past a large mountain ash. The tree has extraordinary roots springing out some four feet aboveground, surrounding the trunk like a monstrous spider. Next to the ash stands an old oak whose hollow trunk has been taken over by a colony of bees. Cherished by Poles for many centuries, beehives were especially prized around churches, offering as they did an endless source of much-needed candlewax. In the fifteenth century, a law was accordingly passed to protect natural beehives. Anyone caught damaging one, or just stealing honey, was taken to the scene of crime, publicly disemboweled, and left to die amid the swarming bees.

Like many Polish forests, Świętokrzyski's too once sheltered partisans. Primo Levi, in his *If Not Now, When?*, writes about anti-Nazi resistance on this very mountain, but it had also known anticzarist activities, culminating in the January Uprising of 1863.

The Benedictine abbey was founded in the early twelfth century and has undergone several reconstructions, most recently in the eighteenth century. This, as usual, betokens a variety of disasters: fires, invasions, death. In 1260, the Tatars looted the monastery and destroyed it, killing all the monks. It was eventually rebuilt and resettled, only to be closed down in 1825 by the proselytizing Russians. The complex became a local prison, which the Nazis in time took over, turning it into a Russian prisoner-of-war camp. Six thousand prisoners are said to have perished here, the Germans having reportedly let them starve to death. There are, Michał tells me, old camp signs on display in the monastery, forbidding cannibalism!

I don't get to see any of the interiors for myself. Once more it is Monday; once more, the doors are closed. Today's abbey is run by the Oblates of St. Mary of Immaculate Conception, a missionary order whose museum displays include African artifacts. Anna tells me that there are also underground crypts at Święty Krzyż with caskets enshrining the preserved remains of a local prince and some of the rebel aristocrats involved in the 1863 January Uprising.

Though thousands of pilgrims are said to stop here on the way to Częstochowa, we are all alone on the mountain just now, overlooking the surrounding forest and beyond it the deep valley arched over by a splendid rainbow. Another exhilarating moment on a deserted mountaintop, with neat farms laid out below, ringed by undulating hills. Eventually, we come upon a vast tract of broken gray rocks; heaps of them scattered between two mountain peaks. The Kielce region is the only area in Poland where rocks from every geological age are to be found, from the Precambrian to the Quaternary. This gray expanse of quartzite rock is singularly desolate and mysterious, and I am not surprised to hear that a local legend is associated with it. The devil, they say here, was flying over this area, carrying a large boulder with some sinister purpose when, suddenly, he heard a rooster crow. Since devils are famously wary of dawn, the devil panicked and dropped the boulder on this mountaintop, seeing it shatter as he vanished into the fading night.

The sun is beginning to set as we make our descent, passing the statue of a supplicant pilgrim who, according to another legend, moves at a pace of one grain of sand a year. When he reaches the summit, they say, the world will come to an end.

I laugh at this, telling Anna that I have heard more legends in one day in Kielce than in my entire time in Poland. Whether this is because there are more of them here or because Anna is good at recalling them is difficult to say. Michał's English is rather limited, but Anna is keen to practice hers and offers many quaint bits of information about the region and its mythology. When, a little later, we pass a roadside shrine under a linden tree and I remark on the great number of these trees in Poland, Anna tells me that the *lipa* is a sacred tree in her country. According to tradition, anyone cutting it down ran the risk of seeing a beloved family member die soon after. The linden was considered sacred because the Virgin Mary was believed to be fond of hiding in its branches, revealing herself only to poor children. Roadside shrines were often built under linden trees to allow passing villagers to pray and take shelter during sudden storms. It was believed that a linden tree was safe from lightning, and also that tea made of linden blossoms was effective in fighting fever. Anna adds that rural Poles were famously dedicated to herbal medicine, knowledge of which was often a matter of life and death in such regions. Now health-food stores are springing up all over Poland, and educated Poles are suddenly showing interest in ancient herbal remedies.

Stopping at a local village, Anna points to another tree with religious associations and medicinal purpose: the black lilac. Dried in the sun and crushed, the black lilac's berries were commonly used in the treatment of stubborn coughs, but otherwise were shunned by most Poles. It is believed, says Anna, that Judas hanged himself on the branches of a black lilac tree.

Though antisemitism has strong roots in the traditional depiction of Jews as Christ killers, the blood libels that inspired so many antisemitic pogroms predate Christianity. As far back as the Hellenic era, Jews were said to kidnap an occasional Greek, fatten him up for a year, and then sacrifice him in a religious ritual, partaking of the victim's flesh. In the second and third centuries, Christians too became frequent victims of ritual murder accusations, battling against the prevailing belief that the Eucharist involved human sacrifice. Once Christianity became a mainstream religion, the suspicions began to fall on various heretical Christian sects—and once again on Jews.

Invariably aimed at social minorities, blood libels were an obvious expression of hostility and mistrust, but the form they took appears to have had its roots in ancient, even primitive, attitudes toward blood. It was because of the prevailing belief that blood possessed the power to heal and wound that so many pagan religions adopted blood sacrifice. Ironically, though the Torah expressly forbids such practices, it was the

Jews who would throughout the centuries bear the brunt of blood ritual libels.

The accusations were not necessarily believed by everyone, but they were often used by unscrupulous regimes as convenient weapons in rabble rousing. A testament to human potential for cruelty and credulity, blood libels were first used by Christians against Jews in 1144, giving birth to a growing belief that Jews used Christian blood in their Passover rituals. The alleged timing appears to have been linked to Christ's crucifixion, a motif current throughout the Middle Ages. On the eve of their expulsion from Spain, converted Jews were forced to confess to the custom of assembling in a cave to crucify a Christian child after torturing and humiliating him as Christ had been.

The preponderance of children in these accusations was perhaps meant to sharpen the contrast between the victims' innocence and the perpetrators' alleged evil. It was, at any rate, a powerful image, successfully passed down from the Middle Ages to the modern era. Not surprisingly, blood libels multiplied in times of political and economic upheaval, surfacing even in China where, around the turbulent turn of the century, the Chinese aimed similar accusations at the foreigners in their midst. The Nazis of course aimed them at the Jews, devoting an entire issue of *Der Sturmer* to their propaganda, with articles ostensibly written by respected scientists. "[T]here remains only one question," one of them concludes: "for what purpose did the Jews use the blood?"

Though much of this I will learn only on returning home, the subject begins to engage my interest on my second day in Kielce, when Anna takes me to see the site of the 1946 pogrom. It is a small, three-story block overlooking a picturesque canal and, I note for myself, it has no cellar. The building, as well as the former synagogue, have recently been refurbished in preparation for the ceremonies marking the pogrom's fiftieth anniversary. The event was attended by some three thousand dignitaries, including Polish Prime Minister Cimoszewicz and the Nobel laureate Elie Wiesel. Even before Wiesel's controversial comments, there had been much ado about the proposed ceremonies, which local authorities agreed to only under pressure from the capital. Many Kielce citizens also opposed the plans, phoning a local call-in radio program with their objections. There were those who were against the unnecessary expense; others who feared that the ceremonies might trigger hostile acts from extremist groups, and that these would further besmirch Kielce's name abroad. Many of the callers simply felt that there was no point in dredging up the past. Even the Pope's reference to the pogrom during his visit to Kielce offended many people. "Why should we feel responsible for what happened a long time ago?" they stated. No one apparently saw fit to point out how many generations of Jews have been held responsible for Christ's crucifixion.

Though Kielce's citizens are hardly unique in preferring to let sleeping dogs lie, it was in fact the Soviet regime that had placed a gag order on the subject of the Kielce pogrom. It is said that three-quarters of Poles had never heard of it before the 1980s when Solidarity finally cracked the journalistic silence. Eventually, a trilingual commemorative plaque was put up by Wałęsa at 7 Planty Street, stating, "In memory of the forty-two Jews murdered on July 4, 1946, during antisemitic riots."

Crossing Kielce's lovely English landscape park, with its streams and bridges and gigantic willows, Anna and I talk about the contradictory evidence surrounding the pogrom, and I tell her about a young village woman in postwar Łódź, the live-in maid of my parents' friends who, every year, just before Passover, would insist on going back home for about ten days, having heard that Jews routinely used Christian blood in their Passover rituals. When reproached by our own somewhat more sophisticated maid, the girl claimed that her grandmother had heard about such things in the parish church.

"The priest wouldn't lie about such things, would he?" the country girl had argued.

Though the Polish Church has in recent years officially repudiated antisemitism, and even acknowledged some responsibility for having nourished it with its past teachings, the legitimacy that antisemitism was given by the Church will take time to fade. Anna will, later in the day, show me a newspaper article alluding to the existence of a cathedral in the town of Sandomierz, one of whose old frescoes reportedly shows Jews engaged in the ritual murder of a Christian child.*

---

*In the same church, however, Jews were hidden from the Nazis, with the knowledge and cooperation of local Poles.

Anna remembers the article as we approach the local cathedral standing across from the Italian-designed Bishops' Palace. From around the end of the eleventh century until the late eighteenth, Kielce was the property of the wealthy Kraków bishops who used the town as an administrative center for their vast estates. The cathedral was built in the twelfth century and has been rebuilt several times since then. It is a cool, dim place with a sumptuous Baroque interior, but I am struck above all by the unexpected evidence of the Church's determined campaign against abortion. A large, color display of excellent photographs stands at the entrance, showing the development of the human fetus. All the major political forces in Poland, states Anna, are aggressively playing on the issue of abortion for their own ends.

"It's one of the most serious issues dividing the country right now," she says, a little surprised to learn it's no less divisive in North America.

We stop for a late lunch at a local hole-in-the-wall, the only place serving a specialty called *pyzy* (cheeks). The large, soft dumplings look indeed like cheeks, very pale ones, stuffed with ground meat and onions. This is the only place in Poland where I come across them, and they are delicious. Anna reminds me that her mother is expecting us home for an early dinner, so we each have only one, then go on with our sight-seeing.

Kielce is a compact town with a pleasant center largely made up of eighteenth- and nineteenth-century mansions. Though some of the elegant facades are still in a state of post-Communist disrepair, Kielce too is quickly being transfigured. It now has Western-style shops, cafés, and restaurants; its youth wear mostly jeans and T-shirts, the young men sporting American baseball caps. Anna, who is very slender, wears a pair of striped jeans she bought in London, changing only the color of her T-shirt. She has long, fair hair, and, taking a snapshot of her, I am struck by the fact that hers is a true Madonna face: heart-shaped and pale, with a widow's peak and calm gray eyes gazing back with grave, delicate composure.

Having shown me around the national museum, Anna takes me to see the former Kielce synagogue. It is a modest building, currently used as an archive center, freshly painted pastel blue and white. It overlooks a stone wall with a plaque put up in honor of the twenty-seven thousand Kielce Jews who died in the Holocaust. It is signed, "The people of

Kielce." There is, in this dishonored town, a new movement headed by a local psychologist and a literature professor, seeking reconciliation with Jews abroad. Despite its notoriety, Kielce has had its share of heroic citizens, eighty of whom have been given the Israeli government Righteous Among the Nations Award. There is a new memorial to honor them too. It bears all their names and a quote by the Israeli poet Chaim Chefer: ". . .I try to think about the people who saved me," it says. "I keep asking myself, in God's name, if I were in their place, would I be able to do as they did?"

Teresa Bąblewska and her children live in a high-rise block on one of the suburban hills surrounding Kielce. Her husband having died of a heart attack in his midforties, Teresa has raised her three children mostly on her own, somehow contriving to make their home one of the most pleasant I am to see in Poland. Airy and flooded with light, its rooms are decorated with huge ferns, the living room wall lined with oil paintings. The paintings were done by Teresa's husband who had been an amateur artist and whose sudden death, I sense, Teresa has never quite recovered from.

My second day in Kielce has been an exceptionally hot one, but returning home with Anna, I am surprised by the pleasant breeze sweeping through the hilltop flat. The windows are all wide open, their curtains billowing. The radio plays Mozart's "Laudate Dominum." The kitchen gives off delicious cooking smells.

Teresa is a tall brunette with unusually dark eyes, in turn wistful and impassioned. It is easy to imagine her young, with dark glossy curls and flashing eyes. She welcomes us warmly, having come straight from work to produce a wonderful Polish meal. Schnitzel, I know by now, is standard guest fare in Poland and Teresa's is as good as any, accompanied by matchless homemade Silesian gnocchi. Anna is not much of an eater, and Teresa keeps nagging her to eat more. This is one of several occasions when I find myself reflecting on the fact that the Yiddishe Mama stereotype is in fact applicable to most Eastern European mothers. We talk about stereotyping over dinner, a subject that eventually leads Teresa to tell me that all through her postwar childhood, there was only one Jewish family living in Krynica. The man had a small shop in town, and his family did rather keep to themselves, but there was never any expression of antisemitic sentiments that she remembers. The only other Jew she has ever known was a survivor of the Kielce pogrom who was still around in the early 1970s. He was clearly mad, however; a familiar figure on Kielce streets, walking about, barefoot, in his ancient black caftan, carrying his shoes and muttering to himself. I ask what happened to him, but Teresa shrugs. One day, he just wasn't there any more; he must have died—Kielce's last Jew.

At this point, Michał arrives, having had dinner with his own family but come in time for dessert. He is a gentle young man with the face of a nineteenth-century poet, gaunt and faintly melancholy, with dark, longish hair. He and Anna are visibly devoted to each other, but it will be a long time before they are in a position to marry. Michał has an occasional gig with a local rock band, while Anna, who has only recently begun to teach, earns only 300 złoty a month—less than a school crossing guard, she points out indignantly, and much less than a policeman. The latter, moreover, can retire with a pension after fifteen years, while teachers must work for thirty. The average two-income Polish family lives on about 1,000 złoty a month, I'm told (about $500), most of it going toward rent, food, and utilities. The Poles' ability to stretch a złoty is as astonishing as their generosity. I have, passing several bakeries and candy shops with Anna and Michał, commented on the fact that Poles seem to consume a lot of baked goods and sweets but comparatively little fruit and vegetables. Anna has perhaps repeated the comment to Teresa, for dessert here includes not only a gorgeous multilayer cake but a platter full of apples, plums, apricots, cherries. I too am urged to eat more than I am used to, though Anna keeps trying to stop Teresa's determined mothering. We are, it occurs to me, roughly the same age, but in Kielce I feel the way I did as a young woman, coming home from my vagabond's life to an immaculate bed, a hug, my favorite homemade dishes. In Poland, I miss my lost mother over and over.

On my third day in Kielce—the day I was to leave—I awake to find myself barely able to get out of bed. The pain—I suspect it to be sciatica—radiates from my waist and down my left leg, bringing agony with the slightest movement. What am I to do?

"It's obvious you're in no condition to go anywhere," says Anna with uncharacteristic firmness. "You must get back into bed and rest." She telephones Teresa, who tells her to reassure me I am welcome to stay. They are certainly not about to let me go traipsing around the country until I have recovered. "And that's that," says Anna, repeating her mother's message.

Intensely moved by their solicitude, I am nonetheless quickly lapsing into despair. I have heard of sciatica taking weeks to heal. What about the remaining places on my itinerary? What about the extraordinary imposition on these generous strangers?

"Don't worry about anything," Anna keeps telling me. "I have nothing much to do with myself right now anyway."

She spends much of her time sitting with me and talking about books, politics, life in Canada. She is curious about North American Poles, most of whom (some four million) emigrated from impoverished rural areas between the end of the nineteenth century and World War I. Eventually, Michał arrives and joins us in the sunny bedroom, to answer my questions about music. Among Polish youth, the most popular music today is something called Disco Polo, a genre that combines disco music with rural and prison folklore. In 1995, more than eighty million Disco Polo cassettes and records were sold in Poland, despite frequent claims that the Disco Polo market is largely controlled by the Mafia. In recent years, hip-hop has also enjoyed popularity among the young, as has American rap. The British too are widely imitated, especially groups like Oasis and Stone Roses.

"Do any of them give concerts in Poland these days?" I ask.

They do now, but for many years rock stars habitually skipped Poland on their tours because the country had a flourishing pirated music industry. Also, until recently, Poland quite simply did not have the facilities for megaconcerts.

"People used to go to Prague in the old days, just to hear someone like Pink Floyd," says Anna, smiling. When she sees me wince with pain, her smile promptly fades. She remembers I am *a patient.* Before the day is over, having read Michael Ondaatje's novel, she begins to refer to me as the Canadian Patient. Certainly, the care and solicitude I am shown could not be more exquisite were my injury truly grave. Teresa goes on feeding me, Anna keeps me company, and Michał runs around to buy a hot-water bottle, a mustard plaster, various medications. The pills require prescriptions, for which he must go to considerable trouble. Fortunately, he knows a nurse, who naturally knows doctors, one of whom agrees to provide a prescription for the housebound Canadian Patient. Before the first day is over, Michał arrives with anti-inflammatories and muscle relaxants and painkillers. Anna runs a hot bath for me; she fills and refills the hot-water bottle. Three days later, the pain is tolerable; on the fourth, controlled by painkillers, sufficiently mild to enable me to resume traveling. When it's time for me to go, I find myself thinking of an article I read in the paper about two villages in the Kielce area, one called Niebo (Heaven), the other Piekło (Hell). The two villages had for years had separate municipalities, but recently, regional authorities have decided that the two must merge. The problem lay in the name to be given the new entity. Each village insisted on the adoption of *its* established name, but after considerable squabbling, Niebo finally won.

Odd as it sounds (why would people name their village Piekło in the first place?), the story happens to be both true and truly emblematic of my own Kielce experience. I have come to this town through a chance encounter, carrying a mental image of hellish suffering, only to have it superseded if not by heaven, then at least something I would have had as much trouble believing in: the selfless, exquisite, unforgettable—and wholly undeserved—comfort of strangers.

CHAPTER 16

T HE ARABS BELIEVE it all began with Noah's great-great grandson, a man named Baz who acquired a reputation for capturing and taming wild horses. Though scholars disagree about the date of the horse's earliest domestication (some say 3000, and others 5000 B.C.), it is generally believed that the first breed of horses with a surviving lineage was in fact established by the Arabs. Certainly, horse breeding was well developed in Arabia by the seventh century, as suggested by the Koran's injunction against the cross-breeding of Arabian horses.

The horse was valued by the people of antiquity* as much for its labor potential as the advantage it offered in organized warfare. Starting in 1500 B.C., when it was first used in Mesopotamia, until World War I, the horse was an indispensable feature in various nations' warfare. Alexander the Great's spectacular conquests in 330 B.C. were largely due to his rejection of clumsy chariots in favor of light, swift horses. Similar breeds also facilitated the eighth-century Mohammedan Conquest, and the thirteenth-century establishment of the Mongol Empire.

In the culture of medieval Europe too, horses and knights became the norm on the battlefield. By then, however, heavy armor was in common use, a fact that explains the emergence of the European warhorse. Much larger and sturdier than its predecessor, the warhorse was able to carry its own, as well as its master's, armor. It was only in the 1300s, after the introduction of gunpowder, that the warhorse was replaced in Europe by the swift, light steeds bred in Arabia.

---

*An interesting exception is the case of the early Hebrews who resolutely failed to exploit the horse. Moses, speaking of a king's appointment, says: ". . .but he shall not multiply horses to himself, nor cause the people to return to Egypt."

Among European nations, Poland's military history has long been distinguished by its celebrated cavalry regiments, particularly the winged cavalry of the Hussars. These fierce warriors traditionally wore wooden arcs bristling with eagle feathers, which rose over their heads like two wings. Not only did these prevent the Tatars from lassoing a rider as they were wont to do, but also, in conjunction with the tiger or leopard skin worn as a battle cloak, often succeeded in frightening the enemy's own horses. The Hussars were largely responsible for the Poles' triumph over the Turks in Vienna, as well as over the Teutonic Knights. Having survived one such battle against the Polish Hussars, a German knight was shaken so profoundly that he waxed remarkably poetic, writing:

> . . .As they drew near, galloping in the wind, the feathers began to mourn, or to chant like old women at a funeral, or like witches at a false Sabbath, and then to shriek as the wind tore at them. I got frightened by the weird sound and the hellish echoes, but my horse became terrified. He reared and whinnied and the effect on the other horses was the same, so that by the time the Polish Hussars reached our battle line, all was in confusion.
>
> I can state without fear or apology: the Polish cavalry did not defeat us in fair battle. They sang us to death with those damned feathers.

Interestingly, the great power of the "wings" on the battlefield came as much of a surprise to the Poles as to their enemies, for their intended purpose was far more modest. It was quite simply an expression of Poles' obsession with military splendor. In Poland, horses were traditionally associated with warrior status, but they were also symbols of aristocratic wealth, their number in a nobleman's stable a common indicator of the family's status. Whatever their number, an aristocrat's horses were habitually pampered and glorified and shown off in public, often accompanying their owner on his various outings. On special occasions, a nobleman might have his horses dyed some bright color, but they were always as lavishly decorated as the nobleman's means permitted. In addition to wings and feathers, a horse might be covered in resplendent silk or velvet, its saddle and bridle embroidered in gold or studded with precious stones.

Given this extraordinary reverence for horses, it is not surprising that Poles have been breeding Arabians longer than anyone else in Europe.

Famous in the equestrian world, they take great pride in their dedication and expertise, their current satisfaction inflated by the fact that the Arabs, who had virtually stopped breeding horses when oil was discovered, are now forced to buy their Arabians from Polish stud farms.

There are four such farms in Poland, the most celebrated of them situated in the small eastern town of Janów Podlaski, right up against the border of Belarus. The farm was established in 1816 by czar Alexander I who wished to ensure a personal supply of top-quality Arabians.

Bred for desert conditions, Arabians are prized above all for their stamina and speed, but also for their beauty, intelligence, and good temper. Ancestral to many of today's light breeds, Arabians belong to the southern stock of hot-blooded horses, as distinct from the northern cold-blooded one. So valued are these horses and so highly prized those bred at Janów Podlaski that the farm is an annual mecca for international horse enthusiasts. Some of the world's most prestigious championships have been won by Polish-bred Arabians, an occasional one purchased by celebrities such as Jane Fonda and the Rolling Stones' Charlie Watts.

There are no celebrities the day I arrive at Janów Podlaski, but I am treated like one, having been invited to visit by Andrzej Krzyształowicz, the outgoing director. Krzyształowicz is a man whose life has been dedicated to horses. He has worked at the stud farm for fifty-three years, thirty-three of them as its highly respected director. He is a tall, distinguished-looking man, elegantly dressed in suit and tie despite the summer weather. It is, in fact, a hot, sunny day, but Krzyształowicz shows no sign of discomfort or fatigue. Emanating Old World charm and courtesy, he shows me around the farm, sharing some of his impressive knowledge. He tells me that the ancient Greeks wrote about horsemanship as far back as 400 B.C. ("and we still follow their principles today") and quotes a Bedouin saying: "Every grain of barley given to a horse is entered by God in the Registry of Good Deeds."

To Krzyształowicz, working with horses is clearly nothing but a labor of love. Though I have never been much of an equestrian fan, Krzyształowicz's enthusiasm is almost infectious. It is the day before the annual Janów Podlaski auction and some five hundred spectators have come to the show, the judges sitting under canvas awnings, the visitors on bleachers in the glaring sun. They will sit here for hours, some sheltered beneath parasols and newspaper hats, others squinting against the afternoon light, turning tomato red.

Not all the spectators are potential horse buyers. Sixty to eighty horses are sold annually at Janów Podlaski, most of them to Germans and other Europeans. Poles are seldom in a position to buy an Arabian, but many of them are horse enthusiasts. In recent years, horseback riding—once the aristocrats' exclusive domain—has become so popular in Poland that travel agencies have begun to offer vacation packages advertised as Holidays in the Saddle.

"Look at the mane! Look at that arched back!" a spectator exclaims in an awed voice while Krzysztalowicz smiles with a paternal blend of pride and determined modesty. In a "breeding" show (as opposed to "performance" or "horsemanship" shows), the horses are led in by the handler and made to trot around the ring. Eventually, they go past the panel of judges, who will rank them on "conformation"—the physical qualities most representative of the breed.

Arabians are compact, relatively small horses with a gazellelike skull, flaring nostrils, short back, and a light, bounding gallop. I concede they look splendid, but Krzysztalowicz reminds me that they are equally good performers, capable of covering almost 100 miles a day.

How much would one have to pay for an Arabian? Krzysztalowicz raises his gray eyebrows: not all Arabians are born equal, it seems. A mare typically costs $4,000 to $5,000, says Krzysztalowicz, but the prices vary greatly. "Charlie Watts from the Rolling Stones bought one for $75,000, but you could buy one for your daughter for as little as $1,000."

The reference to my daughter startles me a little because, as it happens, I too have been thinking of Ranya, remembering how, at the age of nine, she informed me she wanted a horse for her birthday. A horse! I was a single parent who somehow managed to pay for private schools, violin lessons, Disney World, mountain bike—but I could not buy her a horse. I explained this to her and she understood, she said. But all the same, having seen me fulfill every one of her previous wishes, she went on hoping for a horse, drawing it all over her school workbooks, talking to it in her dreams. Eventually, *horse* became the word for her dawning knowledge that no matter what your blessings, no matter how much someone loved you, there would always be something unattainable; a longing you simply had to learn to live with.

In recent years, the price of Arabians has dropped all over the world, reflecting a sharp decrease in American demand. This has been largely due to the introduction in the U.S. of a new tax on luxury horses, the decline of the American dollar, and general rise in related expenses. On the other hand, the Poles no longer have to worry about Soviet competition; nor, for that matter, the Egyptian. Desperate for foreign currency, the latter have oversold their best horses to Americans and are, at least for the time being, out of the international market.

"So what is the secret of Janów Podlaski's success?" I eventually ask Krzysztalowicz.

"The secret?" He smiles complacently. "What can I tell you? It's not an exact science. We Poles just seem to have an instinct for breeding speed and endurance. We've been at it for so long, you see."

All the same, Janów Podlaski has had its ups and downs. Badly decimated by Germans in World War I, the new stock was taken over by the Nazis in World War II, and shipped over to the Reich. Many of Janów Podlaski's finest Arabians eventually died in the 1944 Dresden bombing.

I learn all this while Krzysztalowicz shows me the elegant stable complex, designed in the 1830s and '40s. The horses in the stables will be sold in a silent auction and there is a constant flow of visitors, some with children, pausing to scrutinize the animals. Krzysztalowicz overhears a child ask whether horses sleep and stops to tell him that these horses sleep standing up, often dozing with their eyes wide open; in the wild, horses lie down to sleep.

"What about the salt?" asks the child, pointing. "Why do they eat so much salt?" Horses, explains Krzysztalowicz, lose a great deal of salt while sweating and so require frequent replenishment.

This reminds me of a Bruce Chatwin book in which he wrote of the odd phenomenon of Arabian horses occasionally "sweating blood." There was, the book stated, some speculation about a small parasite causing the bleeding, but none of the English or German breeders I met earlier ever heard of it.

"That's because they've never seen Arabians in the desert," Krzysztalowicz says, chuckling. He says the phenomenon has nothing to do with parasites, only with extremely high temperatures that cause the horses' skin to crack, their blood mingling with their perspiration.

Is it true, I wonder, that a horse will often eat to the point of death, not knowing when to stop?

"Not an Arabian," Krzysztalowicz says. "They're too intelligent for that." The horse apparently has a small stomach and requires light, frequent feedings. All horses tend to overeat, especially if given oats, which they all adore. "That's why we usually give them hay to start with, to discourage them from eating too much too fast."

I ask Krzysztalowicz about a horse's lifespan, which turns out to be about eighteen; an Arabian's is twenty-five, with an occasional one living to the ripe old age of thirty-five, says my host.

Throughout my visit, Krzysztalowicz has been repeatedly stopped and warmly greeted by both Poles and foreigners. On our way out of the stables, he runs into a woman who owns a stud farm in Austria. This reminds him of the time when a horse the Austrian had purchased fell somewhat ill and could not be immediately transported across the border. The Austrian came every day and fed her ailing horse, giving an occasional carrot to the Arabian foal in the adjacent stall. Two years later, at an international auction, the Austrian found herself greeted with a great show of excitement by the now-adult Arabian, who still remembered the carrots it had been given in its youth.

"That's an Arabian for you," says Krzysztalowicz as we cross the lawn. "It forms strong attachments to us foolish humans, and once taught something, it never forgets."

CHAPTER 17

NOT KNOWING ANYTHING about Arabians, my mother used to tell her friends that her daughter had the memory of an elephant. She herself had a rather poor memory, and even as a young woman was often astonished by my recollection of childhood events in Poland, some of which had taken place before my brother's birth when I was three years old. But all that was in Israel, when I was still very young. Eventually, most of these memories got buried by the dust of time, and it is only now, after all these years, that they have started to resurface. Since my visit to Łódź, everywhere I go something reminds me of my childhood, and the Pomeranian town of Toruń is certainly no exception.

I don't know how old I was when my mother bought me a monkey for a pet, but I know it was Christmastime, in Łódź. What reminds me of it is an organ-grinder I come across at the Toruń train station—a wizened, dark-complexioned man, perhaps a Gypsy—with a small monkey sitting on his shoulder. The monkey looks much like mine did: a brown, half-grown creature resembling a bewildered infant. It has small, brown eyes, closely set under a low forehead, and a long, curly tail. It chews on its fist and wrinkles its forehead at a group of jovial boys.

How did my mother come to buy me a monkey? I don't know, though I will, on returning home, try to jog her atrophying memory. She will not only fail to recall the monkey, she will not even understand my question. "Monkey? What's a monkey?" she will ask, looking as bewildered as my childhood pet.

All I know is that my mother bought me the monkey as a Christmas present. We had never celebrated Christmas before, but my mother—a lively, impulsive woman—must have been swept along by the spirit of

Polish celebration. She did not think of it in religious terms, but the monkey came with a small Christmas tree, and I am not sure which of the two shocked my father more, the monkey swinging in its cage, or the decorated tree beside the piano. He was speechless for much of the evening, saving his rage until I was asleep, when their quarrel woke me up. Not for the last time, my mother was mystified by my father's anger; she would never understand his apparently contradictory attitudes toward his own religion. She was not yet thirty and it seemed simple to her: he did not appear to bear any allegiance to Jewish traditions, so why should he object to an ornamented tree? My mother was the sort of person who loves celebration and, living with my father, was deprived of both Jewish and Christian opportunities. The Christmas tree had to go; the monkey stayed for some weeks but then, having bitten a neighbor's child, was also given away.

I give the organ-grinder a coin, then head for the bus, which will take me to a town I am about to fall in love with. Founded early in the thirteenth century on the Vistula, Toruń is the best-preserved Gothic town in Poland, and one of the most beautiful. Though here, too, there are the usual nondescript suburbs, the town has an extraordinary historic core. I have no contacts in Toruń, but have managed to reserve a room at a very modest hotel with a glamorous past: Peter the Great and Jan Matejko are both said to have stayed at the Three Crowns. Unsure of my stop, I seek directions from a group of young people sitting across from me on the bus. They are also getting off in the center, they tell me, and will show me the way. They turn out to be students at the local Nikolaus Copernicus University, an institution named after Toruń's most celebrated son. As we walk toward the market square, I inquire about the Copernicus Museum, unexpectedly finding myself in possession of a scoop. One of my guides, a local history student, tells me that a Polish academic has just discovered that the building housing the Copernicus Museum is not in fact the eminent astronomer's birthplace as is widely believed. The actual birthplace is on our way, and the student points it out to me, saying I may well be the first foreigner to hear about it.

The putative birthplace is half burnt down and crumbling, but the official one, which I eventually visit, is an exquisitely restored redbrick Gothic mansion with period interiors; an elegant residence typical of a wealthy merchant family living in Toruń when the town was a prosperous member of the Hanseatic League. If the history student's information is correct, this house did belong to the Copernicus family, though not in 1473, when Nikolaus was born. He spent his childhood and adolescence in Toruń, leaving it to pursue studies in Kraków and then Italy. Ordained as a priest, Copernicus turned out to be a true Renaissance man, working as an administrator, doctor, lawyer, architect, and soldier. He moved around so much that Poland's travel brochures speak of the Copernicus Route, each town boasting its connection with the man who "stopped the sun and moved the earth." His longest residence was in Frombork, where he built an observatory and pursued his astronomical studies for thirty years while serving as canon of the local cathedral.

The Toruń Museum is rich in Copernicus artifacts, including astronomical instruments and a 1617 edition of *De revolutionibus orbium coelestium.* The first treatise to set forth the theory of a heliocentric universe, it was published when Copernicus was on his deathbed, having finally completed the work that would form the foundation of modern astronomy. One does not normally go to museums to be entertained, but in Poland this often happens in unexpected ways. Tourists arriving at Warsaw's Royal Castle, for example, are amazed to have to leave their shoes behind and don a pair of slippers in order to protect the shiny parquet floors. The slippers come in various sizes, kept in a large bin at the entrance. The day I was there, a large group of Elderhostel tourists was sitting on the benches at the entrance, taking off their shoes and calling out to each other, "Have you got a right-foot seven? I've got a *left*-foot seven and a *right*-foot nine!" This went on for a good while and seemed to be more fun than the castle's opulent interiors.

I am allowed to keep my shoes at the Copernicus Museum but it occurs to me this is only so that the museum staff can hear my footfall. The attendants stand on the threshold to each room and, hearing approaching steps, hasten to turn on the lights—and promptly turn them off again the moment a room is vacant.

Though the Copernicus Museum has been meticulously and authentically restored, many of Toruń's mansions are undergoing less orthodox architectural transformations, combining familiar Gothic elements with ultramodern features such as metal and glass. This recent trend is a controversial one in Toruń, most of the renovations having been undertaken by banks and insurance companies. Some of the handsomest restoration work has gone into the creation of hotels and restaurants housed in ancient mansions, which before 1989 no one had the funds to salvage. I decide to have lunch at one of them, situated in a splendid fourteenth-century town house with high wooden ceilings and Gothic brickwork. Having finished a delicious dish of duck with apples, I linger over my cappuccino, with a Chopin sonata playing in the background, and the sun streaming in through the tall, diamond-paned windows.

Eventually, I go back to sight-seeing, making my way through the Old Town, founded in 1233, and the so-called New Town, added on thirty-three years later. Toruń was largely built by the Teutonic Knights, as an outpost against the Poles. So rapid was the growth of this riverside town that newly arrived merchants and craftsmen found themselves forced to settle outside the city walls. Thus the New Town. In time, the Teutonic Knights' heavy-handed rule brought about a revolt, which, triggering a thirteen-year war, effectively ended the Teutons' rule in Toruń. The town remained a major center of Renaissance culture, religion, and academic life but fell into decline through the Swedish wars and internecine conflicts between Protestants and Catholics. With the Partitions, the city was annexed by West Prussia, where, with one brief interlude, it remained until 1919. It was the Versailles Treaty that returned Toruń to Poland as part of the Polish Corridor—one of the towns Hitler was determined to reclaim for the Reich.

Miraculously, the town emerged from the war intact and has managed to preserve its highly evocative center. Though the Teutonic castle is mostly in ruins, Toruń's fourteenth-century fortification walls are still standing along the river, bastions and buttresses supporting the imposing, well-preserved city gates. Toruń's ancient center is a bewitching maze of crooked medieval streets and alleys, with magnificent churches, granaries, and fine museums housed in exquisite historic buildings. The town also has charming cafés and sweetshops specializing in local gingerbread. Known by its German name—*Pfefferkuchen*—gingerbread made Toruń famous as far back as the Middle Ages, when the town vied with Nuremberg for a monopoly of the confectionery trade. So fierce was the competition between the two towns that in the sixteenth century, a formal agreement was finally signed, permitting each city to sell the other's product. I buy an ornate, Copernicus-shaped cookie at a fragrant Toruń bakery and munch on it while promenading down the fifteenth-century bridge. Eventually, I arrive at one of Toruń's landmarks: the Leaning Tower. A fourteenth-century defense structure, the tower leans somewhat like that of the more famous Pisa, due to the instability of the ground. This prosaic explanation, however, has in no way stemmed the proliferation of local legends. A girl's purity, they say here, can be put to the test simply by standing her with her back up against the Leaning Tower. If her purity has been compromised, she is bound to fall flat on her face, I'm told.

The person who tells me this is a local artist named Janusz Bogacki. He has an attractive gift boutique in the Leaning Tower but when I first see him is so absorbed in his work that he seems utterly oblivious to the browsing shoppers. Among other things, the boutique sells a good deal of handblown glassware made by Bogacki. Though most of the items on sale are aimed at the tourist trade, my interest is caught by several glass pieces of astonishing beauty. Fragile as icicles, the polymorphous sculptures capture in glass something elusive and inexplicably poignant; they are the sculptural equivalent of a haiku. Later, I will be shown more of them and will learn that Bogacki's work has been exhibited all over Poland. I would love to have one of them but can't imagine getting it safely to Montreal.

And so I leave the boutique and go to explore the tower, finding myself shortly in a dim upstairs pub. The place is deserted, except for a friendly waitress who, when I ask questions about the tower, tells me to sit down and wait while she makes a phone call. To my surprise, the person who appears soon after is Bogacki himself: a tall, Nordic-looking man in his late thirties with fair hair gathered into a ponytail. There is something about him I find vaguely intriguing, a rare air of self-containment and quiet pride, touched by melancholy.

He sits down to have a beer, having left his young daughter in charge downstairs. I soon learn what is apparently behind the gravity: Bogacki's wife died in a car crash in 1992, and he has been raising his three young children alone. Though it can't have been easy, Bogacki tells me about his wife without a trace of self-pity. A quiet dignity informs his speech and movements. The only time I see him smile is when he narrates one of the legends associated with the tower.

Once upon a time, a soldier was standing guard on top of the tower when he spotted a beautiful girl in one of the windows across the narrow street. Smitten, the soldier kept leaning toward her window, gradually taking the tower with him.

After a while, Bogacki takes me up a winding staircase to the top of the tower, where he proposes to show me a unique bird's-eye view of Toruń. My heart in my throat, I follow him up a creaky ladder toward the roof, waiting unsteadily while he opens up a trapdoor to reveal a breathtaking vista of red-tiled roofs and lofty Gothic steeples outlined against a spectacular orange-streaked sky. Down on the tiny street, children are playing ball, Bogacki's son among them. The sun is beginning to set, the shops to close their shutters. Swallows are swooping under ancient eaves while, somewhere behind us, a turtledove calls and calls.

"So, what do you think of Toruń?" Janusz Bogacki asks.

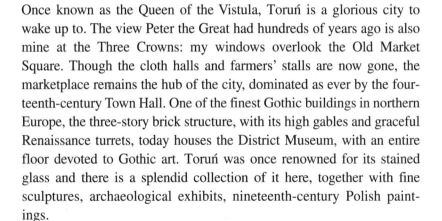

Once known as the Queen of the Vistula, Toruń is a glorious city to wake up to. The view Peter the Great had hundreds of years ago is also mine at the Three Crowns: my windows overlook the Old Market Square. Though the cloth halls and farmers' stalls are now gone, the marketplace remains the hub of the city, dominated as ever by the fourteenth-century Town Hall. One of the finest Gothic buildings in northern Europe, the three-story brick structure, with its high gables and graceful Renaissance turrets, today houses the District Museum, with an entire floor devoted to Gothic art. Toruń was once renowned for its stained glass and there is a splendid collection of it here, together with fine sculptures, archaeological exhibits, nineteenth-century Polish paintings.

Having stopped for breakfast, I walk about the Old Town, admiring the stately burghers' mansions with their high parapets and ornate facades. There is a monument to Copernicus in the square and, a little farther on, a fountain with bronze frogs overlooked by the statue of a young violinist. The fountain commemorates another legendary event, one that began with the arrival in town of an unwelcome witch. Turned away, the witch put a curse on the town, bringing on an amphibian invasion of calamitous proportions. Desperate, the mayor offered a sack of gold and his daughter to any man who would rid Toruń of this pestilence, a feat finally accomplished by a young peasant who reportedly led the frogs out of town with his violin. In Poland, it seems, not only rats but frogs too are susceptible to musical magic.

I have been walking aimlessly for about an hour when I find myself at the end of a narrow side street, distracted by nearby shouts. Turning the corner, I find a young woman standing alone on the sidewalk, her eyes raised toward a pseudo-Gothic tower. She is, I see, carrying on a conversation with someone in one of the top windows. The person in the tower is barely visible, but answering my question, a passerby tells me this is the local jail. Having for years heard my parents disparage the cushy Canadian penal system, I waste no time in trying to find out how things are done in a Polish jail. I arrive at the entrance along with a harried-looking lawyer and present my press card. Is there by any chance someone who might have a few minutes to spare, I ask the uniformed guard.

I am ushered in, presented to another guard, asked to wait while phone calls are made. I sit in front of the barred fence, thinking of some of the things I have recently read about Poland's judiciary system. With urban crime ever on the rise, Polish courts are said to be groaning under the weight of unresolved cases. Sometimes litigants are in court longer than they are in prison. This is only partly due to the rising crime rate. Much of it has to do with the high dropout rate of Polish judges. Since the average judge earns between 1,000 and 1,200 złoty a month (about $500 to $600), many ambitious men and women are leaving the courts to practice corporate law. In recent years, Poland has lost more than 25 percent of its judges, while the number of court cases has increased by over 20 percent.

Eventually, a woman comes out to greet me. The prison psychologist, she has an appointment in fifteen minutes but will gladly answer my questions until then, when the warden will take over. The Toruń jail, she tells me, was built in 1856 and is a short-term institution. Those who receive prolonged sentences end up getting transferred to other jails. Her job is to assess each prisoner as he comes in, and to encourage rehabilitation. For many, this means learning a trade or finishing high school; for others, enrollment in a drug rehabilitation program.

What are the most frequent crimes around here?

"Oh, mostly robberies and burglaries and car theft. Increasingly, failure to pay alimony."

I have read that every forty minutes, a woman is raped somewhere in Poland, but the psychologist says that since most rapes go unreported, these are estimates whose accuracy is difficult to gauge. Sexual crime is definitely on the rise, though. Poland even has its own serial killer now, a notoriously sadistic one convicted of some fifty sexual murders.

The psychologist is curious about my reasons for visiting the jail, so I tell her about the views of people like my parents who feel that Canada would have fewer repeat offenders if only they spent time in a real jail instead of a resort. "I wanted to see what a real jail looks like," I say, eliciting a sudden smile.

Toruń's jail is, of course, different from high-security jails, says the psychologist, but things have changed in Poland since 1989. Only recently a Russian arrested for armed robbery stated that compared with a Russian jail, a Polish one is like a spa. In Russia the system is still largely punitive, but in Poland— "Well, we are trying hard to learn more humanitarian ways."

At this point, the warden comes in, rather surprising me. He is a mild-featured, gentle-mannered man, more easily imagined teaching high school than running a penal institution. He listens attentively and speaks with an air of quiet amusement. Would I like a tour, he asks.

I follow the warden up a spiral staircase surrounded by bars to a large recreation area with a pool table, a VCR, a small library. The librarian says the books are mostly pre-Communist and of little interest to the prisoners. There is great demand for horror and crime fiction.

I ask the warden whether there are special prisons for women, impressed to learn that Poland now has remote penal communities where women can live and work, the mothers among them permitted to keep their children until the age of three. Even in old jails, conditions have improved in recent years. In 1989, for example, the Toruń jail housed three hundred inmates; today, it has half as many, only two to five in each cell.

We stop and look into one of them through a peephole, something I have never done before. Two young men in jeans are sitting at a small table, playing cards, looking no different, and no less jovial, than students in a Canadian cafeteria. There are bunk beds with rough blankets, a toilet with a curtain, a large poster of Madonna. Also, a television, which, the warden hastens to tell me, was provided by the family.

I ask whether it's true that prisoners are better fed than hospital patients, and he says quite likely. Authorities know that patients' families will see to it that they are properly fed, whereas this is seldom true of prisoners' families.

"How do Poles feel about capital punishment?" I ask when the warden, too, mentions the serial killer. Three-quarters of them are in favor of the death penalty, which is still officially on the books. "In actual fact, no executions have taken place in Poland since 1989," states the warden. "Not a single one."

I think I detect a note of pride but can't be sure. The warden hastens to tell me that though they do everything they can to improve prison conditions, Polish sentences are tougher than in Western Europe. A thief, for example, might get anywhere between six months and five years, a murderer a minimum of fifteen years. As the warden ushers me back to the reception area, I remember having read recently about a Warsaw pickpocket, a woman who had been sentenced to a year in jail as well as a fine, and tried to appeal the sentence. "Your Honor," she argued, "I am sure my conscience would be just as easily touched by a lighter sentence." Criminals, it seems, have caught on to the newly benign spirit of the judiciary system. All the same, the pickpocket was not successful in her bid.

Out on the street, across from the jail, there are two women now, one of them young, the other ravaged-looking. The older woman is carrying on a conversation from the corner—a tirade, really, against someone named Andrzej. She stands among passersby, her head flung back, cursing at the top of her voice, while the teenager leans on her shoulder, pale and thin faced, silent tears rolling down her face.

I did not, I must confess, find the jail particularly depressing. The older woman's jaded face and the young woman's tears get to me, however, possibly because their appearance opens the door to yet another childhood memory.

I was perhaps eleven and living in Israel when my father was arrested on suspicion of dealing in stolen merchandise. It was all a terrible mistake. He was soon vindicated and released, but not before the news appeared in our small-town newspaper; not before everyone I knew had heard about it. It took no more than two or three days, but by then I knew what it was like to be a criminal's daughter. To be talked about in whispers. To see my mother's face collapse in the grocery, and hear her muffled sobs late into the night.

The last thing I do in Toruń before catching the train to Poznań is have a late-afternoon dinner. I have spent much of the day visiting Toruń's churches and museums and, walking through the New Town, come across a place named For Your Last Penny. It is a tiny eatery that, my guidebook tells me, offers tasty Polish cuisine for under $3. I go in to have a look, and find myself being hailed by the history student I met on my first day here. He is sitting in the corner with two friends and cordially invites me to join them. One of his companions is his girlfriend; the other a thin Palestinian engineering student named Belal. The girl's name is Luisa, and she is studying political science, hoping for a career in national politics. Why politics?

"Either that or journalism," Luisa says. "Something that might help improve the lot of Polish women." Luisa is an intense young woman with flaming red hair, and relevant statistics at her fingertips. Women earn about 30 percent less than men in the same occupations. They are more likely to be fired or laid off, especially given the current rate of unemployment. Her sister recently had a baby but so feared losing her job that she decided against taking a maternity leave. "Something she is entitled to by law," points out Luisa.

I must look somewhat incredulous, for Jurek, the history student, says it is not at all uncommon these days. To tell the truth, Polish women are being encouraged to drop out of the workforce altogether, mostly in hopes of eliminating the job competition. Many Poles still feel that a man needs a job more than a woman. All of which has given birth to a new Polish trend—a move back toward "traditional family values."

Jurek draws the quotation marks with his fingers, looking at me through his round spectacles. His statement comes as something of a surprise, given Polish propensity to emulate Western trends. It seems even more surprising in light of the fact that in the Communist bloc, women were expected to join the workforce as a matter of course, often taking up occupations traditionally held by men.

"Yes," says Luisa, "yes, but the truth is they seldom attained top positions in any of these countries." What's more, having been subjected to half a century of Communist pressures, Polish women are feeling a certain nostalgia for traditional female roles.

"It's ironic, isn't it," elaborates Jurek, "but there seems to be a sort of reaction to all that Communist sloganeering." Equality for All may sound great, but the idea is so charged with Soviet associations that there is a grassroots tendency to reject it out of hand.

At this point I suddenly remember Beata, the Białystok prostitute, and her open hostility toward Polish feminists. I am curious to know what my companions will make of it. To my surprise, Luisa says she understands Beata's reaction; it is not at all an unusual one in Poland. What many Polish women resent these days is the pressure from high-powered, privileged feminists urging ordinary women to eschew their dependence on their men; to hold on to their jobs, to report violent husbands. "What they don't understand," says Luisa, "is that for lots of women, dependence on a man is preferable any day to a backbreaking job that brings in a few miserable złoty and takes them away from their children."

"What I think people don't understand," says Belal, who has been silent so far, "is that Polish women are quite simply tired. All those years of working from morning to night, of lining up for food, of worrying about arrests. People think women in the Muslim world have it bad, but if you ask me, women in Eastern Europe have been much worse off, and many of them still are."

"Oh, I don't know about that," says Luisa, "but you're definitely right about the fatigue." Millions of Polish women spend their days at some wretched job that is supposed to make them feel liberated, only to rush home to shop and raise their children, and take care of all the domestic chores. "They don't have husbands who do the dishes, or dishwashers and such. You can't really blame them for shutting their ears to feminist propaganda, can you?"

Jurek tells me he has an aunt married to a man who beats her up whenever he gets drunk, which he apparently does with some regularity. She hates the feminists because they make her feel guilty for putting up with him. Her feeling of inadequacy, of weakness, is worse than the beatings. Jurek shrugs at this. "But what is she supposed to do? Where is she supposed to go with three young children, I ask you?"

Domestic violence, says Luisa, is a serious problem in Poland. Every fourth family reportedly experiences some masculine aggression aimed at a woman. Unfortunately, authorities usually choose to close their eyes to the evidence, treating it as a private "family matter." And though there are some new women's organizations founded to help female victims, they are hardly in a position to provide all the support needed.

"What's needed," says Belal, "is a social structure that takes care of women's and men's needs. When men are unemployed, they lose their masculine pride and, well, they end up taking their frustrations out on their women."

The comment arouses Luisa's pique, and they argue for a while while I finish my cutlet and crisp potato pancakes. When they finally calm down and I ask Belal how he likes living in Poland, he looks faintly discomfited.

"It's okay," he says. "I'm getting a good education anyway."

Jurek makes a vaguely scornful sound, glancing at Belal, and then addressing me. "You know," he says, "we Poles are no more enlightened about minorities than we are about women. We do have laws against harassing people because of their religion or race, but there are still a lot of hooligans in Poland, even in a university town like Toruń."

I look at Belal for a moment. "Are you harassed here because you are an Arab?" I ask pointedly.

"From time to time," he says. "It's not as bad as it is for African students, but it does happen."

I have seen only two Africans in Poland, but I am told there are hundreds of them, and that they are sometimes taunted in public. In Poznań, two black basketball players were recently beaten up in a bar. "People keep trying to provoke us," says Belal, "and sometimes they succeed."

"It's like this," says Jurek. "Many Poles suffer from low self-esteem, you see; it's not their fault, but they do. And so they look for someone they can turn on. If it's not the Jews, it's Third World refugees or students. That's how it is."

At this, Belal smiles wryly. "The difference," he says, "is that anti-semitism is not politically correct any more, is it, while prejudice against Arabs is still out in the open."

Here he is right, of course, and not only about Poland. Having stopped in London, I know that there are anti-Muslim sentiments among the English too, fueled by the popular notion that all Arabs are either terrorists or oil tycoons.

Though I say goodbye soon after, I continue to dwell on this conversation long after I board the train to Poznań. I sit looking out the window at the fading countryside, recalling Sartre's famous statement that antisemitism lets any idiot feel a member of an elite. I think about this because of Jurek's views on Poles' low self-esteem, but no doubt too because two skinheads happen to be sitting across the aisle from me, looking very pale and quiet but somehow conspiratorial. They pay no attention to me, or anyone else on the train, but their presence makes me vaguely uneasy. Antisemitism may not be politically correct in some circles, but I shudder to think what these two might do if they happened to see me reading a Hebrew book, for example. Fortunately they soon fall asleep, looking all at once young and tired and vulnerable, like two overgrown children dressed up for Halloween.

It is dusk by now, and the windmills in the distance are all shrouded in eerie mist, with a violently red sun setting on the horizon. Here and there, a lone farmer stands raking, or gathering vegetables; a peasant woman walks her cow home; children climb a plum tree, vanishing behind a passing train. The train whistles and flashes by, giving way once more to enveloping mist. I think of the books on my shelves, the pictures on my walls, the plants at my windows; above all, of my distant daughter. They all exist, I remind myself, as do my friends, my parents. Beyond the mist, the forests, the trains, is my own home. I remind myself that I too have one.

CHAPTER 18

COUNTESS MARIA WALEWSKA was eighteen when she met Napoleon Bonaparte, and had been married for three years to a Polish nobleman, living on his ancestral estate outside Warsaw. Ever since the Third Partition in 1795, Warsaw had belonged to Prussia, but after his 1806 triumph over the Prussians, Napoleon swept into the Polish capital, soon establishing the Grand Duchy of Warsaw—a sovereign Polish state made up of a tiny part of Prussian-annexed territory.

After the victory over their mutual enemy, Napoleon was positively revered by the francophile Polish aristocrats, Maria Walewska among them. The countess was married but Napoleon, unable to father an heir with Josephine, had had his own marriage annulled. For the next three years, he had numerous trysts with his beautiful Polish mistress, in Warsaw as well as Paris. The romance finally came to an end when Napoleon remarried in 1810, the same year in which Walewska gave birth to Napoleon's son. Christened Alexandre Walewski, the boy was an orphan by the age of seven, having lost first his adoptive father and then his remarried mother who died at age twenty-eight. Napoleon fully acknowledged his paternity, bestowing both land and title on his Polish progeny. At age fourteen, determined to avoid conscription into czarist Russia's army, Alexandre Walewski escaped to London, then made his way to Paris.

After Tadeusz Kościuszko's failed 1794 insurrection, thousands of Poles had taken up residence in revolutionary France, plotting Poland's independence. The expatriates included luminaries such as Adam Mickiewicz and Frédéric Chopin, who was never to see his beloved

Poland again. In 1830, many intellectuals, including Napoleon's son, joined another anticzarist uprising, Walewski soon going to England to plead Poland's cause. When this revolt also failed, Walewski returned to Paris, where he eventually had an illustrious career in politics and diplomacy, while also writing for the French press and stage.

Though it is sometimes said that Countess Walewska had been encouraged by the Polish aristocracy to ingratiate herself with Napoleon on patriotic grounds, another view holds that she was seduced by the unscrupulous Corsican along with the rest of her people.

"I want to see whether the Poles deserve to be a nation!" he had declared on entering Poznań, and the Poles kept flocking to join his armies, convinced he was to be their savior. They fought his battles in Europe, and in distant lands like Haiti, where a Polish legion had been sent to crush a slave revolt, only to perish from swamp fever. Eventually, there would be the doomed 1812 Russian campaign, for which many more Poles would give their lives, Napoleon himself managing to escape with the protection of a Polish light cavalry.

Throughout all this, only Kościuszko had serious doubts about Napoleon, whom he saw as a megalomaniac out to exploit Poland. Having declined to command the Polish legions, Kościuszko would soon have the bitter satisfaction of finding himself vindicated. To this day, Poles speak rancorously of the fact that Napoleon toyed with their desperate ancestors, dangling the prospect of independence while he needed their participation, but losing interest after making peace with Austria and Prussia. When, in 1815, the Congress of Vienna was set up to organize post-Napoleonic Europe, the decision went against an independent Poland, including the short-lived Duchy of Warsaw.

Poland's French connection is first explained to me in Poznań, to which Napoleon had transferred his imperial headquarters from Berlin. The person who acquaints me with this particular chapter of Polish history is Dorota Fabré, whose husband happened to be a descendant of one of Napoleon's cavalry officers. Pani Fabré is the mother of lovely Alicja who, with her husband Adam, accompanied me to the Old Believer village outside Augustów. Having found a room at a Poznań pension, I called the two numbers Alicja had given me, to find one of them answered by her mother. Alicja and Adam were both in Ukraine, she informed me, having left recently on business. Retired, Pani Fabré was baby-sitting her two grandsons. Would I like to come over for afternoon tea?

Dorota Fabré lives in what seems to be one of the few private homes in the city. It is a two-family art deco dwelling, the top floor of which belongs to Alicja's widowed mother. Overlooking a formal garden with fruit trees and a goldfish pond, the flat is truly beautiful, full of inherited antiques and Turkish rugs, palms, books, pictures. Pani Fabré had worked as an art historian, and the walls are covered with many fine paintings, some by Polish artists who have become well known. Though Polish art is beginning to command increasingly high prices, most artists are not finding it easy these days, confirms Pani Fabré. In the old days, the state would organize exhibitions and sales, find suitable studios, and in general promote Polish artists' work. Alicja, who is a photographer, would be in dire straits today if it weren't for her husband's successful enterprise.

Adam Gutowski is in the pharmaceutical import business, a joint Polish-Swiss venture. He had intended to open a pharmacy, but so many Poles apparently had the same idea that, in 1991, he decided to take the plunge and start importing Swiss medications to Ukraine.

"Why Ukraine?"

"Well," says Pani Fabré, "it's a much better market than Poland, you see." Not only does Ukraine have a population of sixty million, but approval for new medications is far more easily obtained there than it is in Poland. The beginning was extremely difficult, however. Adam had to wait for three years before making his first transaction. Now, at last, the venture is going well, so well that Pani Fabré confesses to feeling somewhat uneasy. She has another daughter, also married to a businessman, and she is frankly ambivalent about their new prosperity. On the one hand, she is glad her daughters no longer have to scrimp and save; on the other, she can't quite get over her inner conviction that there is something undignified about a life dedicated to the accumulation of capital.

Dorota Fabré herself is nothing if not dignified. A white-haired, ramrod-straight matron, she has a probing blue gaze and what I have come to think of as typical Polish energy. Though she is in her sixties, her movements are both brisk and elegant. A daughter of the former landed gentry, she too is dismayed by the quick disappearance of traditional values, the growing vulgarity among Polish youth, the obsession with sex and consumerism. She is able to laugh at herself, though, pointing out that even Socrates used to complain about the youth of his day. She is bemused by the fact that young people who can barely spell are turning out to be technological wizards. It irks her, she admits, that they all seem to be able to master computers and cars whereas she, a woman with a doctorate, has twice failed her driver's test.

At this point, Pani Fabré's grandsons, who have been doing their homework in the kitchen, come into the living room for more cake and cookies, and have their manners corrected before being allowed to leave with replenished plates.

The children are dimpled, identical-twin boys of ten who strongly resemble their fair-haired mother. Actually, says Pani Fabré, they look exactly like her own father. She shows me a prewar sepia photograph of a youngish man, a dashing Poznań physician who, along with thousands of other Polish officers, was killed in the Katyń forest.

Some fifteen thousand officers are said to have lost their lives in Katyń, after being captured in the 1939 Soviet invasion of Poland. Most of them were not professional soldiers but reserve officers from the upper echelons of Polish society. In April 1943, more than four thousand of them were found dead in the Russian forest, all the others having disappeared without a trace.

"Out of fifteen thousand, only one escaped," Pani Fabré says, "and then only because he had been in Moscow, undergoing interrogation when the massacre took place." For years, the KGB claimed innocence in the Katyń affair. Pointing to the fact that the officers had been killed with German bullets, they insisted that the Nazis had committed the murders sometime in the winter of 1941. Though it was quickly pointed out that the Katyń corpses were all wearing summer uniforms, it was 1990 before the Soviets finally admitted their "error."

"Between the Germans and the Russians, we've lost Poland's crème de la crème," Pani Fabré states.

Although hostility toward the Germans is common enough among the elderly in Poland, there are those in Poznań who concede that their city, one of Poland's leading commercial centers, has derived certain benefits from the Prussians' 125-year rule. It is said to have left Poznań with a highly developed industrial base and infrastructure, as well as a strong work ethic. There is, in this part of Poland, a palpable pride in industriousness and efficiency; above all, in belonging to the capital of what is often referred to as "the cradle of Polish statehood."

The term refers to the central-western region known as Wielkopolska (Greater Poland), the lowlands that formed the original core of the Polish nation. The name *Poland* itself has come down from the local Polonians—a Slav tribe whose leaders, the Piasts, ruled the country for the first five centuries of its existence.

Poznań was founded in the ninth century, its strategic position on the east-west trade routes ensuring rapid economic development. By the tenth century, it was the most powerful stronghold in Poland and had the country's first house of Christian worship. Cathedral Island, where it all started, is still there in the Warta River, inhabited today only by priests and monks but attracting thousands with its renowned Basilica of Sts. Peter and Paul. Having been transferred to the left bank, Poznań flourished during the Renaissance, gradually becoming one of the most important and prosperous cities in Poland. Like Toruń, it embraced both humanism and the Reformation and, like the Pomeranian city, fell into decline with the Swedish invasions, to be annexed by Prussia in 1793.

Under Prussian rule for over a century, Poznań became a rallying point for Polish nationalism, the anti-Prussian sentiments finally flaring up in the 1918 Wielkopolska Uprising, an event that brought about a reunion with the resurrected Polish state.

Between this historic event and World War II, Poznań flourished anew, boasting a new university as well as an immensely successful International Trade Fair. Ever since the Middle Ages, there had been a tradition of out-of-town merchants coming to Poznań on St. John's Day (June 24) and the annual trade fair eventually took up that tradition. Today, the fair remains the focus of foreign commercial interests, with a million visitors attending it every summer.

That Prussian hegemony was, in less than three decades, replaced by the Russian is of course one of the bitter realities of Polish history. Once again Poznań proved resistant to foreign domination, giving birth to the first major uprising against Communism. Breaking out at the height of the 1956 International Trade Fair, the uprising began as a massive strike involving some twenty thousand workers but quickly turned into an armed revolt, with impassioned demands for more food, housing, free-dom. The unprecedented defiance of Poznań's protest took the regime by surprise, but the next day Soviet tanks rolled into Poznań, leaving more than seventy workers dead and some six hundred wounded. And yet, brutally crushed though it was, the Poznań uprising did succeed in bringing about significant changes in Communist leadership and is gen-erally regarded today as the precursor to Solidarity.

On my second morning in Poznań, Pani Fabré shows me the mas-sive monument to the victims of the Poznań strike, and the one to the Poznań army, which resisted the 1939 German invasion for three months. Following Polish defeat, the Nazis embarked on a new pro-gram of Germanization, the citizens' resistance leading to frequent arrests, executions, deportations, and extensive destruction.

"Our emblem, as you know, is the white eagle, but it should really be the phoenix," declares Pani Fabré.

With her grandsons at school, Alicja's mother has offered to accompany me on my walking tour through the Old City, and I once again congratulate myself on my good fortune in having landed such a keen, cultivated guide. Poznań, with its population of 600,000, is a city with a highly developed cultural life. It has its own opera, ballet, theater, and orchestra; museums, art galleries, music festivals. With its reconstructed historic center, its river and vast artificial lake, it is an attractive city, with numerous architectural gems ranging from the Romanesque to the Neoclassical. What with churches, fountains, palaces, and botanical gardens, I walk my feet off on my second day in Poznań, as awed by my elderly guide's stamina as I am by her knowledge. All over Poland, one comes across the uniquely Polish funerary artifacts known as *coffin portraits,* but it is only after the visit to the Gothic Cellars in Poznań's Town Hall that I learn something about their background.

Coffin portraits first appeared on the Polish aristocratic scene in the sixteenth century, becoming ubiquitous in the seventeenth and eigh-teenth centuries when noblemen's funerals were characterized by great pomp and ceremony. So resplendent were these occasions, and so lav-ish the accompanying feasts, that months, and sometimes even a year, might elapse between an aristocrat's death and his funeral. The time was spent in feverish preparation involving craftsmen, decorators, cooks, and artists hired to paint the final portrait of the deceased. Executed on wood or sheet metal, the hexagonal portrait would eventually be attached to the coffin to enable the deceased to participate, if only symbolically, in his own funeral. Accompanied by the family's coat of arms, the portrait was removed before burial, thereafter to be displayed on local church walls along with the deceased's heraldic shield. The occasional aristocrat preferring a more modest funeral had to remember to write it into his will.

"And even then his wishes might be circumvented," adds Pani Fabré. He would certainly get his modest funeral as requested, but the family might still hold the lavish one *they* preferred." She laughs.

This conversation, which takes place over a cup of a superb coffee in the Old Market Square, eventually leads to a discussion of another historic Polish oddity—a political one known as the *liberum veto*.

In the sixteenth century, when Polish kings began to be elected, the electorate came to include the gentry and clergy—about 10 percent of the population, Pani Fabré tells me.

"Ten percent were eligible to vote?"

"Yes, about 800,000 Poles. It doesn't sound like much, I know, but in fact it was the largest percentage of voters anywhere in Europe."

What made the system so remarkable was a utopian law demanding unanimous approval of any bill brought before the *Sejm* (parliament). This was the *liberum veto*, a practice that permitted any one of the 800,000 voters to veto a bill, or a king's election, effectively paralyzing the *Sejm*. Naturally, this led to heavy bribing of minor deputies, some of whom grew wealthy supporting an interested magnate's royal candidate.

"So who was the best king Poland ever had?" I ask Pani Fabré.

"In my view, Kazimierz the Great, but that was back in the fourteenth century."

"And he died without an heir, didn't he?"

"That's right." This reminds Pani Fabré of another funerary ritual. When the deceased happened to be the last of his line, the custom was to destroy both his symbols of office and his coat of arms. The custom was applied even to Kazimierz the Great, though in his case it certainly did not lead to historic oblivion. So many of Poland's castles and fortresses and towns were built by this intelligent, enlightened king that it is often said he was born into a country made of wood, but left it made of stone.

The layout of Poznań's Old Market Square has not changed since 1253, when the original Town Hall was built. To this day, a dozen streets lead out from the square, all lined with gabled mustard- and peach-colored burghers' houses. Today most of these restored dwellings are occupied by boutiques, banks, and cafés; some by quaint museums. It being close to noon when we leave the café, Pani Fabré suggests we hang around the Town Hall for a few minutes. At precisely noon, two metal goats make their appearance above the Town Hall's clock, butting their horns together twelve times. The goats appear on Poznań's coat of arms, in commemoration of a local legend in which two goats are said to have stood with locked horns on the front steps, drawing attention to an unsuspected fire inside the Town Hall.

Just outside the Town Hall stands an executioner's statue and old pillory, where public floggings and executions routinely took place. The pillory is a 1925 copy of the original found at the Historical Museum, a stone structure put up with the help of proceeds from fines levied on immodestly dressed prostitutes!

In Poznań, most museums are open until five in the evening, but by two-thirty, both of us are tired and hungry, and I invite Pani Fabré to join me for dinner—perhaps a Chinese one, I suggest, having sensed a certain interest in the exotic. Has she ever had Chinese food?

Pani Fabré hesitates. Poznań has a good number of foreign restaurants—Chinese, Indian, Korean—but she confesses she has never tried any of them. She is tempted, she admits, but has to pick up her grandsons and feed them soon. On the other hand, if she can get hold of her elder daughter, perhaps the twins could have dinner with their cousins. "Try it," I urge her. "Please."

She does, and it all works out, everybody being delighted with the arrangements. Which is how Pani Fabré becomes acquainted with orange beef and General Tao chicken and—her favorite—tender black Chinese mushrooms served with crisp water chestnuts and bamboo shoots.

"I haven't traveled since my husband died," she tells me, eating a lichee fruit, "but it looks like the world is coming to me instead."

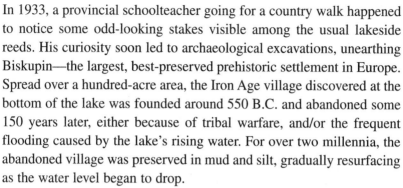

In 1933, a provincial schoolteacher going for a country walk happened to notice some odd-looking stakes visible among the usual lakeside reeds. His curiosity soon led to archaeological excavations, unearthing Biskupin—the largest, best-preserved prehistoric settlement in Europe. Spread over a hundred-acre area, the Iron Age village discovered at the bottom of the lake was founded around 550 B.C. and abandoned some 150 years later, either because of tribal warfare, and/or the frequent flooding caused by the lake's rising water. For over two millennia, the abandoned village was preserved in mud and silt, gradually resurfacing as the water level began to drop.

The emerging village was once inhabited by the Lusatians, a Slav tribe engaged in farming, animal husbandry, and fishing. Situated on an island, the settlement was made up of timber-paved streets with oak-log dwellings linked through their gables, and surrounded by a twenty-foot-high palisade with an oak-log watchtower. Partially reconstructed in recent decades, the village huts consist of two rooms, one originally occupied by small farm animals, the other by an extended family. The iron used in the Lusatian culture is said to have come from Transylvania, but there are other objects—weapons, jewelry, religious artifacts—from as far away as Egypt, Italy, and the Black Sea region, indicating brisk Iron Age trade.

At this point I must sadly confess that the above information has been culled entirely from books. I never got to see Biskupin, though it wasn't for lack of trying. Not only had I been given erroneous information about rail service, but I arrived in Biskupin after three hours' travel to find the Archaeological Park about to close—two hours earlier than indicated by my guidebook!

Having wasted the better part of a day, I give up on Biskupin on hearing the following morning's weather forecast. I decide to have breakfast at a nearby milk bar, then go back to the pension for my luggage before catching the morning train to Wrocław. By the time I finish breakfast, it is pouring in Poznań, and the only taxi to come by turns out to be occupied by a driver from Gniezno and his wife, here on holidays. They express their regrets and drive off, only to turn around and come right back to say they will take me after all. They have taken pity on me, they say, given the bad weather and the fact that I am a foreigner.

"How did you know I was a foreigner? Was it my Polish?" I ask.

"It was more your smile," says Maryna Płonka. "It's not often we see teeth like these in Poland," she adds rather sadly.

I can hardly claim to have a Farah Fawcett smile, but Maryna, who is in her late twenties, is missing at least one tooth and keeps trying to smile with her mouth shut. Though I have been told that taxi drivers make a good living in Poland, the Płonkas apparently don't.

"We have Swiss taxes and Mozambique salaries here," Dariusz states as we approach the railroad station. By now I know that Maryna is an unemployed secretary and that Dariusz is supporting her and her four-year-old son from a previous marriage; *they* know I am in Poland to research a book and the fact seems to intrigue them. We are almost at the station when Dariusz turns to his wife and says, "What would you say to spending the day in Wrocław?"

"Wrocław!" I say. "It's two hours away, isn't it?"

"It is," he says, "but. . .well, we are on holidays. It's raining and—"

"Yes, let's go," interjects Maryna. "What can we do in this weather anyway?"

I insist on at least paying for the gas, and my offer is gratefully accepted. And so I end up leaving Poznań by taxi instead of train, driving toward Silesia with a couple of impulsive strangers from Poland's first capital, bemused as so often on this trip by the manifest rule of the unexpected. Back home, I probably would not have accepted a ride from perfect strangers, not even such a harmless-looking pair. Dariusz has a face as close to being angelic as it is possible for a grown man's to be, and Maryna too is gentle featured, her sleepy brown eyes studying me with frank curiosity.

Both of them are intensely interested in my Canadian life but eventually get around to answering my questions about Poland. Not for the first time, I am surprised by how articulate and well informed ordinary urban Poles are, compared with their North American counterparts. Though only 7 percent of the Polish population is university educated, the literacy rate is 98 percent here, and those with a high-school education—compulsory in Poland—often seem as knowledgeable as college graduates back home. This is in good measure because, until recently, Poland was a nation of dedicated readers. Now, Dariusz says, people are mostly dedicated to maximizing their income. In the old days, being poor didn't seem to matter. Not only was everybody in the same boat but there wasn't much to buy anyway. Now that the shops are full of attractive goods, everyone is suddenly on the make. Dariusz is frankly dismayed by taxi drivers' famous tendency to fleece passengers, especially foreigners like me. He smiles at me in his rearview mirror. At the same time, he concedes, it is difficult to make an honest living, given all the expenses involved in driving a taxi. He is thinking of getting out and doing something else—perhaps going into the computer service business.

As he tells me this, Dariusz notes an oncoming car blinking its headlights in what is apparently a common signal here, warning drivers of lurking highway police. He slows down a little, swearing at the ceaseless rain, and then at the sudden, pervasive smell of sulfur.

"We're in Silesia," says Maryna, grimacing back at me.

Silesia, Poland's southwest province, is the most heavily populated, industrialized, and polluted region in Poland. In Upper Silesia, the infant mortality rate is almost twice that of Western Europe; the number of children born with congenital defects is 60 percent higher than in the rest of Poland. There have been studies indicating lead poisoning in some 35 percent of Upper Silesia's children, many of whom also suffer from various respiratory problems.

Historically, however, Silesia has been one of Poland's most frequently disputed regions, the claimants being Prussia, Bohemia, Austria, and Poland. It is a vast basin of steelworks and factories and coal mines. And of gold too, it seems. Polish scientists, Dariusz tells me, are convinced that there are large gold deposits in the Sudeten Mountains, where digging has at last started. Maryna says there are also rumors of treasures hidden in the Sudeten by the retreating German army. This reminds Dariusz of the recent uproar over "Nazi gold."

"Did you know they stole over $4 billion worth?" he asks, glancing at me over his shoulder. The Allies managed to recover only $360 million, some of which is said to be in Britain to this day. What has enraged the Poles is the fact that only a small percentage of the recovered gold has come down to them.

"Poland! The country that's suffered more than any other in

Europe!" says Dariusz in an indignant tone. "If anyone's going to get the short end of any stick in international affairs, you can be sure it's going to be Poland."

Maryna's point of view is more optimistic. She has read that the Allies were quite simply reluctant to pay vast sums of money to Communist regimes. Perhaps some of these things will be corrected now?

"Ach, don't count on it. Just look at our history." The statement is followed by a bitter litany against the superpowers' cavalier treatment of Poland. Not only did they hand Poland over to Stalin at Yalta but sat with their arms folded while the Nazis ravaged the country. "I won't say anything about the stupidities at Versailles, but what followed—the indifference—that's what's so hard to swallow."

These are far from being unusual sentiments in Poland, though I have yet to hear them expressed with such fervor. To add insult to injury, Dariusz says after a moment, Wałęsa even got excluded from the ceremonies marking the fiftieth anniversary of the end of World War II. "The Big Four were all invited, but we—we who lost more of our soldiers than France—we weren't even asked!" Dariusz honks his horn rather furiously.

Maryna pats his shoulder. "The only time Dariusz gets excited is over politics," she says. And then she smiles at me over her shoulder. "Are you going to write all this in your book?" she asks, watching me jot something in my notebook.

"Who knows?" I say. "I might."

At this, Dariusz makes a vaguely scoffing sound. "Do you really think anyone's likely to be interested in reading about Poland?" he asks.

"I certainly hope so," I say.

"I don't know," he says. "I can't see what you find so interesting in Poland."

"Well," I say, "this conversation is interesting. Your history and—"

"Ah yes, our history," interjects Dariusz. "Foreigners are crazy about our history." One day, he tells me, he picked up a fare at the Gniezno cathedral. "A rich man from New York married to a Polish woman. 'Every stone is historic here,' that's what he said to me. Well," concludes Dariusz in a tired voice, "to you it may be historic; to us it's just something we keep tripping over."

CHAPTER 19

I T IS OFTEN SAID that Jan Matejko, the celebrated Kraków painter, has shaped all Poles' historic imagination, having managed in a comparatively short life (1838-1893) to capture on canvas all the pivotal events of Polish history. Monumental in size and passionate in spirit, his paintings are on display in Poland's major museums, with modest reproductions commonly found in ordinary Poles' homes. One such painting hangs in the living room of the Dłutek family, from whom I have rented a room for my two nights in Wrocław. Titled *The Third of May* (Poland's national holiday), it captures both the fervor and the turmoil of an event all Poles are intensely proud of: the proclamation of the Polish Constitution.

Taking place in 1791, nineteen years after the First Partition, the momentous occasion saw the birth of the first codified constitution in all of Europe, second in the world only to that of the United States. Though Poland was to remain a monarchy (henceforth hereditary), the progressive new constitution introduced political innovations abolishing the counterproductive *liberum veto*, and social reforms aimed at improving the lot of Poland's disenfranchised bourgeoisie and serfs. Tragically, though hailed throughout Europe, the radical reforms outraged Catherine the Great, who wasted little time in summoning her troops. Not only was the new constitution forcibly abolished, but the inevitable conflict precipitated the Second and Third Partitions, through which Poland saw its entire territory split up among Russia, Prussia, and Austria.

The eradication of their country was a staggering price to pay for lofty aspirations, and the Poles did not pay it without a heroic fight.

One of the most spectacular battles of this period was fought in 1794 against the Russian army at Racławice, where Tadeusz Kósciuszko led his Polish troops to stunning victory. Though the ensuing revolt was ultimately crushed by Russia, the Racławice battle, in which peasants were for the first time allowed to take up arms, has always been celebrated as a testament to Poles' patriotic will. For over two centuries, it has inspired works not only by Jan Matejko, but numerous other painters, poets, writers. Toward the end of the nineteenth century, with the approaching centenary of the famous battle, a group of Polish patriots in the Austrian-occupied city of Lwów undertook to commemorate the historic event by commissioning an extraordinary public painting whose fate was to be closely linked to that of Poland itself. Roughly half the size of a soccer field, it weighed about seven thousand pounds and was hung in a new rotunda especially constructed to display the circular masterpiece: the Racławice Panorama.

A new European invention, panoramas were on the way to becoming the most popular form of mass art on the Continent. By the nineteenth century, almost every large European city boasted at least one, famous battles being the most common theme. In its first six months alone, the Racławice Panorama recorded over a million visitors, an enthusiastic Emperor Franz Jozef among them. It remained a major attraction for half a century—until 1944, when a German bomb destroyed the renowned rotunda. When the war was over and Lwów had been swallowed up by the U.S.S.R., the eastern city's Polish population was shunted to ravaged, depopulated Wrocław, one of the major cities in the newly acquired western territories. Though Wrocław had been a German city for over two centuries, the Poles from Lwów transplanted much of their Eastern culture with them, including the severely damaged Racławice painting. Understandably, the Soviets were not eager to restore a work celebrating an anti-Russian revolt, so the monumental canvas lay in storage until 1980, when the rise of Solidarity made it possible to contemplate its public display in Wrocław. After five years of painstaking restoration, the Racławice Panorama was open to the public in a new crownlike rotunda, a Polish attraction second only to Częstochowa's Black Madonna.

I visit the Racławice Panorama on my first afternoon in Wrocław, expecting to see a vast, circular painting, but finding myself instead a participant in an extraordinarily powerful illusion. Admitted in a group of mostly Polish spectators, I circle about the darkened viewing platform, scrutinizing the images on the vast, ingeniously lit canvas. The canvas, it turns out, is not only invisible but promptly forgotten as I gradually lose myself in the simulated experience of witnessing a major historic event. The effect is that of standing on top of a hill, gazing for miles at the surrounding rural landscape. There are fields, woods, hills, ravines, and a small village whose illusory proximity and depth are cleverly heightened by the addition of authentic accessories between the viewing platform and the painting. It is springtime and the sky is blue, the meadow in bloom, the pastoral village submerged in a scene of burgeoning nature. Eventually, however, as one circles the panorama, the bucolic landscape gives way to the unfolding battle. But it is one thing to celebrate a historic triumph, another to witness the unleashed furies after Tadeusz Kośziuszko leads his troops into the fray. I remind myself that I am merely looking at a clever painting of a grisly battle, but the scene nonetheless leaves me quite literally weak-kneed. It depicts a swirling mass of peasants, soldiers, and horses, intertwined in a tumultuous struggle into which I feel myself slowly, helplessly drawn. I am one of those people who, even in the cinema, usually look away from a scene of extreme brutality. At the Racławice Panorama, the scythes and cannons and blood seem so immediate, so overpowering in their staged authenticity, that I feel myself truly threatened; about to be swallowed up by the breathtaking carnage.

It feels like the narrowest of escapes; one mercifully followed by the far more sedate pleasure of visiting Wrocław's renowned Town Hall. Poland is nothing if not rich in ancient town halls, but even after visits to the best of them, Wrocław's is truly astonishing in its magnificence. Rising above a vast market square built in the 1240s, the Gothic building was begun in 1322 and took three centuries to complete, acquiring Renaissance features in the process. The central facade, with its prominent 1580 astronomical clock, has a richly adorned triangular gable with exquisite pinnacles, but the southern is the more elaborate. It includes Renaissance windows crowned with spirelike roofs, carved figures, stone corbels, and two intricate friezes. Somehow, this spectacular architectural achievement survived World War II intact, though 70 percent of Wrocław had to be rebuilt after the retreating German army set fire to what remained in the aftermath of battle. It had been one of the largest, longest battles of the entire war, the Germans being reluctant to relinquish what was by then one of their most prominent cities.

The conflict between Poles and Germans had started as far back as 1109, when a battle was fought just outside Wrocław, ending in German defeat. In subsequent centuries, there were Tatar invasions, Bohemian and Austrian occupations, followed in 1741 by Frederick the Great's conquest. It was then that Wrocław became Breslau, a Prussian city second only to Berlin. By the end of World War II, when it finally reverted to Poland, Wrocław had been German for over two centuries.

Capital of the province of Silesia, today's Wrocław is Poland's fourth-largest city; a major industrial, commercial, and cultural center whose Polish origins go back to the ninth century. Situated on the Oder River, it is a vibrantly resurrected city whose architecture reflects its historic permutations. There are massive Germanic brick churches, Flemish-style Renaissance mansions, Viennese Baroque palaces, and early-twentieth-century public buildings—all surrounded by the grim, ubiquitous apartment blocks. Despite the latter, and the city's highly developed industry, Wrocław boasts a beguiling historic center, remarkable for its elegant parks, gardens, and above all bridges. After Venice and St. Petersburg, Wrocław has the largest number of bridges in Europe—almost one hundred of them, spanning the city's fifty-six-mile network of canals and river tributaries. A city with a long cultural tradition, it has an exquisite eighteenth-century university (which Frederick the Great converted into a prison), a seventeenth-century library with precious collections, an opera house, orchestra, internationally renowned theaters. Wrocław also has the distinction of being the city where, in 1475, the first book in Polish was published.

As one walks through Wrocław's center, it is impossible to forget the city's turbulent history. For one thing, German signs are common in Wrocław, its shops and cafés and restaurants eagerly catering to German tourists, many of them former Breslau citizens whose families had lived in this town for generations. But there are also Russian tourists, several of whom I see at the local Soviet soldiers' cemetery, searching for the graves of male relatives killed in the three-month battle against the Germans. Outside, on a busy intersection, there are two Soviet tanks, looking menacing and incongruous at the cemetery gates.

On my second day in Wrocław, I come upon a band of young Polish men in gaudy capes, boisterously climbing onto the tanks for snapshots, then marching off, arm in arm, singing with great gusto.

As it happens, my host, Captain Dłutek, is a local army officer, and it is he who eventually tells me the young men in the colorful capes were Polish soldiers celebrating their recent discharge from military service. Poland has an army made up of ninety career officers and some 135,000 draftees who serve between fifteen and eighteen months. Polish university students are exempt from service, and in 1996 as many as half of the army's recruits succeeded in having their draft date deferred. I have been told elsewhere that the army has been rather lax in its drafting policies because its resources are inadequate to support a larger force. Captain Dłutek categorically denies this, saying that young men are often released on grounds of impaired physical or mental health. He adds that there have been a few notorious incidents of brutality, but says nothing of the rumors that criminal elements have penetrated the army ranks. He does admit that current hazing practices have many Polish parents taking steps to get their sons exempted.

All the same, Captain Dłutek assures me, the army enjoys greater prestige in Poland than any other institution, including the Church. This, I will eventually learn, has hardly been true since World War II, but Poland boasts a well-trained force, with over 120 years' experience in international peace missions. One of its great weaknesses, however, is the lack of foreign language skills among its officers, a liability that Dłutek too suffers from to this day.

Captain Dłutek, who is almost forty, is a square-jawed, broad-shouldered man with a sonorous voice and a nervous manner. Though he has readily agreed to answer my questions, he seems oddly restless, crossing and recrossing his long legs and repeatedly glancing over his shoulder as he speaks. With Polish hopes set on joining NATO before the end of the century, he tells me, the country has been energetically engaged in adapting its military structure to NATO standards. It is widely felt that NATO membership will ensure peace and stability in the region, but many fear that Yeltsin, who is against NATO expansion, may yet undermine Poland's chances.* All the same, Poland has chosen to adopt a positive

---

*Poland has since been officially invited to join NATO.

course, investing vast energy and resources in revitalizing its military. One of the many post-Communist innovations has been the army's transfer to the Civil Defense Ministry's jurisdiction, a move that has entailed drastic organizational changes, including some in military leadership.

But the greatest challenge, it turns out, lies in changing deeply entrenched attitudes. Under the Communists, the most trivial procedures were effected in a spirit of great secrecy, the Party controlling every aspect of the vast, byzantine system. "Well, we've been trying to change all that, but this is our legacy. We must reform not only the military's structure, but the mindset impeding the necessary reforms."

Nonetheless, the captain is optimistic. He himself is taking an English course and keeps trying to get his elder son to practice his own English. In fact, Pani Dłutek made clear to me at the outset, it was only their wish to expose thirteen-year-old Staszek to foreigners that has led them to register with the local tourist bureau, which has referred me to them.

The Dłuteks live in a bright, spacious high rise, close to the city center. Theirs is the first apartment I have seen where the children each have their own bedroom, smartly furnished à la IKEA. The younger son being at camp, there is a free bedroom, currently rented out to me.

Pani Dłutek, an attractive *zaftig* matron, is a full-time housewife whose energy is largely expended trying to secure her two sons' future. There *is* no future in Poland without foreign languages, she tells me when I finish interviewing her husband. Having already arranged for me to have breakfast alone with her son, she now invites me to join the three of them for supper. I had planned to go out on the town this evening, but it is once more raining, and so I finally yield and sit down in the kitchen to a light meal of wieners, herring, cheese, and tomato salad. This morning, over a leisurely breakfast, I managed to bring Staszek out of his shell, but in his parents' presence, he seems determinedly tongue-tied, so the captain and his wife do most of the talking. My questions about their family lead my hostess to tell me about one of her nephews, an only son and a brilliant medical student who has just married a girl of Gypsy origin.

"We're not, any of us, prejudiced against anybody," she says, "but . . .well, the fact is my sister and her husband had hopes in other directions."

We speak about Gypsies for a while, and Pani Dłutek assures me most of them are not nearly as badly off as they like to make out. She personally gave a young Gypsy woman an apple and bread roll one day, only to see her fling them into a waste bin with an angry gesture.

"Of course, my nephew's bride is not from that class at all; she's a nursery school teacher, but. . .oh, families are a complicated thing, aren't they?"

The young couple is on their honeymoon in Prague, a place that the Dłuteks have also visited. It is, the captain concedes, a beautiful city, but one that to him seems frankly tainted by Czech spinelessness. Whereas Poles sacrificed *their* capital on the altar of freedom, the Czechs chose to surrender to the Germans, saving their capital but not their soul.

This is not an uncommon sentiment among Poles, who tend to see themselves as a nation of romantic heroes and the Czechs as petty bureaucrats shaped by German sensibilities. But Pani Dłutek waves it all away, saying Poles are simply envious of Czechs because the latter are better at blowing their own horn and also more industrious and orderly than the majority of Poles.

"What they are," says her husband, "is just more pragmatic. We Poles are stirred by lofty principles, the Czechs by the principle of sheer survival." He agrees with his wife, however, about the Czechs' superior ability to promote themselves. The little resistance they put up against the Nazis, for example, has been blown up out of all proportion. "In Poland, such acts of resistance were everyday events!" he says sententiously.

And so it goes throughout supper, with occasional pauses during which Staszek is urged to quiz me in English about Canada. The boy smiles at me shyly but remains obstinate in his silence. With his fair hair, hazel eyes, and high cheekbones, he reminds me of my brother, who was roughly the same age when we arrived in Canada. My brother too was slightly built and rather shy, and used to run away when asked by Hasidic Jews to come in on the Sabbath in order to light their stove. He ran away, he would tell me in later years, because, having grown up in Israel, he felt offended to be mistaken for a gentile. At the same time, since we did not observe the Sabbath, he was clearly in a position to oblige the Hasidim. If he ran away, it was because their request left him confused about his identity. It was a problem neither of us would ever quite outgrow, rooted as it was in our father's ambivalence toward his own religion. On the one hand, my brother had been circumcised in Łódź; on the other, he never had a Bar Mitzvah. Oddly enough, it was my mother who tried to observe Jewish holidays, cooking gefilte fish and matzoh balls and berating my father for never going to the synagogue, for playing cards on Yom Kippur. She accused him of having no respect for his dead parents, of depriving his children of a sense of identity and tradition. She was certainly right there and, years later, reminded him of her warnings when—quite unreasonably, I felt—he was dismayed to find both his children married to gentiles.

As for Staszek Dłutek, he seems a little cowed by his overbearing father, speaking self-consciously even in his native Polish. When we finish eating, however, and Captain Dłutek, emboldened by vodka, thanks me in English for having joined them, Staszek impulsively corrects his father's pronunciation. He is perfectly right, but my host mock-glares at him across the table and jokes, "Don't teach your father how to make children!"

It is a common enough Polish saying, but it makes thirteen-year-old Staszek blush with embarrassment.

"The problem with Staszek," Pani Dłutek says to me the next day over breakfast, "is he's not aggressive enough." It has both her and her husband a little worried: how can you get anywhere in the new Poland unless you have gumption? Her younger son has it; he's a go-getter, but Staszek is still a bit tied to her apron strings. Perhaps it is her own fault—she had given up her nursing job to be a full-time mother.

"But what's the use of having a car and VCR and such things if our children end up being raised like orphans, I ask you?"

Pani Dłutek presents her case in a breathless, confiding voice. The two of us are alone this morning, sitting in the sunny kitchen over coffee, discussing parenthood, while I wait for the long-distance operator to place a call to Greece. Despite her decision to stay at home, Pani Dłutek wants me to understand that she is a thoroughly modern woman. She is emphatically pro-sexual equality, she tells me, and even pro-choice. She herself has had an abortion in Dresden, something she feels she can tell me but not her own mother, with whom she does not see eye to eye on many contemporary issues. She had to fight with her over breast-feeding, for example, something that she personally believes in but that the Communists managed to brainwash millions of women against. It was part of their concerted campaign to lure women into the workforce, but the negative attitudes toward lactation are proving difficult to eradicate.

And then there is the issue of divorce. Her mother won't even discuss it, though one of her own daughters in Łódź is secretly contemplating it. Pani Dłutek is in her late thirties, and among her generation, she says, divorce no longer carries any stigma. According to official statistics, there were thirty-eight thousand divorces in 1995; in 1993, the number of divorces exceeded that of marriages and, states Pani Dłutek, there would likely be even more of them if housing were not such a serious problem in Poland. Recently, she has read that 10 percent of all divorced couples are forced to go on living under the same roof indefinitely.

"Because of the housing shortage," says Pani Dłutek, "my sister may end up getting a divorce without my mother ever finding out about it!" She is about to add something when the telephone rings, the operator informing me my daughter is on the line.

I say goodbye soon after. I have only the rest of the day for Wrocław and plan to spend it exploring the city, before having dinner and catching the bus to Kłodzko. Kłodzko is where Magda's elder daughter lives, and I am expected there this evening. Pani Dłutek shakes my hand warmly. She asks permission to have Staszek write me in English. She asks me to drop them a line to say I have arrived home safely. She presses some homemade cake and an apple on me and has tears in her eyes when I turn to go.

The last interesting thing I see in Wrocław is huge graffiti scrawled across the wall of a local supermarket called HIT. It is a German-owned store whose publicity slogan—BUY FROM HIT—has been amended to read DON'T BUY FROM HIT-LER.

The person who explains what it's all about is a young student waiting on tables at a lovely restaurant called Chopin, where I am to have

my last meal in Wrocław. The Germans, he tells me, have been investing heavily in Silesia, and some local Poles are beginning to worry
about losing Wrocław once more. There are, all over Poland, many
people who seem unable to come out from under the past's shadow;
who seem determined never to forgive or forget. He's as good a patriot
as anybody, he says, but he does not think it is in the Poles' interest to
keep nursing old grievances. "We have to look to the future," he says,
"to try to be a normal society again."

The longing for normality is a compelling one in Poland, though it
swings, depending on whom you speak to, between westward aspirations and a nostalgia for a long-vanished Polish past. Surprisingly, the
latter is encountered not only among the very elderly, but also the generation of middle-aged Poles raised on parental nostalgia for the
interwar era when the country was ruled by Marshal Józef Piłsudski.
Having in 1918 declared Poland sovereign for the first time in 123
years, Piłsudski is generally regarded as the father of national independence, and a great war hero—to many, the very last great Polish hero.
He has always been a somewhat controversial figure because of his
often dictatorial stance, as well as his insistence on a tradition of ethnic
and religious diversity. Nevertheless, Piłsudski's memory is cherished
for defeating the Russians in the Polish-Soviet War (1918-1920) and
for bringing stability and prosperity to post-World War I Poland.

Though no one could have predicted the fifty calamitous years that
would follow Piłsudski's death, his passing in 1935 left most people in
Poland feeling deeply bereaved, none more so than the country's three
million Jews. If they feared that the benevolent Piłsudski's passing
might rekindle antisemitic sentiments current earlier in the century,
they were soon enough proven right. Ironically, what has reminded me
of their subsequent plight is Wrocław's anti-German graffiti, echoing
as they do the aggressive campaign to boycott Jewish shops in prewar
Poland.

"Poland for Poles!" and "Patronize your own!" were the watch-
words after Piłsudski's death, but the sentiments had had their genesis
in the late nineteenth century when the National Democrats first
formed a right-wing movement increasingly committed to racial and
political violence. Had they succeeded in taking power in the 1930s,
say historians, their regime would have strongly resembled that of

Hitler and Mussolini. Fortunately, they failed, but not without leaving a tenacious legacy of radical nationalism, largely fueled by the identification of Jews and Marxists as Poland's enemies. It was this legacy that, in the late 1930s, inspired a new law forcing merchants to post their names outside their shops for all to see. In Gdańsk, Anita Górniak told me that her grandmother would often recall having been repeatedly—physically—discouraged from shopping at her favorite Jewish store by ultranationalist bands. It was through such measures that by the time the Nazis invaded, a third of all Polish Jews found themselves wholly dependent on American charities.

I think about all this as I eat my dinner, managing nonetheless to enjoy both the music and the splendid dish of mushroom-stuffed beef rolls in sour cream. The restaurant has been playing nothing but the work of its namesake, and my thoughts of boycotted merchants eventually give way to the memory of my recent visit to the composer's birthplace. Though I have always enjoyed Frédéric Chopin's music, I have to admit I had not fully appreciated it until I began to read up on Polish history. Chopin may have been half French, but his lyrical, often melancholy, works, with their sudden musical storms, capture not only the upheavals of his own short life but the deep longing and turbulent echoes of his beloved homeland.

This must have been all too apparent to the Nazis, for they not only dismantled the composer's monument in Warsaw, but declared the death penalty for playing his music. Defiant as ever, the Poles played it anyway, in private and in public, taunting the invader. When the war was over, the famously hideous monument was rebuilt in Łazienki Park, and soon public concerts were taking place in Żelazowa Wola, the Mazovian village where Chopin's father worked as French tutor to a local aristocratic family. It was there, in the exquisite garden of the Chopins' country manor, that I too sat one balmy Sunday, listening to the mournful notes of the B Flat Minor Sonata. The work, with its famous funeral march, had been written when Chopin knew himself to be afflicted with tuberculosis, the disease that was to kill him in 1849, at age thirty-nine. He was living in France by then and had for many years enjoyed spectacular renown. His polonaises and waltzes and mazurkas were the favorite music at every European court, though perhaps few of the guests bothered to discern what Robert Schumann, speaking of Chopin's music, called the "cannons obscured by flowers." The Poles, on the other hand, were keenly aware of them, none more so than those present at Chopin's last performance, a benefit concert for Polish refugees. He died in Paris soon afterward and was buried there, with Polish soil from Mazovia strewn over his grave. Before his death he had requested that his heart be taken back to Poland, where it rests to this day in a cherished urn at Warsaw's Church of the Holy Cross.

CHAPTER 20

ONE OF MY LAST Polish photographs, dated the summer before our departure for Israel, was taken in a small forest village where my family spent two weeks every summer, along with various acquaintances from Łódź. In the photograph, seated before a lake, are six children of varying ages, my brother and I among them. Two of the others are Magda Stein's daughters: five-year old Anita and seven-year-old Roma; the former fair and curly-haired and smiling, the latter dark-haired and pugnacious-looking, staring into the camera's eye with mysterious displeasure. When, on my second day in Kłodzko, I show the photograph to the middle-aged Roma, she reacts with a frown, a smile, a little snorting sound accompanied by a shake of her graying head. "We grow up, we grow old, but we hardly change, do we?" she says musingly. She looks at the photograph for another moment, her dark eyebrows knitted in a characteristic scowl. Her forthrightness, I would soon find out, is equally characteristic, allied with a fierce determination to call a spade a spade. On this occasion, our first tête-à-tête in Kłodzko, it leads her to confess that she is, as the photograph suggests, something of a misanthrope—in contrast with her sister who has always had the gift of seeing the very best in people. She repeats that it is a gift, one Anita inherited from their mother along with her Polish beauty.

Roma takes after her Jewish father. She is tall and broad-shouldered and dark, with short, bluntly cut hair. Her manner has a brusque, no-nonsense quality somewhat unusual in this country. Polish women of her generation and class commonly aim for a light, old-fashioned sort of graciousness. Perhaps because she has little free time, Roma, who is an obstetrician and gynecologist, seems permanently set in her harried professional mode. She is under particular pressure this week because a close colleague has had an accident, and Roma has been forced to take over his caseload. Ironically, the colleague was supposed to cover for Roma this weekend, a time she had planned to spend showing me around. As things worked out, she picked me up at the bus station last night in her OR greens, dropped me off at her apartment with an injunction to make myself at home, then rushed back to the hospital to deliver a Kłodzko woman's twins.

Roma lives in a small, turn-of-the-century apartment building where her stepfather was born. It is an outwardly somewhat shabby building, but the flat is exquisite, having high ceilings, large windows, and a ceiling-high, tiled wood stove, which, now that central heating has been installed, is merely decorative. Living alone as she does, Roma has an amount of space unusual in Poland: two bedrooms and a large living-dining room furnished with fading sofas, solid-looking antiques, and many books and objets d'art picked up in years of travel. Like many educated Poles, Roma speaks several languages, and since her English is clearly superior to my Polish, we quickly abandon the language of my childhood in favor of what I have come to refer to as my "step-mother tongue."

It is my first morning in Kłodzko, and though she had come home in the small hours, Roma got up early to prepare a lavish breakfast, with excellent ham, eggs, several kinds of cheese. As I was heading for the shower, she quickly ran out for fresh rolls and fruit, waving away my expressed dismay at all her exertions. No, she does not need to sleep more than a few hours, she presently tells me; you don't take up obstetrics if you can't do with minimal sleep. In fact, until very recently, you didn't go into medicine at all unless you were prepared to work very hard for very little in Poland. All the years she has been in practice, most Polish doctors earned as little as policemen, and sometimes as little as hospital cleaners since, under Communism, the salary structure was based on seniority rather than job category. Seven years after the fall of Communism, the public sector is still operating under extreme constraints. Just the other day, ten thousand doctors from across Poland took part in a March of Silence in Warsaw, demanding increased spending on health and social services, as well as higher wages.

Of course, Poland does have a private sector now, and doctors who go into it are finally able to make a respectable living. But private medicine is still new in Poland, and not everyone is prepared to take on its risks and challenges.

I ask Roma whether it's true that Polish doctors routinely accept bribes, and she admits they do. Either that or they hold two positions or, like herself, play the stock market to make ends meet. Having no dependants, she is in a stronger financial position than most of her colleagues, but much of her income goes toward travel, her avowed passion.

For the most part, Poles still have to be prepared to grease a few palms to get prompt high-quality medical care. In provincial towns, hospitals are often poorly equipped and inadequately staffed, a problem bound to get more severe as, increasingly, young doctors opt for private practice. Interestingly, despite the new opportunities in the private sector, the application rate for admission to medical schools is steadily dropping. In the old days, there used to be nine to ten applications for every available slot in the medical faculty; this year the number is down to three. "Private doctors may end up making a lot of money," says Roma, "but it takes many years and Poland now offers other, much more lucrative, opportunities." There are other deterrents: the growing awareness of inevitable risks, for example, as malpractice suits become more common. In Poznań recently, a surgeon engaged for a gallbladder operation had left a surgical bandage in a patient's abdomen and was successfully sued to the tune of 50,000 złoty. In her own field, there is still an exceptionally high incidence of premature births and infant mortality. These are due mostly to pollution, but also to poor nutrition and general awareness. Twice as many people die of cancer in Poland as in the West, in good part because more than half of them seek medical attention when it is too late. Things are improving, though, in medicine as in other areas. Many towns now offer prenatal care, for example, with large urban hospitals showing a growing concern for pregnant women's and newborn infants' welfare.

At this point, the telephone in the hallway rings, and Roma comes back to tell me she must head back to the hospital. She leaves me to linger over coffee by the sunny window, listening to Bach and musing on my own daughter's birth in a well-equipped Montreal hospital where a fetal heart monitor alerted attending doctors to my child's distress, and a pair of forceps saved her from fatal entanglement in the umbilical cord.

And then I think of my brother's birth in a postwar Łódź hospital, an event almost miraculous in its ease and swiftness. Though I was only three when it took place, I vividly remember the subsequent visit to the maternity ward: my mother's blue satin kimono, the cross over her bed, the pervasive smell of cabbage. My mother, who had already had an abortion in Poland and would have two more before we left, was deliriously happy. She had a daughter and a son now, the latter so beautiful that for years strangers would stop her on the street to admire his features. I admired him too, and loved him with a passion no less fierce for being muddled by frequent jealousy. I never wanted to have a second child, for fear that my daughter would end up feeling similarly abandoned.

Though this particular worry did not appear to cloud my mother's joy at the hospital, another would surface within days when she returned home to learn that Mrs. Blum, my father's partner's wife, had leapt to her death in her absence. Did my mother's pregnancy serve as a catalyst in this suicide? It is possible, but in truth, Mrs. Blum had been visibly deteriorating for some time, ever since she and her husband finally got news of their daughter's fate. Many years would pass before I learned the full details of the Blums' tragic story, but despite everyone's efforts to keep me in the dark, I somehow managed to gather what Mrs. Blum had done. When my father realized that I knew, he pleaded with me not to tell my mother while visiting her in the hospital. I didn't, but the suppressed knowledge must have left its weight on my subconscious, where birth and death would come to seem inextricable. Years later, while I was expecting my own child, Mrs. Blum suddenly began to haunt my anxious dreams. Over and over, I would watch her fall to her death, whirling in space, her long hair billowing, her limbs flailing as she suddenly glimpsed the inexorable gray pavement. I could feel her abrupt terror in my bones for hours; the accelerated racing of her chaotic blood. Now and then, just before I awoke, the spinning black image would begin to shrink, gradually transformed into a newborn child; a fair-haired infant propelled out of some mysterious source toward a cold, shiny floor, its mouth forming a small, silent O of bewildered pain.

❁

I have come to Kłodzko for the sole reason of visiting Roma, but the town turns out to be such a lovely surprise that I soon find myself making small-scale comparisons with the far more glamorous Prague. This is when I remember the Dłuteks' comments on Poles' relatively poor self-promotional skills. Who in the world has heard of Kłodzko? How many visitors to Warsaw ever think of coming to see it? True, the town still has a somewhat tattered look, but a charming one nonetheless.

Tucked up against the Czech border in the south of Poland, the thousand-year-old Kłodzko is set on a hillside, crowned by a fortress overlooking two rivers and the Sudeten Mountains. Situated on the main trade route between Bohemia and Poland, it was from the start a bone of contention between the two countries, passing back and forth between them several times before the Hapsburgs took over in the sixteenth century, and the Prussians in the eighteenth.

Having arranged to meet in the Old Town in the early afternoon, Roma and I make our way up to the ancient fortress, pausing to look at an exhibit of regionally manufactured crystal. Since the eighteenth century, the Kłodzko region has been renowned for the quality of its glass, sought well beyond Poland's borders. The crystal service for the coronation ceremony of Queen Elizabeth II came from this region, where several glass factories still operate. Above the courtyard, in the Wall of the High Bastion, there is a stone sculpture of Wałeska, a legendary Czech princess reputedly strong enough to break horseshoes with her bare hands. Captured by her enemies, however, she was immured alive in the Kłodzko fortress.

Originally a timber stronghold, the current fortress was undertaken by the Austrians in 1662 and completed two centuries later by the Prussians. One of the largest fortresses in Europe, it is an impressive structure endowed with casements, bastions, and dungeons; one offering a superb view of Kłodzko and its environs. The vista, it is said, is strongly reminiscent of Grenoble's: steep rooftops, towers, distant hills, and the winding blue ribbons of the Nysa Kłodzka and Młynówka Rivers. There is an islet called Piasek in the latter river. It has a Franciscan church and monastery and is connected to the town with a picturesque thirteenth-century Gothic bridge whose longevity is attributed to the use of mortar made with egg whites! A century in the building, the bridge was constructed of sandstone, in time acquiring Baroque statues of limestone saints piously gazing heavenward.

The bridge is one of the features that puts me in mind of Prague. The other is Kłodzko's hilly situation; the medieval charm of its sloping streets and steps, which wind around the old market square, running into each other. Cobbled as far back as 1376, these streets have genuine Gothic, Renaissance, and Baroque buildings, some with well-preserved architectural features: lovely portals, vaults, armorial sculptures, elegant balustrades. The greatest tourist attraction seems to be the dense network of underground tunnels excavated by prisoners-of-war during the Prussian era. Branching out from the fortress, the excavations run underneath the Old Town's streets and squares, linked up in places with medieval cellars. In peacetime, this subterranean system provided local merchants with vast storage space, but its main purpose was to provide wartime shelter. In 1743, a Dutch engineer came up with a plan that turned the tunnels into a unique labyrinth of explosive mines designed to destroy enemy artillery. Divided into small units, the tunnels were loaded with gunpowder and set to blow up whenever the enemy moved its guns above a given section. This, says Roma, was why Napoleon never succeeded in storming the Kłodzko fortress. She suggests I might want to join a guided tour of the underground Millennium Route, something tourists apparently like to do. When I learn that some of the passageways are so low that they require crawling, I decide to pass. I opt instead to visit the fourteenth-century Parish Church of Our Lady—one of the most spectacular Baroque church interiors in Poland—and then to accompany Roma on a brief shopping trip. She only needs a few last-minute items for dinner, but tells me she is glad I decided to come when I did. Had I chosen to visit her in the 1980s, she would hardly have been in a position to receive me properly. One summer, expecting French colleagues she had met at a medical convention, she grew positively desperate, driving to the country in search of fresh produce, buying children's crepe paper to cut up for the toilet.

"I won't tell you what we had to use now and then in those days." She sighs. In the butcher shop, she tells the owner she has a guest from Canada and must have something fit for the occasion. She winks at me and the butcher grins, showing a few gold teeth. I can't help noting that despite her self-avowed misanthropy, Roma is warmly greeted everywhere we go, by merchants, neighbors, patients. At the entrance to the greengrocer's, she is stopped by one of the latter and, after a brief consultation, takes out a pad and writes out a hasty prescription. When I express amazement at the casualness of all this, she says Polish doctors don't yet take themselves as seriously as their colleagues in the West. Since most of them work on a fixed salary, moreover, there is no incentive to encourage unnecessary office appointments. This reminds Roma of a professional joke. A doctor is walking through a cemetery when he hears a voice calling out to him. "Doctor! Doctor! Would you by any chance have on you a good cure for worms?"

The Kłodzko region may be in Silesia, but it is in the southern, decidedly more salubrious, part of the province. One of the most captivating, least known, parts of Poland, it is a region of green hills, deep valleys, and mineral springs renowned as far back as the Middle Ages. Surrounded by the Sudeten Mountains, the Kłodzko valley boasts ancient forests, immense pastures, winter resorts, and several well-known health spas to which Silesians flock to recover from the perpetual pollution in the north. One of the most famous (it was once visited by Winston Churchill) is called Kudowa-Zdrój and rests in a deep valley sheltered from the north winds by the Stołowe (Table) Mountains. These unusual tabular mountains offer a labyrinth of gorges, ravines, spectacular rock formations, and stalactite caves with ice-age animal bones. But the most extraordinary thing I see in these parts, or anywhere in Poland, is a small chapel just outside Kudowa-Zdrój, ghoulishly decorated with human skulls and bones. More than three thousand skulls surround the modest altar, nestling against each other in vertical formations, with crisscrossed bones closely lining the entire length of the chapel's ceiling. It is a stunning collection put up in 1776 by the chapel's priest, whose own remains rest in a glass case beside the altar, along with those of a gravedigger involved in the enterprise. The dour nun who acts as tour guide explains all this to the small group of Polish tourists, making everyone gasp when, a few minutes later, she bends down to open a trapdoor to a deep cellar, where twenty-one thousand additional skulls have lain piled up for over two centuries.

I am as stunned as the others, thinking uneasily of Tamerlane, the ruthless Mongol conqueror who, after capturing a town, would slaughter thousands of its defenders, then build pyramids of their skulls. The nun is quick to point out that the local priest was not impelled by either vindictive or morbid impulse but rather by the altruistic desire to provide a memorial to hapless plague victims. People in the region had been dying in such numbers, she explains, that most of the dead had been left unburied, with wild animals feasting on the abandoned corpses. It took the priest and his devoted assistant eighteen years to complete the collection, but they died satisfied in the knowledge that the dead would not be forgotten. The nun shuts her eyes, looking suddenly like a live icon.

The plague had swept through Poland five times in as many centuries, the last one hitting the country in 1717. An acute febrile disease caused by a bacterium transmitted by fleas from infected rats, the plague often caused death in three to four days, sometimes before any symptoms had manifested themselves. The first known European plague had appeared in Athens in 430 B.C., but the most widespread struck in 1334, originating in Constantinople and spread throughout Europe by returning Crusaders and trade caravans from China. The mortality rate being as high as 90 percent, the twenty-year plague killed three-quarters of Europe's and Asia's populations, with far-reaching and sometimes little-known ramifications. Scholars have suggested, for example, that the decay of Latin as the lingua franca of Western Europe's educated elite was precipitated by the widespread death of the clerics and scholars who had long kept the language alive. The plague also gave rise to the Flagellants, who aimed to appease God's wrath by ruthless flagellation. In the fourteenth century, bands of European Flagellants would march from town to town, stopping in public places to bare their backs and mercilessly flog themselves and each other while exhorting the watchful public to repent their sins. It is fascinating to note that while the Flagellants, and others, regarded the plague as a manifestation of God's will, this did not stop them from holding Jews responsible for the pestilence. Western European Jews were widely accused of poisoning Christian wells, and the attacks on them grew so frequent, and so pervasive, that they brought about a gradual shift of European Jews toward the east. This was how, in the fourteenth century, thousands of Jews began to make their way toward the uniquely hospitable Poland.

That evening, I tell Roma about my visit to the Chapel of the Skulls and end up involved in another discussion of Polish-Jewish relations. It starts with a reference to King Kazimierz the Great (1310-1370) who, having welcomed the persecuted Jews to Poland, is often credited with saving them from probable extinction. Poles like to cite this as a testament to their own tolerance and generosity, and Roma does not quite refute this. Kazimierz was in fact a wise and enlightened king, but he was not quite as altruistic as Poles like to make out. The truth, she says, is that Poland, whose population had been diminished by Tatar invasions and by the plague, desperately needed new human resources. In the Middle Ages, Poland had only two classes—the aristocracy and the peasantry—and the Jews in particular were needed to develop local trade and industry, for which neither the peasants nor aristocrats had any aptitude.

When I tell Roma that Poles still seem to me somewhat deficient in business acumen, and that most people I met have blamed this on the Communists, she makes an impatient gesture. Communism certainly did not help develop Poles' commercial skills, but these had never been Poles' forte anyway. In fact, she would go so far as to say that much of the antipathy between Poles and Jews has to do with their radically different sensibilities. Poles, as history shows, are generally impulsive, romantic, tempestuous, whereas Jews are prudent, farsighted, analytical. Since most of the Jews Poles came in contact with were merchants, moreover, Jews inevitably became identified with typical mercantile traits.

This prompts me to tell Roma about a Canadian friend whose elderly mother reportedly said in recent years that she used to think only Jews were cunning and crafty until the recent influx of merchants from the Middle East and the Orient.

"That's how it is," says Roma. "The less experience you have of the world, the more likely you are to entertain false notions." This, she adds, is what must be understood about the Poles. The country was, until recently, made up largely of backward, rural folk with an almost medieval mentality. They were not only superstitious but rather simple-minded. "Peasants, really, for the most part, and easily outwitted by the much shrewder Jews."

Naturally, there has been a good deal of resentment, but there are always resentments toward ethnic minorities. Even Poles from different regions have negative views of each other. One of the things Roma has observed about the Jewish character is a tendency to blow everything out of proportion. Poles call Ukrainians "throat slitters;" the Scots, like the Jews, are said to be tightfisted. And so on. Jews are, it seems, more thin-skinned than most people. Don't I agree, she asks.

"Well," I say at length, "perhaps if it were only a question of words rather than pogroms and gas chambers, Jews *would* be less sensitive to antisemitic innuendo."

Roma concedes the point but goes on to reiterate her sister's view that Jews were not usually attacked *qua* Jews but rather because they were perceived as top dogs. But there was something else, which she feels Jews don't really understand. *They* may have thought of Poland as their home, and of course it was, but they had their own religion and their customs and the Poles themselves never stopped seeing them as aliens who gradually succeeded in gaining disproportionate economic power. "Well, you know how passionate Poles are in resisting *any* foreign control. Their feelings toward the Jews were not all that different from those aimed at the Teutonic Knights," she states. Eventually, she too mentions Communism. Any compassion Poles had felt following the Holocaust was dissipated when Jews assumed power under the Soviets, she reiterates.

I have been thinking about this ever since my talk with Anita, and presently tell Roma that though I certainly understand Poles' feelings on the subject, it seems unfair to regard Jews as traitors when many high-minded, patriotic Poles were equally bewitched by Communist ideology. "Someone like General Jaruzelski," I say, "was nothing if not a true believer, and he was as Polish as they come."

"He certainly was," says Roma, "but then there are many Poles who see Jaruzelski too as traitor, and want to see him punished."

This is followed by a brief thoughtful silence, during which I muse on a postwar Łódź rabbi rumored to have been a secret police agent, and on the Soviet officers on the streets of Łódź, resplendent in their khaki uniforms. And then Roma, perhaps feeling she has failed to make her point, says with renewed energy, "Look, let's take Israel, for example. Imagine—just imagine—that Israel became occupied by the Russians, and that Israeli Arabs, feeling maligned and promised better conditions, began to collaborate with the alien regime. Wouldn't anti-Arab sentiments flare up among most Israelis?" she demands.

"I'm sure they would," I say.

"There you are," says Roma. One of the things that steams her up, she then adds, is people's blindness to their own double standards, the Jews' included. Israel is a perfect example of what bothers her. Why is it, she asks, that Arabs fighting for a free homeland are terrorists, while postwar Jews fighting the British mandate in Palestine are to this day seen as heroic? What about all the innocent people killed in the attack on the King David? For that matter, what about Ben-Gurion's orders to sink a ship carrying one thousand Jews just to prevent arms going to the Irgun? Roma looks at me, then makes a vaguely disgruntled gesture, accompanied by a sigh. Have I heard about the controversial issue of restitution for lost property in Poland, she inquires. Hearing that I have, she goes on to say, "Well, what about all the Palestinians who lost their homes, their land? Are the Israelis planning to compensate *them* for their losses?"

As these are facts that have troubled me as well, I sip my brandy in silence, interrupted by another of Roma's little snorts. "I once had a similar conversation with an Israeli doctor whose family had come from Poland. He accused me of being an antisemite." She gives me a crooked grin. "I told him I'd have to be crazy to be an antisemite with my looks. I assured him I was quite simply an old-fashioned misanthrope. I would have gotten on very well with Jonathan Swift, I think."

When I chuckle and say she certainly seems to have frequent lapses, she smiles through a ring of smoke—she is a heavy smoker—and says that may well be true, but in general she is disgusted with human beings' selfishness and cruelty; above all, with their self-delusions and the inclination to try to whitewash the past. "It's as true of the Poles as it is of the Jews," she points out, "though I have to say that as a group, Jews seem to me especially sanctimonious."

Here, Roma goes on to echo Hania Gwiazda's views on Jewish resentments against Poles' failure to stick out their necks on Jews'

behalf. On the other hand, she states, not all Poles who did were moti-
vated by heroic impulse. Some were, of course; many must have been,
but the truth is that Poles, like most threatened human beings, thought
above all about their own survival. Some who would not have risked
their own lives did so because they were paid and were desperate
enough to accept the risks.

Interestingly, many Poles who did save Jews insist today on remaining anonymous, some fearing antisemitic neighbors, others burdened
by far-fetched anxieties. In recent years, a Polish filmmaker interviewing country folk for a wartime documentary reportedly met a woman
who had sheltered Jews but was anxious to keep her identity a secret.
"What if someone broke into my house, hoping to find hidden gold?"
she asked the filmmaker.

Roma tells me all this with an expression of suppressed disdain. All
the same, she insists, Jews have not given Poles enough credit for their
heroism. She thinks Jews are perfectly justified in holding Poles
responsible for prewar antisemitism but certainly not for their unwill-
ingness to risk their own lives during the Occupation. She is troubled
too by the frequent perception of Poles as Nazi collaborators. To be
sure, there were Poles who collaborated with the Nazis, but they were
a tiny minority; the same sort of people who betrayed Polish aristocrats
to the Russians. "Jews naturally don't like to be reminded of this, but
after all, there were Jews, too, who grew desperate enough to betray
their own people, right?"

I concede there were, reminded of Peter Wyden's *Stella*, a book that
tells the extraordinary story of a German Jew who acted as a Gestapo
"catcher" in wartime Berlin, hunting down hidden Jews with unparal-
leled dedication. When I tell Roma about Stella Goldschlag, she says,
"You see? Like I say, Jews are no better and no worse than others, but
neither are the Poles." On the whole, she thinks, Poles have been getting unfair press in the West. In her travels she has met people who had
got the absurd impression that the Poles were almost as guilty as the
Germans for the Holocaust. Nathan Leipciger, chairman of the
Canadian Jewish Congress Holocaust Remembrance Committee, is
equally dismayed by this widespread view. "How can you say that?" he
is quoted to have exclaimed in a recent interview. "I was in camps
where ninety percent of the inmates were Poles. . . . Most of this [anti-

Polish] feeling is just based on myth."* In fact, points out Roma, the Polish government was in exile in London, helping the Allies and promoting ŻEGOTA, while the French were certainly collaborating in Vichy. "But you hardly ever hear about French antisemitism, do you? Whereas Polish antisemitism is still a hot issue in the West, isn't it? All those books published in the U.S. alone—" She pauses abruptly, suddenly remembering my portable tape recorder. "I suppose you're going to report on this conversation in yours?" She looks at me with her dark, mildly ironic eyes.

"Almost certainly," I say.

"In that case," she says, "just so readers don't end up accusing me of antisemitism too, I'd like to go on record stating the things I do like about the Jews."

I was about to turn the recorder off, but I stay my hand, curious. "Tell me," I prod.

"Well," says Roma, "the first thing will probably surprise you, given my personal experience, but I do admire Jews' devotion to family and community, their extraordinary ambition for their children. And of course their gifts. When you think of Jewish contributions to world civilization—it's totally out of proportion to their numbers." She pauses.

"How about sheer tenacity?" I ask.

"Well, tenacity," she says. "The Poles are also tenacious. But there is something else, and it's seldom mentioned. Of the three monotheistic world religions, Jews are the only group that never tried to force their religion on anybody else. There's all that biblical talk about being the light to the goyim and so on, but it was always light, never the sword, with Jews."

---

*See "Poland Striving to Shake Off an Anti-Semitic Past," *Globe and Mail,* May 29, 1992.

CHAPTER 21

THERE WAS, in prewar Kazimierz Dolny,* an old
Jewish legend which had it that every year, on the eve of Yom Kippur,
the town's synagogue would light up suddenly on the stroke of midnight,
echoing with prolonged lament. This, according to the legend, marked
the annual assembly of Jewish souls who had died unnatural deaths.

It is a week before Yom Kippur when I finally visit my father's
hometown, to find the synagogue housing a Polish cinema. I have seen
Jewish synagogues converted into everything from banks to swimming
pools in Poland, so a cinema does not come as much of a surprise at
this point. But it is an unlikely venue for a phantom congregation, and
much too small nowadays: three thousand local Jews died in the Nazi
death camps, my father's entire family among them. When I arrive in
Kazimierz, I still don't know where any of them died, or whether my
father knows. While we lived in Łódź, he made several visits to the
Jewish Agency offices, hoping to find a familiar name on one of the
survivor lists. There were no survivors other than my father, and he
never went back to Kazimierz. He too had heard rumors of Jews
attempting to go back to their prewar homes, only to be killed on their
own thresholds. Not that my father discussed any of this with me. He
was, throughout my childhood, an unusually taciturn man, discourag-
ing all questions about his lost family. In Kazimierz, I can't stop
thinking about them. I have been in many Polish towns famous for
their prewar Jewish communities but none, not even nearby Lublin,

*Dolny means Lower, distinguishing this town from Kraków's Kazimierz, which is on the upper
Vistula.

270

immortalized by I. B. Singer, seemed to me so powerfully haunted. The fact that this was my father's *shtetl* may have something to do with it, of course, but Kazimierz's atmosphere is the stronger reason.

I arrive in Kazimierz in the evening, getting off the bus on the main road from Puławy, unnerved by the pervasive darkness. I would be terrified were it not for the handful of passengers heading toward the marketplace. Astonishingly, even the square has no streetlights but the Dom Architekta, where I am to stay, turns out to be smack in the market square. The walk takes barely five minutes, but on this first visit to Kazimierz, this dark and autumnal evening, it is long enough to transport me backward, to a shadowy world I know only from photographs, films, fiction.

It is September by now and drizzly, the floating moon obscured by swollen, low-lying clouds. There is the distant sound of barking dogs and of footsteps retreating on the cobblestones; the smell of charcoal wafts out of the only open restaurant. The restaurant is lit up but the only other illumination comes from the small windows clustered around the square. Oddly, the shafts of light piercing the darkness only contribute to the eeriness of the scene. There is the outline of what looks like a village well; the shape of a tree swaying in the wind. On any journey, but especially one undertaken alone, there are flashes of occasional loneliness, but in Kazimierz I experience a moment of desolation so acute that it is a physical ache deep within my chest. Nor does it quite vanish in the bright, comfortable room I am given on the second floor. Despite its name—Architect's House—the Dom was built as a refuge for Polish artists and intellectuals, who have always been partial to Kazimierz. What with its central location, tasteful interiors, and excellent dining room, the Dom will prove to be one of my best accommodations in Poland. But on this first evening, none of it seems to register, so absorbed am I in the melancholy contemplation of a vanished past. It is the beginning of the Jewish new year, a fact that perhaps contributes to my meditative mood. I think of my faceless grandparents preparing for the High Holidays, of men in black gabardine caftans and bewigged matrons heading toward the synagogue, of the reedy sound of the shofar. I try to imagine my father, small and dark-eyed, with a yarmulke and earlocks, led up the street by his older sisters, or trudging through snow toward the local heder. He was a bright child and his parents envisioned him as a celebrated talmudic scholar; with some luck perhaps even a rabbi. Once in Warsaw, however, he abandoned his parents' Orthodox ways, the war bringing the final break with his traditional background.

The man who chased Russian shiksas is not, I confess, easily imagined as a pale-faced yeshiva scholar, so after a while my mind travels toward Kazimierz the Great, the king who gave the town its name,* and also its synagogue, built as a birthday gift for his Jewish mistress. Like her biblical namesake, the local Esther had somehow gained favor with the great king and may well have enhanced his kindly disposition toward the Jews. The synagogue he built for her, at any rate, became renowned throughout Poland, some of its stones reputedly having come from Jerusalem's Wailing Wall. Rebuilt in the eighteenth century, it was still in use when World War II broke out, only to be desecrated by the Nazis. Kazimierz the Great also built a hilltop castle for his Esterka, whom he visited through a secret tunnel linked up with the town's own fortress.

And now the synagogue is a cinema and Esther's castle a picturesque ruin, but Kazimierz the Great is still revered for having transformed a small riverside village into a mercantile town so prosperous that it came to be known as "little Danzig." He did so by giving it its first municipal charter and by promoting a trade in grain, much of which was channeled through Kazimierz's Vistula port. The town thrived until the seventeenth century but was not spared the usual historic calamities: fires, plague epidemics, foreign invasions. Its decline, like that of other Polish cities, began with the Swedish Deluge, exacerbated by several natural and political disasters. After the Partitions, Kazimierz too fell under Hapsburg rule, and it was only in the nineteenth century that its grain trade began to flourish anew, having gradually passed into Jewish hands. By then, the town was predominantly Jewish, with a renowned Hasidic rabbi attracting disciples from all over Poland. My grandfather was a fanatical scholar, so perhaps it was this, as much as the town's burgeoning economy, that led my grandparents to move here from a nearby village. He did not prosper

---

*This is the prevailing view, but some scholars believe the town was actually named after an earlier king, Kazimierz the Just (1138–1194).

here either—he was much too wrapped up in the Talmud for that—but the town continued to flourish, aided perhaps by another *liaison d'amour.* It is said that an Austrian commandant fell in love with the beautiful daughter of a kosher butcher and that this apparently led to growing bureaucratic benevolence in Kazimierz, with unprecedented privileges for its Jewish community.

The Jewish slaughterhouse and timber butcher shops are still standing behind the Kazimierz synagogue, blackened by time and long since abandoned, one of them having been converted into an art gallery. There is a square in front of the butcher shops, with posts and metal hooks from which the carcasses must have hung on market days. Eventually, I will learn that merchants from nearby villages still come to display their wares here, but today, my first morning in Kazimierz, all the action is in the main marketplace, just outside the Dom Architekta's arcaded entrance.

I have awakened to find a rural market day in full swing below my windows, astonished to see the dark, desolate square transformed into a bustling, colorful scene. I must have slept like the proverbial log, for the din below is considerable. There is the honking of geese and squawking of chicks, children's squeals, merchants' cajoling voices. The square is teeming with regional farmers, and Belarussians selling pottery and hand-embroidered blouses. There are trucks and cars and long wooden carts with farm horses swishing their tails at the squeezed shoppers. The shoppers are mostly women, carrying baskets and knotted bags and pausing to examine the displayed produce with studied disdain. They handle the merchandise, and bargain, and stop to gossip by the village well as women did for centuries, coming to draw water.

It is an ancient wooden well sheltered by a shingled roof and, today, surrounded by makeshift stalls piled high with cabbages and onions and wild mushrooms. There are baskets with apples and pears, and trays holding currant jam, buttermilk, country cheese, and sausage. A man in a faded cap announces his pears to be the juiciest in the region, and at the next stall, a woman with parchmentlike skin throws back her head and laughs theatrically.

Some of the women are standing stoically, others sitting on the sidewalk next to enormous sacks bulging with grain, beans, flour. They are all wearing babushkas and keep looking up at the overcast sky with grim, anxious faces. I have read that these market days have been taking place here since the sixteenth century but have trouble imagining Hasidic fur hats and wigs in this Polish crowd. And yet, having read books by Sholem Aleichem and I. B. Singer, I know that Poles and Jews attended the same country markets, milling together amid horses and cows, bargaining in Polish, Yiddish. For the first time, I find myself wishing I had come years earlier, when there was still a chance of running into someone who remembered my father's people. Half a century after the end of the war, the only Kazimierz Jews history recalls are corn merchants like the Lustigs and the Fuersteins; fabulously rich men who built mercantile dynasties in Kazimierz, buying up the sixteenth- and seventeenth-century granaries and some of the town's best mansions.

Though Kazimierz is described everywhere as a town, its population (four thousand) and compact layout give it the feel of a village. What distinguishes it from other villages is its famed Renaissance architecture. Personally, I find some of it distinctly pretentious, the facades too aggressively sculpted, the stone parapets more opulent than any seen in my travels. The oldest and perhaps grandest of them was built in 1630, but like other historic buildings in Kazimierz, it has been destroyed and reconstructed several times, today housing the Town Museum.

There are several competing mansions in Kazimierz, but also countless, far more modest, dwellings whose architecture is unlike any I have seen so far. They are whitewashed stone houses (the area is rich in limestone), with black, sloping wood-shingled roofs, often exceptionally low. Some of the houses have wooden arcades, others two-tiered roofs with projecting eaves supported by oak pillars. There are dormer windows and even balconies and, now and then, small mouthlike openings built into the roof for ventilation.

And then there are the historic granaries, perhaps the strangest structures to be seen in Kazimierz. In its heyday, the town had almost fifty of them, most of them on the river. Today only ten remain, four of them in ruin, two converted into quaint hotels. They are strange, imposing stone edifices, two- to four-stories high, boasting fanciful gables modeled on local Renaissance churches. Compounding the architectural oddity are the small, sometimes round, windows that, set into the immense, flat facades, give the granaries the look of gigantic, gaping faces.

The trade in grain made Kazimierz a surprisingly cosmopolitan town, accustomed to dealing with buyers from Italy, Scotland, the Netherlands, Greece, and Sweden. Some of these men ended up settling in Kazimierz, raising families and polonizing their names, though one of the homes built by the Italians to this day bears quotations from Seneca on its facade.

But none of these, I know, ever belonged to Kazimierz's poor, so I keep walking up and down the narrow, tortuous streets, looking for the forgotten past. The Jewish past may be uncelebrated—Polish historians speak with occasional bitterness of Kazimierz having become largely Jewish—but the town is justly prized. The current population includes rural folk, but also artists, poets, and various urban luminaries with country homes in Kazimierz. Some of these homes are quite grand, but most are modest cottages with charmingly tangled gardens, back lanes overgrown with apple and pear trees, and jasmine creeping up picket fences. Eventually, I do come upon some old timber houses, dark and crooked and uncharacteristically shabby, but those were built after the war, it seems.

I learn this from an elderly woman heading home from the market with a little violet-eyed child. There is not much more she can tell me; she is only here to visit her son and his family. The beautiful, dark-haired little girl gives me a toothless grin and holds up a loaf of bread shaped like a rooster for me to see. "*Koo-koo-ri-koo!*" she cries, exactly as my mother, young and playful, used to do, all those years ago.

"They still have bread in the breadbox, but they want fresh bread," says the grandmother, clearly disgruntled. "A new loaf every day. Is this how it is where you come from?" she asks. And then she realizes she doesn't know where I come from and asks me, blinking up at me behind thick spectacles. When I tell her I am from Canada, she sighs and says, "Ach Canada! In Canada, the pigeons must eat better than some Poles do." And then she resumes walking without another word, followed by the skipping, vivacious child.

I eat very well at the Dom Architekta, which has a bright spacious dining room with a wall of windows facing the market square. As the tables are all large, and I am alone, the hostess soon asks permission to seat another solitary diner, an elderly woman from Warsaw who introduces herself as Ela Nowacka. I have gone out of my way to chat up Kazimierz's elderly citizens without much success, but my first dinner at the Dom takes a somewhat unexpected turn.

Pani Nowacka was raised in nearby Lublin, but occasionally came to Kazimierz for visits with her parents. She is a well-dressed, gray-haired woman with grave features and careful manners—Jewish, I suspect, possibly because, with her olive complexion and aquiline nose, she strongly reminds me of an Israeli friend's mother. She is an amateur photographer and never stops being surprised at what she brings home from Kazimierz. Have I seen the photographs at the local museum, she asks. I have, and go on to express amazement at how little Kazimierz seems to have changed. There is a wartime photograph of the market square, for example, with soldiers lined up stiffly in two parallel rows. The soldiers are German, but the market square looks exactly the same, doesn't it?

This observation makes Pani Nowacka sigh and say a town can be rebuilt, but the damage to people's psyches is more difficult to mend. She herself lost her father in the war. He was shot by the Germans for resistance activities, and her mother was never the same after that. She raised her two daughters alone and, both of them being dark, never let them leave the house. "To the Germans, anyone dark was automatically a Jew." Pani Nowacka sighs.

After a moment's pause, she asks where my parents originated, and when I tell her, she stops with her fork and knife poised in the air and looks at me intently. "I never thought you might be Jewish," she says in a lowered voice.

Another crypto-Jew, just as I suspected; one understandably haunted by the past. After dinner, sitting in the handsome lobby, she tells me about her family. The first Nazi death camps were all in the Lublin area—Majdanek, Bełżec, Sobibór—and many of her relatives perished in one or the other. She had a newly married aunt in Kazimierz whose house still stands behind the marketplace. The aunt went into hiding in Lublin and survived the war, but her husband didn't. Someone, she says, denounced him to the Nazis for a sack of sugar. The aunt never came back to Kazimierz. She too had heard the warnings in the wake of the Kielce pogrom and ended up emigrating to Palestine.

"That's how it was," Pani Nowacka says. "But I'll tell you one thing—many Poles will confirm this: the life went out of Kazimierz after it lost its Jews. It's been regaining its vitality in recent years, but after the war, it. . .well, it just seemed to have lost its soul." She falls silent for a moment, then gets up and tells me she must go have her afternoon nap. She shakes my hand and gives me one of her rare, melancholy smiles. "Happy new year," she says.

"God created Kazimierz on Sunday, when He had had some rest," the locals like to say, and my personal connection to the town notwith-standing, it is easy to see the reasons for the conceit. Endowed with rich soil and riverside location, Kazimierz nestles in a lush, narrow valley, surrounded by wooded hills and crisscrossed by ravines. On my second day in the area, the weather improves briefly, and I go for a long walk in the early morning, past plum and apricot orchards and along the meandering river. The hills, one of them topped with the fortress destroyed by the Swedes, have begun turning red and gold, and so have the trees around me. But I have seen photographs of Kazimierz in spring and they seemed nothing short of Edenic: the cherry and apple trees in extravagant bloom, the gardens lush with flowering lilac, the fields and ravines spotted with wildflowers, and newborn lambs graz-ing by the blue river.

The river is rather gray today, but the morning is ethereal and serene, the small town just beginning to awaken, the heavy mist to lift from the Vistula. There are gigantic weeping willows all around the river, and swampy meadows with gliding white ducks, and dripping birches, oaks, beeches. As always, the fragrance of soaked earth speaks to me, all the more so with fall in the air. It is somehow different from Montreal's autumn air, more like that of my childhood, which smells seem to evoke more keenly than anything else in Poland.

But there is nothing else in the Kazimierz surroundings to recall grimy Łódź. The area has virtually no industry and its pastoral setting offers only fields of hops and corn, a windmill on one of the riverbanks, beehives, grazing sheep and cows. And silence. The silence feels like a gift this morning, broken only by the cawing of crows, an occasional rooster call.

I run into a woman walking her dog and engage her in conversation despite the suspicious growls of her German shepherd. In recent years, with more and more Poles moving into their own homes, and insurance premiums remaining high, large dogs have become common in Poland, especially in the suburbs. There have been many reported cases of canine attacks and an occasional public outcry at the mildness of the sentences imposed on the owners. The German shepherd soon comes around, but his mistress, it turns out, has lived here only since her retirement and can't answer my questions. She was an art teacher and painter in Warsaw but got tired of the noise and the pollution. We chat for a few minutes, and then she says goodbye and turns to go, suddenly spotting a man walking his dog in the grassy distance. "Ah, there's someone who has lived here all his life!" she exclaims, and offers to introduce me. We walk over and the painter greets the man, explaining I am from Canada and writing a book about Poland. Perhaps he can tell me something about local history?

The man shrugs and nods, though he looks none too enthusiastic. He is a man in his midseventies—almost exactly my father's age—but looks at least a decade younger, with fading red hair and small, raisin-like eyes set in a freckled face. I tell him he is the first person I have met who has lived here since before the war. I wonder what life was like in those days. Has Kazimierz changed a lot?

It has certainly changed since 1989, he says, when people began to invest in hotels and restaurants and what have you. But the greatest changes were brought on by the war, when much of the town was damaged and people lost friends and relatives. It was a terrible time, but at least they got rid of the Jews, he states, truly startling me. Not that he was happy to see what the Germans did to them, but it was good for Kazimierz to be Polish again. "There were thousands of Jews in those days," he adds. "Bloody-minded people."

"What made them bloody-minded?" I ask, carefully neutral.

"Oh, madam, you should have been here to see for yourself. They were the most aggressive people you can imagine. They suffocated the local Poles, they did."

"How exactly?"

"Madam, they were so wily. It's difficult to imagine. They cut prices and did everything they could to gain control of our commerce. Did they care that they were ruining the Poles? Oh, madam, I could tell stories till the sun goes down and still not be done. They all grew rich at our expense, they did."

At this point, he pauses, lets his Labrador sniff the hedge, then turns back toward the center. I experience a wild moment wondering what would happen if, all alone here on the riverbank, I were to tell him that my father was one of those bloody-minded Jews; that, quite possibly, they attended school together. My father went to the Jewish heder but also to a Polish school. After a while, thinking of my grandparents, I say, "But surely not all the Jews were rich in Kazimierz. There must have been a few poor ones, weren't there?"

"Ah, them!" The man makes a contemptuous gesture. "They lived down there—" He motions vaguely. "They were more like Gypsies, those Jews. They lived in timber huts, their houses were filthy and infested with rats—just like true Gypsies."

"And who lives in those houses now?" I ask as we leave the river.

"Oh, those were not houses, they were hovels, madam. They collapsed or burnt down long ago. Who'd want to live in them?" He spits into a raspberry bush, then pulls out a handkerchief and blows his nose. After he stuffs the cloth back into his pocket, he wags his head silently, then turns and looks at me with dawning curiosity. "Why is madam so interested in the Jews?" he asks.

"Oh," I say, "I'm interested in everything. I'm just trying to understand Poland."

"What's there to understand?" he says. "We Poles were the Jews' blacks—it's as simple as that. Only *we* were in our own country—we let them in and let them do it to us. That's what we can't forget! That's what you must tell your readers!"

The hateful words echo in my ears the next day as I browse in the market square's tourist shops, looking for souvenirs and postcards. I am also in search of a book about Kazimierz but am told there are none in English—or any language other than Polish—though the town gets a fair share of Western European tourists. When I do find one, it is in a Polish bookstore off the main drag, where foreigners are unlikely to go looking. And so I find myself thinking of Greece, where every kiosk and souvenir shop routinely stocks books in English, French, German.

I remind myself that the Greeks have been in the tourist business much longer than the Poles, but all the same, I can't help wondering what would happen if tomorrow a Greek or Jew or Armenian opened a souvenir shop in the market square and was savvy enough to sell foreign books and etchings and good-quality photographs of Kazimierz? There is no doubt about it: he would, before too long, become far more successful than his complacent competitors. He would quite possibly meet the fate of a Montreal businessman who started a chain of cut-rate dry-cleaning stores, only to have the central warehouse burnt down to the ground. Success, as Ambrose Bierce once said, is the one unpardonable sin against one's fellows.

All this continues to preoccupy me as I go on with my explorations, still searching for something, some confirmation that my grandparents lived here just over half a century ago. Outside the pharmacy, I run into an amiable-looking woman who launches a litany of her physical ailments; another who tells me a story of woe I can barely follow—something about the bureaucratic red tape connected with her son's application for a liquor license. Eventually, though, I do get lucky. I have been walking some of the town's back streets when I come upon an old, picturesque timber house smothered by Virginia creeper. Next to it stands a small stone house in a state of arrested renovation, its roof covered with a plastic dropcloth. Suddenly, an elderly woman appears at the door, wiping her hands on an apron.

"I see madam is looking at my wreck of a house," she says, sounding at once mournful and ironic. "I'm ashamed: everybody's looking at it, but what can I do? There's not enough money to pay the roofers just now." She makes a vaguely hopeless gesture. It was a good house once. Her husband's family had bought it from a Jewish tailor in the late thirties. Her father-in-law was a tailor too and had been friendly with the Jew. They got a good deal on it because the Jew and his family were anxious to escape. "And good for them," she says. "All the others—" She makes a vague, melancholy gesture, waving her palm outward. And then she points to another house, farther down the street. "They, on the other hand, are from Skowieszynek. They moved in after the Jewish owners went into the ghetto. Now the son, the Jewish son, is demanding restitution and my neighbors are mad. But the Jews are within their rights, aren't they?" she says. "It was their home after all, wasn't it?"

I am intrigued to hear this point of view from an elderly villager and ask whether she is old enough to remember the war. I think she may well be but have run into Poles who looked years older than their age and don't wish to give offense. As it turns out, my question makes her laugh.

"What does madam take me for—a spring chicken? I'm over seventy, dear lady. I was fifteen, a woman already, when the Germans set themselves up in the Franciscan monastery—the one on the hill." She points, going on to tell me about the first Poles shot by the Nazis, the first rounding up of Kazimierz's Jews.

"When did it happen, exactly?" I ask.

"It happened—" she starts, but breaks off abruptly. "Since madam is so interested, why not come in and have a cup of tea? This dampness does no good to old bones, does it?"

I go in and sit in a tiny, cramped kitchen, to be served tea and poppy-seed cake by someone—I am having trouble assimilating this—who was here when the first SS jeep rolled into town; someone who has seen it all. Pani Wiatr serves the tea in glasses and drinks hers with a sugar cube in her mouth. She sits across from me at a small table covered with an oilcloth, warming her hands against the tall glass. The Jews, she tells me, were forced into the ghettos in 1940, not long after the Jewish tailor had escaped with his family.

"Ghettos?" I say.

"There were two of them—one near the Jewish bathhouse and one over on Nadrzeczna Street. You ask if I remember, dear lady—how could one forget? Some of them were killed even before they got to the ghetto; herded they were like cattle, dear lady, with whips and everything. People we'd known our whole life—neighbors and even friends." She sighs, running her hand through her wispy hair.

"So the Poles had friends among the Jews?" I ask, looking into her faded blue eyes.

"What a question!" says Pani Wiatr. "They lived in Kazimierz for centuries, did the Jews. Some of us—even my father-in-law—learned to speak Yiddish." She waits for this to sink in, then surprises me by saying they often attended each other's weddings, in church and in synagogue. "Sometimes Jews would even come to church with us on Christmas Eve, dear lady."

"The Jews would go to church?" I echo, incredulous.

"Some of the young ones, madam, just to be with their Polish friends."

I am frankly skeptical, and so is my father, who left for Warsaw as an adolescent and whom I finally question on my return. Research at Montreal's Jewish Public Library, however, will eventually confirm most of Pani Wiatr's statements. But this is still in the future. In Pani Wiatr's kitchen, what I find myself thinking of are the Holocaust survivors killed by local Poles on returning home to Kazimierz. When I try to share this with Pani Wiatr, she quickly interrupts me. They were *not* locals, those murderers, she insists, but peasants from nearby villages. They didn't know any of Kazimierz's Jews and didn't want to know. As soon as they heard that the Jews had been ordered to vacate their homes, they rushed in from the countryside, even stopping the poor Jews from taking their own possessions. "Can you imagine?" she says, squinting her rheumy eyes. "People behaved like animals, worse than animals." She wags her head sadly, then urges me to go ahead and eat her poppy-seed cake. "But it wasn't the locals," she adds after a thoughtful moment. "No, no, no."

Sometime after the Nazis had taken over, the still unmarried Pani Wiatr went to live with her aunt in nearby Puławy. Her own parents had seven children, and she was sent to live with her aunt whose husband had been killed early on. The aunt was a seamstress, and it was hoped the girl would pick up a trade.

"But truth to tell, I had two left hands in those days, I did. Just didn't seem to get the hang of it. She would show me something, my aunt would, and then, a week later, she'd have to show me all over again. I was a good pupil at school, but stupid as a shoe when it came to the needle."

And so she returned to Kazimierz and, ironically, soon got engaged to a tailor's son, who became a tailor himself. "And, well, sure enough, I ended up having to help him, didn't I? I learned to work that needle after all. Such is life." She chuckles, smiling at me from within a web of tiny wrinkles.

I ask how long she spent in Puławy, and she says not very long; something like a year. After that, one of her younger sisters took her place and she pleased her aunt much more.

"So you were back in Kazimierz when the Jews were finally deported?" I have already learned from Pani Nowacka, the crypto-Jew at the Dom, that all of Kazimierz's Jews ended up at nearby Belzec.

This is confirmed by Pani Wiatr, who personally witnessed only the last transport in the spring of 1942. There had been several of them, but this was the only one she saw with her own eyes. By then there were only three hundred, maybe four hundred, Jews left in the ghetto. They were all ordered into the market square and herded onto carts. "Like animals," she repeats in a thinning voice. "Forced onto the horsecarts by those German sadists—shoved and beaten and whipped, and some forced to walk." Pani Wiatr raises a frail, spotted hand and wipes away a tear. She suddenly remembers it was the first day of Passover, and also that at the last moment, just before leaving, Kazimierz's rabbi ran to the synagogue and took some of its most sacred objects.

"I can still see him," she says, "clear as day, walking beside the farm cart as it turned the corner out of the market square, wearing the Jewish shawl they used to wear and chanting Hebrew prayers. That's how it was. That's how it all ended," she says, and heaves one of her deepest sighs. And then she looks at me, her blue eyes probing my face.

"Madam is of Jewish origin, I suppose?" she says.

I had planned to spend only three days in Kazimierz but have stayed for four, with barely two days left for Warsaw before I leave Poland. On Friday, my last day in Kazimierz, the sun comes out for the first time since my arrival, and with the approaching weekend, the town undergoes a sudden transformation. All over the market square, the restaurants and bars have put up their striped Coca-Cola parasols, with vinyl tables and chairs set up on the gray cobblestones. Pani Wiatr did not know my father's family, but her graphic description of the Jews' last hours in Kazimierz haunts me as I cross the ancient square. I think, not for the first time, about the maddening imperviousness of stones; that they should offer no hint whatsoever of history's grim weight—the wheels of farm carts groaning beneath their human cargo, the shuffling of elderly feet, and of young children. Only ignorance can make these cobblestones seem simply picturesque.

But Kazimierz is certainly picturesque, as the sudden appearance of painters with easels reminds me. I come across a pair of them on my last walk in Kazimierz, followed by a jogger in a shiny tracksuit—the first one I have seen in Poland—chased by a barking dog. I am on my way to see a memorial just outside Kazimierz, put up in honor of the town's murdered Jews. Long before I get there, however, I recall one obvious question I have been keeping at bay: what would have happened had my grandparents managed to survive the war—to my father, and to his new family? Esterka and the kosher butcher's daughter may have gotten away with their exalted affairs, but I suspect that my grandparents would have quite simply disowned my father, let alone his impure progeny. When he married my mother, my father did not yet know that his family was doomed, if not already dead; he must have known that his parents would rather *be* dead than see him married to a shiksa.

After walking for more than a mile, I finally reach the monument, which stands off the highway, not far from what was once the local Jewish cemetery. Going back several centuries, the cemetery was destroyed by the Germans, who used the ancient tombstones to pave their headquarters' courtyard up on the hill. In 1978, some six hundred stones were reassembled and joined to form an extraordinary sculpture, symbolically—dramatically—bifurcated. Many of the stones are fragmented, but some are surprisingly intact and engraved with menorahs; all bear elaborate, eloquent, Hebrew inscriptions.

It is a stunning, ineffably poignant monument that puts me in mind of the Wailing Wall. For the second time in Poland, I find myself wishing I believed in prayer, though I'm not at all sure what it is I would be praying for, unless it is for my Jewish grandparents' forgiveness. Yom Kippur, after all, is the Jewish Day of Atonement and, by tradition, a day on which antagonists are expected to seek reconciliation. It is only three days away, and I'd like to think that after half a century, my grandparents could find it in themselves to forgive their only son. Even more, that he would forgive himself.

CHAPTER **22**

T IS SATURDAY AFTERNOON, and I am once again in Warsaw, temporarily installed with Stefan Kryński's in-laws. Stefan and his wife are in Kraków but will be back later today. Meanwhile, the job of baby-sitting their son and entertaining their Canadian guest has fallen to Stefan's in-laws. Pan Broda is installing new bathroom tiles, six-year-old Janek is watching TV, and Pani Broda sits with me at the kitchen table, looking at my family photographs, with one eye on her bubbling pots. We have spent part of the day at Łazienki, a royal hunting ground turned in the eighteenth century into an enchanting park, then went on to the seventeenth-century Wilanów Palace—another Polish Versailles—which served as King Jan Sobieski's summer residence. The palace and its grounds were magnificent, but after three months in Poland, I found myself feeling rather saturated by Baroque splendor and am happy to be back in Pani Broda's fragrant kitchen, enjoying a glass of cold Polish beer before dinner.

Pani Broda is a woman in her early seventies, fair-haired (she seems proud that there is virtually no gray) and slender, with large, penetrating slate-gray eyes. She wears a well-cut skirt and pale-gray silk blouse adorned by a Bohemian garnet brooch—a stylish and genial woman, as well as a curious one. She seems, in fact, as curious about me as I am about her. Delighted to have tangible proof of my Polish connection, she studies the old photographs through her silver-framed reading glasses, posing many questions. How did my mother feel about moving to Israel in 1950, she asks toward the end. I don't want to offend her by saying my mother disliked Poland and was happy to leave it behind. And so I say something equally true: she worried about our safety in the Middle East. The anxiety is even evident in her last Polish photograph, one taken just before boarding the Łódź train for Gdynia. It shows an unsmiling young family of four, dressed in coats and hats, carrying bags and bulging suitcases against a dismal background. My mother wears an odd expression here—as if she had, out of sheer habit, started to smile for the photographer, only to be abruptly reminded of her worries about the future. She was, she had recently taken to saying, perfectly capable of living in a tent if necessary, but what of the rampant malaria, what of the Arab terrorists? She had no desire to stay in Poland, yet had doubts about Israel, which she imagined, not unreasonably, as a vast desert populated by hardy and zealous pioneers. She eventually found some reassurance in a letter and photograph sent by Simon Blum who, a year after his wife's suicide, had emigrated to the brand new state of Israel and looked much as he had in Łódź—happier, at that.

Dated May 1, 1949, Blum's photograph shows a wiry-haired man of about thirty, dressed in suit and tie, standing in front of a Tel Aviv café. He is squinting against the sun, smiling. He had wanted to emigrate even before Israel gained its independence, but his wife refused, though by then they knew that their daughter was dead. There was a clandestine organization called Briha in those days, actively promoting escape to British-occupied Palestine. This entailed an illegal crossing into Czechoslovakia, then a few months' wait in Germany or Austria before boarding the ship for the long journey to Haifa. Mrs. Blum was not afraid of the risks involved—what was there to be afraid of now, she would often say—but she refused to set foot on either German or Austrian soil. "The devil kicks equally well with the left as with the right," she cryptically told my mother.

I tell Pani Broda about the Blums, and she studies the Israeli photograph with keen interest. I too am interested, marveling at the tenacity of a man who had survived Auschwitz, lost his wife and child, and still somehow found the fortitude to embrace normality. To stand every morning in front of a mirror, fumbling with unruly hair, tie. Within a year, Simon Blum remarried and went on to have two children, whom I would eventually meet in Israel.

When I tell Pani Broda all this, she sighs and says life must go on. But then she takes me utterly by surprise, pulling off her glasses and looking into my eyes. "How come a woman like you never remarried?" she asks. She knows I have been divorced for over twelve years.

"Oh, I don't know," I say, nonplussed. "All the good men I met were already married, it seemed."

"That's too bad," she says. Pani Broda herself has had three husbands. She has been married to the current one for twenty years, having met him soon after her second husband, the father of her children, left her widowed at the age of fifty-three. Her first husband, a childhood sweetheart, ended up at Auschwitz for resistance activities.

"So you see," she says, "we Poles have suffered too."

"Of course," I say. "I'm sorry."

She seems about to add something but thinks better of it, standing up instead to show me a photograph of her first husband, a shockingly young man with fair, curly hair and ironic smile. She looks at it for a moment, then puts it away, calling out to her grandson to lower the volume. Janek is watching "Sesame Street" and our conversation soon shifts to children's TV programs, reminding Pani Broda of a story she thinks I may find of interest; one connected both with the war and a Polish show called "*Jacek i Agata.*"

Jacek and Agata are TV puppets whose creator was a young female member of the Polish underground. One day, during the Occupation, she glanced out of the window while holding a clandestine meeting in her flat, to see a Gestapo car parking outside her building. There was no time to run, not even to hide the incriminating documents in their hands. They had as long as it took the Gestapo to climb several flights of stairs. Soon the Nazis were ringing the bell, only to find themselves conversing through the door with what sounded like two young children—a boy and a girl—timidly saying their parents had gone out and taken the key with them. They would be back in the evening—would the gentlemen please come back then? The Nazis stopped and thought about it, evidently deciding it would be best to return when the suspects were home. "They left without a word," says Pani Broda, "and that was how Jacek and Agata came into being."

At this point, Pan Broda enters the kitchen and asks his wife to come have a look in the bathroom. He needs her advice with the pattern. Pani Broda excuses herself, and I take this opportunity to call LOT and confirm Monday's flight. Holding on for an agent, I am struck by the coincidence of leaving Poland again in September, though the weather in 1950 was, to judge by our last Polish photograph, far more autumnal than it is on this wonderfully balmy weekend. Pani Broda did not ask how *I* felt about leaving Poland—children adapt after all, and I certainly did; I came to love Israel. But short-lived though it proved to be, the grief of leaving the only home I knew was as keen as it was unshared, compounded by parental distraction and the general chaos of imminent departure. The last photo from Łódź shows me leaning into my mother and clutching my cloth doll with an intensity surprising in a six-year-old.

The doll was important. It was the one purchased during the trip to Kraków, to bribe me into eating at a restaurant. Though I had other, far more glamorous, dolls, it was Zoya I took with me everywhere I went, including this momentous journey. I suspect I found her presence reassuring. She may have served to remind me that my fears were unfounded and that overcoming them could even have its rewards. All the same, my sense of impending loss must have been building up within me, exploding once we were at sea.

It happened on our first night on the boat to Haifa, after my parents had left my brother and me to sleep in the cabin and gone upstairs to dance or to have a drink. That evening, while my brother slept on the lower bunk bed, I clutched beloved Zoya in my shaky hand and slapped her face, and twisted her limbs, and thrashed her wildly against the cabin wall. Many years later, in Canada, there would be a song, "You Always Hurt the One You Love," reminding me painfully of blameless Zoya's end. It did not take long for her worn seams to burst, for the stuffing to start flying, the tears to spring out of my eyes. But I can still feel the texture of rough cotton against my palm, the tingling sensation in my fingertips and, rising up my constricted throat, the acrid, as-yet-unfamiliar taste of compounded loss.

Stefan and Bożena are on their way—they have called from a gas station—and having finished a late-afternoon dinner, I sit in the Brodas' living room, chatting over tea and jam-filled Polish pancakes. Dinner consisted of beet soup with dumplings and a tender veal roast, which only a few years ago would have been impossible for most Poles to obtain, let alone afford. And yet, when I ask my hosts how they feel about Poland's metamorphosis, Pani Broda thinks for a moment before answering.

"It's a different kind of society, this sink-or-swim society my grandchildren are growing up in," she says at length, with a resigned shrug. "It has its good and its bad points, like everything in life. We're still getting used to it, I suppose," she adds.

Though there is nothing new in this statement, Pani Broda's last words lead me to reflect that Poles have spent much of this century getting used to changing realities. First there was World War I and its aftermath, and national independence for the first time in 123 years, and then the German Occupation, the havoc and destruction wreaked by another war, followed by four decades of totalitarian rule. When my family lived in Łódź, everything was blamed on the war and the Communists: housing shortages and rising crime, low wages and high taxes, lack of raw cotton, and malfunctioning toilets. Getting used to postwar life was what all the adults around me were constantly working on. This is why the color of my Polish memories tends to fluctuate between the vivid shades of private pleasure and privilege and the grimness of external realities.

When I share some of this with my hosts, Pan Broda nods sagely. "And now we're getting used to capitalism—only it's capitalism with broken teeth," he says, quoting Agnieszka Osiecka, Poland's most popular songwriter. "You wanted your own home," she used to sing (she died recently), "and you got capitalism with broken teeth." Pani Broda explains all this to me but insists that her husband exaggerates. The song was written in the early 1990s, when the economy was still in a shambles. "Since then, a lot of those broken teeth have been fixed." She smiles. She seems to be generally more receptive to new ideas, and I find myself wondering what, exactly, Pan Broda's position was under the Communists. I have managed to learn only that he was a bureaucrat until 1989, when he finally retired; he seemed a little evasive on being questioned, and I did not persist. I have found it impossible, traveling in Poland, to face elderly men who apparently thrived under the former regime, without wondering what horrors they may have been guilty of.

Pan Broda is a balding, rather burly man with inscrutable eyes and—surprising in this poker face—two rather seductive dimples. Whatever his position before his retirement, he has apparently been successful. The Brodas' flat is a spacious and well-furnished one, with hundreds of books and a piano, which Pani Broda apparently plays. Despite the evident comfort, Pan Broda's conversation is marked by a peevishness of tone, giving way now and then to passionate indignation. He tells me, for example, about former president Wałęsa's refusal to pay income tax on foreign currency received from Warner Brothers for the movie rights to the story of his life.

"One million dollars!" rages Pan Broda. "He insists the money's a gift, not income, the shameless oaf!"

"Money corrupts; it's a well-known fact," Pani Broda says. She admits she is very grateful to have all the recent amenities but all the same can't help lamenting the fact that Poles are becoming more like Americans—obsessed with material things and money. She tells me about an Old Town fortune-teller, all of whose clients used to be women with romantic problems. Now, it seems, 75 percent of them are looking for financial tips and entrepreneurial forecasts.

We all laugh at this, interrupted by little Janek who emerges from the bedroom to inquire when his parents will be back, and to ask for ice cream. There is no ice cream today, Pani Broda says, but he can have some strawberry Jell-O, if he likes. Janek accepts the treat and sits eating it on the living room sofa, utterly absorbed in its gelatinous wonder. I think of the first time I had Jell-O in Israel—the extraordinary vividness of childhood pleasures. When I tell the Brodas about my memory of the ice cream in Łódź, and my failure to find anything approximating it anywhere in Poland, Pan Broda asks whether I have tried the ice cream at Blikle's.

The name means nothing to me, but Blikle's, it seems, is a Polish institution Varsovians are as passionate about as Parisians used to be about LeNôtre. Founded in 1869, the shop is famous mostly for its jam-filled sugar buns, which are Poles' favorite pastry, and which Charles de Gaulle became so enamored of while visiting Poland that he thereafter had Blikle's ship them all the way to Paris. In addition to its superb confectioneries, Blikle's also boasts Gloucestershire sausages, reputedly produced in cooperation with Prince Charles's own sausage supplier.

It is as the Brodas tell me all this that Stefan and Bożena arrive, having gone to Kraków for a friend's anniversary party. When all the greetings and introductions are over, and we are ready to leave for the suburbs, Pan Broda mock-chides Stefan for failing to take me to Blikle's while showing me the Old Town back in July. "How can she go back to Canada without trying Blikle's ice cream?" he asks theatrically.

When Stefan finally gathers what this is all about, he turns to me with a smile. "In that case," he says, "we must definitely stop at Blikle's." I try to argue against. it. After all this hype, I frankly dread the thought of having to conceal what I think of as inevitable disappointment. They must be tired, I say, after the long drive from Kraków. But it's no use. Both Stefan and Bożena insist, aided by Janek's shrill chanting: "Ice cream! Ice cream! Ice cream!"

And so we get into the red Toyota and drive toward fashionable Nowy Świat (New World) Street, where Joseph Conrad, and other luminaries, once lived, and around which I note a remarkable number of Mercedeses and BMWs. Part of the Royal Route, Nowy Świat Street is a long boulevard with lovely Neoclassical architecture and many fine galleries, boutiques, and European cafés. Inhabited as far back as the seventeenth century, the area is rich in landmarks, including a palace occupied by the prewar British embassy. It was on this balcony, at the start of World War II, that the British ambassador stood reassuring a large crowd of Poles, who listened and cheered wildly, convinced that Britain would not let them down.

Eventually, we arrive at Blikle's, only to find a long lineup in front of the ice-cream counter. I try once more to persuade my hosts to go on to Piastów, but Janek protests and Stefan points out there is a good reason for the line: it's the best ice cream in Poland.

He goes to park the car while Bożena and I queue up with Janek, chatting in French, and a little Hebrew, which Bożena has recently taken up because of her work at the Jewish Historical Institute. She is a pretty, vivacious brunette in her early thirties, expecting her second child. Polish children don't start school until the age of seven, but Janek has begun kindergarten and we talk about the pros and cons of waiting to have a second child and of Polish education. Bożena says that their curriculum and textbooks are currently undergoing revision, both having been criticized for their historical inaccuracies and gender stereotypes. The Polish public is becoming extremely sensitive to such issues. When, for example, a Warsaw school attempted to introduce computer classes for boys and cooking sessions for girls, there was an instant uproar. "We're catching up quickly," says Bożena, stroking Janek's hair. Stefan joins us, and I admit to being impressed by the sweet, increasingly evocative fragrance of freshly baked wafers. It is a delicious, tantalizing aroma that conveys a promise I find myself inwardly resisting; one I know cannot possibly be kept.

But it almost is. My vanilla comes in a cone rather than a sandwich, but the wafer is fresh and flavorful and crisp, and the ice cream itself rich and creamy and so delicious that there is no need whatever for me to dissemble. It is, in fact, the closest I come in Poland to a perfect Proustian moment; one trailing an inevitable reminder: tomorrow is my last day in Warsaw.

In the car, I am told to sit beside Stefan while Bożena climbs in the back, chatting with her son. Stefan drives toward Piastów, asking in English about my recent travels. Though we have talked on the phone, this is the first time I get to explain the reasons for my extended stay, telling him in a nutshell where I have been and what I have tried to accomplish.

"And have you figured out what it is Poles want?" Stefan asks with a half smile. At some point, walking that first day through the Old Town, I told him about my in-flight conversation with the ex-Krakovian; the one who had stated he no longer knew what it was Poles really wanted.

I tell Stefan they want all the obvious things: the cars and washing machines and stereos—but they want them all without giving up things that people seem to come by only in times of struggle and deprivation. Stefan asks for examples, and they are not at all difficult to name. "A sense of purpose, solidarity, spiritual growth," I say. "Poles seem to realize that they are on the way to losing something quite precious in exchange for all those flashy consumer goods."

"You mean we all want to eat our ice cream and have it too?" Stefan grins behind the wheel.

"Something like that." I laugh, still thinking about it. The way I see it, many Poles are just beginning to suspect there is no end to wanting. "It was much simpler in Poznań, back in 1956," I add after a moment, "when it seemed that food and housing and civil liberties were all Poles needed to be truly content."

"Hm," Stefan says, pondering as he stops for a traffic light. He then changes the subject, going on to express amazement at how much I have managed to see and do in such a short time. So what do I think of Poland, he asks me at length.

"Ah," I say, "I've been asking myself the same question for days."

"Seriously," says Stefan. "What *do* you think? Be frank."

"Well," I finally say, "I promise to write and tell you, Stefan, but it will take me about a year and roughly three hundred pages."

He grins at that. "Three hundred pages to tell me, or to find out what you think?" he asks.

"Both, I suppose," I say. "Yes, both."

The following day, on my last afternoon in Poland, I call Olga Podlaski in Kraków. I called once before, back in July, and learned from her mother that she had given birth to a girl and both mother and daughter were doing well. Olga was still in hospital at the time, so this is the first conversation I have had with her since we parted in Kraków at the beginning of my journey. Her daughter is almost three months old when I learn that after my departure, Olga and Marek decided to name her Irena—not exactly *after* me but certainly *because* of me. I am reminded that on that first day in Kraków, talking about names over our Greek dinner, I happened to tell them how delighted I had been to find, on first arriving in Greece, that my name meant *peace*.

"We decided we liked that." Olga chuckles into the telephone. "We couldn't think of a better name for a child facing our second millennium. Can you?"

Bibliography

Ascherson, Neal. *The Polish August.* Middlesex: Penguin, 1981.

Ash, Timothy Garton. "Neo Pagan Poland." *New York Review of Books,* December 14, 1995: 10-14.

Benson, Herbert. *Timeless Healing: The Power and Biology of Belief.* New York: Scribner, 1996.

Bliss Lane, A. *I Saw Poland Betrayed.* Indianapolis: Bobbs Merrill, 1948.

Brandys, Marian. *Poland.* New York: Doubleday and Company, 1974.

Brumberg, Abraham. "The Last Jew in Warsaw." *Granta,* Autumn 1996: 243-254.

Buruma, Ian. "Poland's New Jewish Question." *New York Times Magazine,* August 3, 1997: 34-57.

Carroll, James. "The Silence." *New Yorker,* April 7, 1997: 52-68.

Chatwin, Bruce. *What Am I Doing Here?* New York: Viking Penguin, 1989.

Davies, Norman. *God's Playground: A History of Poland.* New York: Columbia University Press, 1982.

Davies, Norman. "The Misunderstood Victory in Europe." *New York Review of Books,* May 25, 1995: 7-10.

Dydynski, Krzysztof. *Poland.* London: Lonely Planet Publications, 1996.

Fedorowicz, J., I. Maryniak, B. Stanosz, and D. Warszawski. "File on Poland." *Index on Censorship.* London: November/December, 1994.

Fénelon, Fania. *Playing for Time.* New York: Atheneum, 1977.

Ficowski, Jerzy. *The Gypsies in Poland.* Warsaw: Interpress Publications, 1983.

Fonseca, Isabel. *Bury Me Standing: The Gypsies and Their Journey.* New York: Knopf, 1995.

Franciszek, Piper. "Estimating the Number of Deportees to and Victims of the Auschwitz-Birkenau Camp." *Yad Vashem Studies:* 21, 1991: 49-103.

Grabowska, Ianina. *Polish Amber.* Warsaw: Interpress Publications, 1983.

Hoffman, Eva. *Exit into History.* New York: Viking Penguin, 1993.

Jahanbegloo, Ramin. "Philosophy and Life: An Interview with Isaiah Berlin." *New York Review of Books,* May 28, 1992: 46-54.

Kaufman, Michael T. *Mad Dreams,*

Saving Graces. New York: Random House, 1989.

Klee, E., W. Dressen, and R. Volker (eds.) *The Good Old Days: The Holocaust as Seen by Its Perpetrators and Bystanders.* New York: Macmillan, 1991.

Knab, Sophie Hodorowicz. *Polish Customs, Traditions, and Folklore.* New York: Hippocrene Books, 1993.

Lukas, Richard C. Bitter *Legacy: Polish-American Relations in the Wake of World War II.* Lexington: The University of Kentucky Press, 1982.

Marshall-Cornwall, J. *Napoleon.* London: B. T. Batsford, 1967.

Marsden, Philip. *The Bronski House.* London: Harper Collins, 1995.

Mierzwinski, M. *Malbork.* Bydgoszcz, Poland: Excalibur, 1996.

McNeil, William H. *Plagues and Peoples.* New York: Doubleday, 1976.

Michener, James A. *Poland.* New York: Random House, 1983.

Miłosz, Czesław. *The Captive Mind.* New York: Vintage Books, 1953.

Paikin, Steve. "Poland Striving to Shake off Anti-Semitic Past." *Globe and Mail,* May 29, 1992.

Pick, Hella. *Simon Wiesenthal: A Life in Search of Justice.* London: Weidenfeld and Nicolson, 1996.

Rosenberg, Tina. *The Haunted Land.* New York: Random House, 1995.

Salter, M., and G. McLachlan. *Poland.* London: Rough Guides, 1996.

Shneiderman, S. L. *The River Remembers.* New York: Horizon Press, 1978.

Sloan, James Parker. *Jerzy Kosinski.* New York: Dutton, 1996.

Steinlauf, Michael C. *Bondage to the Dead.* Syracuse, New York: Syracuse University Press, 1997.

Syrop, Konrad. *Spring in October.* London: Weidenfeld and Nicolson, 1957.

Szermer Bohdan. *Gdańsk, Past and Present.* Warsaw: Interpress Publications, 1971.

Tec, Nechama. *When Light Pierced the Darkness: Christian Rescue of Jews in Nazi-Occupied Poland.* New York: Oxford University Press, 1986.

Tomaszewski, Irena and Tecia Werbowski. *ZEGOTA: The Rescue of Jews in Wartime Poland.* Montreal: Price-Patterson, 1994.

Watt, Richard M. *Bitter Glory.* New York: Simon and Schuster, 1979.

Weschler, Lawrence. "Urban Blight." *New Yorker,* December 11, 1995: 54-69.

Wyden, Peter. *Stella.* New York: Simon and Schuster, 1992.

Zamoyski, Adam. *The Polish Way.* New York: Franklin Watts, 1988.

Ziegler, Philip. *The Black Death.* New York: John Gay Company, 1969.

Acknowledgments

This book would not have been possible without the generosity and support of many individuals and organizations, above all the Canada Council for the Arts which subsidized the project. I am indebted to Stefan Władysiuk of McGill University's Polish Library for help beyond the call of duty, as well as to the Jewish Public Library and Concordia University Library. Many thanks to Irena Bellert, Kajetan Morawski, Elaine Kalman Naves, Arthur and Judy Yelon for reading the typescript and offering helpful comments; to Stan Pappius for providing a cover photograph; to Richard Galligan for sending relevant articles my way; to *Gazeta Inc.* for providing the Polish type fonts; to Michel Benoit for drawing a map; and especially, to Anna and Teresa Bąblewska, and Michał Pastuszka, for taking me in and nursing me back to health. I am grateful to the *Rough Guide* and *Lonely Planet* guidebooks for showing me the way and, along with the *Warsaw Voice,* providing much valuable information. From beginning to end, there have been friends and strangers who have kindly offered hospitality, help, information. They are: Sally Aitken, Stan Asher, Adam Bartosz, Janusz Bogacki, Andrzej Gardziel, Maria Habinowska, Maria Ilków, Stanisław Janicki, Kazimierz and Teresa Kaczmarczyk, Benedykt Kafel, Ula and Wojtek Kłaptocz, Jerzy and Ewa Krasicki, Andrzej Krystałowicz, Andrzej Krysztofowicz, Victor, Denis, and Joan Lehotay, Nathan Leipciger, Renata Linette, Jerzy Lipiński, Marta Łukasiewicz, Beata and Paweł Majewski, Krzysztof Małachowski, Wanda Muszyńska, Andrzej and Eve Nowacki, Ewa and Bogumił Oświęcimski, Hania Pappius, Richard Pooran, Stanisław Pruszyński, Irena and Krzysztof Raźny, Leslie Regnier, Urszula Rzeszotarska, Ilona Sóos and Jerzy Stachowiak, Józef Szydliński, David Tigne and Joanne Giasson, Tamara Tomaszewska, Bożena, Krzysztof, Grzegorz, and Małgorzata Tusiewicz, Sylvia and Bill Wees, Alina Włodarczyk. My heartfelt thanks to all.